C000241093

Making Your Doctoral Research Project Ambitious

This book presents the doctoral dissertation process as not just a way of getting a qualification or even a method of learning how to do research better, but as a substantial and significant piece of research in its own right. The book will inspire current and prospective PhD scholars to take up ambitious and large-scale study projects, dedicating this most important time to a worthy piece of research.

This edited collection provides real and outstanding examples of multiple research design methodologies which will allow doctoral researchers to develop a wide set of research skills, leading to the development of a high-quality academic thesis from which peer reviewed research papers and books can emerge. Each main chapter presents the summary of a doctoral thesis, followed by focused aspects from the projects where the contributors highlight the development of a research design, the process involved in executing the design, and present selected findings with their implications. Each chapter concludes with the researchers' experiences of learning through this journey and the implications of the process for the development of the discipline and their own career.

Ideal reading for doctoral students and supervisors, this book is a source of encouragement and motivation for new researchers seeking to challenge general perceptions in the social sciences that PhD or other doctoral research projects must be small-scale rather trivial studies, but can instead produce robust findings that have real-world implications.

Nadia Siddiqui is Associate Professor and Deputy Director of the Durham University Evidence Centre for Education (DECE), UK.

Stephen Gorard is Professor and Director of the Durham University Evidence Centre for Education (DECE), UK and a Fellow of the Academy of Social Sciences.

Making Your Doctoral Research Project Ambitious

Developing Large-Scale Studies with Real-World Impact

Edited by
Nadia Siddiqui and
Stephen Gorard

Routledge
Taylor & Francis Group

LONDON AND NEW YORK

Cover image: © Getty Images

First published 2022
by Routledge
4 Park Square, Milton Park, Abingdon, Oxon OX14 4RN

and by Routledge
605 Third Avenue, New York, NY 10158

Routledge is an imprint of the Taylor & Francis Group, an informa business

© 2022 selection and editorial matter, Nadia Siddiqui and Stephen Gorard; individual chapters, the contributors

British Library Cataloguing-in-Publication Data
A catalogue record for this book is available from the British Library

Library of Congress Cataloging-in-Publication Data
A catalog record has been requested for this book

ISBN: 978-1-032-05975-4 (hbk)
ISBN: 978-1-032-06245-7 (pbk)
ISBN: 978-1-003-20136-6 (ebk)

DOI: 10.4324/9781003201366

Typeset in Minion
by MPS Limited, Dehradun

Contents

Figures and tables

Figures

Tables

Editor Bios

Dr Nadia Siddiqui is Associate Professor at Durham University. She is leading several projects, and researching early years schooling, disadvantage in education, and evidence use in policy and practice. She supervises postgraduate students and doctoral researchers working on ambitious projects. This book resonates strongly with her own journey as a doctoral researcher supervised by Professor Stephen Gorard, and then embarking on a successful academic career.

Stephen Gorard is Professor of Education and Public Policy, Director of the Durham University Evidence Centre for Education (DECE), and a Fellow of the Academy of Social Sciences. He is passionate about exposing and reducing inequality in education, and improving the quality of education research.

Contributors

Dr Haifaa Alabbad gained her PhD in education from Durham University, UK, on the determinants of absence and exclusion from school. She has more than 15 years experience of teaching English as a foreign language in Saudi Arabia. She is interested in research methods involving secondary data and systematic reviews.

Sophie Anderson is an ESRC funded PhD researcher in the School of Education at Durham University with a background in teaching in the secondary age phase in English schools. Her doctoral research focuses on the academic buoyancy construct and its relationship with school attendance. She is currently employed as a Research Associate in the Department of Psychology at Durham University.

Dr Ismail Aslantas is National Education Specialist at the Ministry of National Education in Turkey. He has a wide range of experiences in the educational sector, including primary school teacher, deputy and school principal. He is interested in education policy, teacher performance evaluation based on student achievement, and educational equality and equity. In his PhD, Dr Aslantas examined the stability of value-added models in estimating teacher effectiveness.

Dr Pallavi A. Banerjee is Senior Lecturer in Education at the University of Exeter. She leads the MSc Educational research programme, teaches research methods to Masters students, and supervises PhD students. She completed a PhD at Durham University. She has a wide experience of teaching in different countries, and leading an international school.

Phanatdao Chantarasiri is a doctoral researcher at Durham University, with a scholarship from Suratthani Rajabhat University, Thailand, where she has worked as an English lecturer in the Faculty of Education. She was a member of the Lower Mekong Initiative Professional Communication Skills for Leaders Community of Practice where members from five countries in Southeast Asia collaborated to help develop English language capacity. Her research interests are co-operative learning, TESOL/TEFL methods, English language research, and teacher training.

Dr Nada El-Soufi teaches at the Lebanese American University. She completed her PhD in education at Durham University. She has 28 years of experience teaching English as a foreign language in higher education institutions in Lebanon. Her research interests include the infusion of critical thinking in the language classroom, research design and methods with a particular focus on randomised control trials and systematic literature reviews.

Caner Erkan is a doctoral researcher at Durham University. He has more than five years of experience as an assistant expert at the Ministry of National Education, Republic of Turkey. He is interested in evidence-informed policy and practice, particularly getting evidence into use. His doctoral research is focused on how to best disseminate research evidence to teachers.

Dr Rita Hordósy is Nottingham Research Fellow at the University of Nottingham. Her research interests revolve around social justice issues in education and post-compulsory education trajectories, and she is currently working on the research/teaching nexus compared across European universities. Rita conducted her doctoral research in education at the University of Birmingham.

Dr Mark Ledger received ESRC-funding to complete a PhD at Durham University. His research is concerned with value-added and the assessment of secondary school performance.

Dr Binwei Lu currently works as a tenure-track Assistant Professor at Zhejiang University in China. She obtained her doctoral degree at Durham University, focusing on academic selection and its impacts on effectiveness and equity. Her research has been widely reported by the UK media, such as the Times, Independent, and TES. She won the Review of Education Early Career Researchers Award 2021 and the judges' commendation in the 2021 BERA Doctoral Thesis Award.

Dr Rebecca Morris is Associate Professor at the University of Warwick. She completed her PhD at Birmingham University on the introduction of free schools in England. Her research interests include education policy, the teacher workforce, widening participation, and literacy.

Dr Thomas Perry completed his PhD study on value-added performance measures at Birmingham University. He is now Assistant Professor at the University of Warwick. His ongoing research concerns supporting students, school leaders, and policy-makers to improve education through evidence-informed policy and practice. Dr Perry's work has been cited widely and internationally including by a UK Parliament Briefing, and UNESCO, and featured in the media, including BBC Radio 4.

Dr Ismail Shafeeu is Dean of the Centre for Research and Publication at the Islamic University of Maldives. He holds a PhD in education from Durham University, UK. He has extensive experience in teaching and managing curricula at both secondary and university levels. He critically evaluates educational policies and highlights various challenges faced by the Maldives in the provision of quality education that is fair to all pupils. Dr Shafeeu also had the privilege to hold several leadership positions in the educational sector, including a key policy level job in the Education Ministry of Maldives.

Pian Shi is a PhD researcher at Durham University. She has been working on service learning and the moral education of youth for several years. She worked for The Public Service Education Research Programme in Beijing Normal University since 2011, and was involved in developing a series of Civic Service Education Courses for students of primary and middle schools in China. She is also committed to encouraging community workers and parents to participate in youth's service learning through developing guidebooks and training programme for community workers and parents.

Yiyi Tan is a PhD researcher at Durham University. Her PhD project evaluates the use of contextual indicators in HE enrolment and understanding inequality in HE participation in China. She is interested in education policy, education equality and equity, and research methodology. She is also interested in understanding the principles of fairness.

Meechai Wongdaeng has been an instructor of English and EFL teaching methods at Prince of Songkla University in Thailand, for several years. He is currently a doctoral researcher at Durham University. His research interests are in the application and evaluation of metacognition, self-regulation, and other learner-centered approaches in EFL pedagogy, and on the use of evidence to inform education policy and practice.

Caiwei Wu is a doctoral researcher at Durham University. She is interested in critical thinking and classroom dialogue. Her PhD project focuses on evaluating the impact of Philosophy for Children on young people's critical thinking and academic performance, in a Chinese context.

Preface

This book is intended to change readers' view of what a PhD or other doctoral study in the social sciences is like. We expect that this book will challenge any general perceptions in the social sciences that doctoral research projects must be mostly weak or small-scale studies. That they contribute to doctoral students' learning experiences without any expectation that they also contribute substantial evidence to the wider knowledge pool. Our experience of supervising masters, doctoral, and new researchers, for around 40 years in total between us, suggests that it is entirely feasible for all of them to conduct studies of real substantive significance. Put another way, completing a thesis or dissertation is not just a way of getting a qualification or even a method of learning how to do research better. A dissertation is, of course, both of these, but more importantly it is a piece of research in its own right. And the research should be both substantial and significant.

The book illustrates what we mean by this through 17 real-life case studies of doctoral research, and additional chapters drawing out their more general lessons. The authors are from around the world, including China, Hungary, India, Jordan, the Maldives, Pakistan, Saudi Arabia, Thailand, Turkey, and the UK. They were studying and writing in English, which was a second or third language for most of them. They did not have it easy. As they discuss in the relevant chapters, they often faced barriers to data access and overcame the challenges of limited resources. Many were researching during the COVID-19 lockdown and still completed their PhD on time in three years. The book should therefore be a great source of encouragement and motivation for other new researchers to be ambitious and realistic, perhaps using multiple approaches and larger datasets, producing robust findings that have real world implications.

This book will be a resource for all current and prospective doctoral (PhD, DPhil, EdD) researchers in the social sciences, for international scholars, new researchers, masters students facing a dissertation, current and prospective postgraduate supervisors, doctoral training centres, councils funding doctoral studies, and anyone interested in improving the quality of social science research more generally. In addition, the chapters are important substantive contributions to social science in their own right.

All of the scholars contributing a chapter have been supervised by one or both of the two editors, and most have have conducted or completed their PhDs since we arrived at Durham University, UK, in mid-2013. The editors and authors would like to acknowledge the assistance of other supervisors and co-supervisors, especially the key contributions of our colleague Professor Beng Huat See.

We all hope that you will enjoy this book.

CHAPTER 1

Thinking bigger: The importance of an ambitious doctoral research project

Nadia Siddiqui and Stephen Gorard

Introduction

This is a book about worthwhile doctoral research projects. It is intended for new researchers of all kinds – those completing or thinking about a PhD, and those in their first research appointment. New researchers include Masters' students doing a dissertation, because the same pleas for ambition and clarity in research that are made in this book apply to them as well. We are also addressing doctoral supervisors looking for examples or advice. In fact, the book will be of interest to researchers at all stages, although the main focus, and all of the case study examples, concern doctoral researchers.

We hope that the words of the 17 new researchers in the substantive chapters of this book will be a source of encouragement and motivation for other new researchers. We want to encourage you to be ambitious and realistic, to use multiple approaches, larger datasets, simple analyses, and clear uncluttered reporting, to produce relatively robust findings that have real-world implications.

What is a doctoral degree?

The number of people studying for a doctoral degree (a PhD, DPhil or a professional doctorate like an EdD) is increasing across all disciplines, worldwide. In the UK, doctoral admissions and completions have increased annually for at least ten years. UK universities attract one of the largest proportions of doctoral researchers, locally and from across the globe. In 2019, UK universities awarded 101,885 doctorates. These new researchers can make important contributions to the research environment of UK higher education (HE), and that of their home countries.

The UK Higher Education Statistics Agency states that a PhD (or equivalent doctorate) is the highest level of standard degree offered by a university (Higher Education Statistics Agency HESA, 2018). There are

DOI: 10.4324/9781003201366-1

many different formats for a research doctorate. They can be full-time (usually three or four years), part-time (usually five to seven years), or a mixture of the two. Some will include compulsory training in research, while others like the professional doctorates may have substantive modules as well, with assignments similar to a Master's degree that have to be completed before beginning the research dissertation. Some actually incorporate a Master's degree, such as an MPhil awarded after one or two years.

In some countries the doctorate is awarded for a thematic collection of new research articles. In the UK, this format of PhD by publication is possible, especially for staff already working in a university. Some doctorates are a combination of coursework and new research. There are also different traditions by subject area or discipline. However, most doctorates involve submitting a long (perhaps 50,000 to 120,000 words) thesis, based on original research, for independent evaluation by a set of examiners. This has been standard for all of our PhD students.

This book focuses on doctorates of this format, which is the most common in the social sciences. However, there is no evidence suggesting that the quality of research undertaken or the training given to new researchers needs to vary because of the precise format of their doctoral studies (Evans et al., 2018; Smaldone et al., 2019). The key to all doctorates, this highest qualification, is generally thought to be the quality of research they report. A successful doctorate should mean that a researcher has met the criteria of submitting an original research piece, examined and passed in a *viva voce* examination led by a selected academic examiner who is independent of the student's institutional affiliation (Quality Assurance Agency QAA, 2020).

The importance of doctoral research

Doing a doctorate by research is expensive, in terms of fees paid to the institution, accommodation and subsistence for three years or more, maybe the cost of books, and fieldwork expenses. There is also the salary foregone, given that you could have had a job instead. Part-time doctorates permit students to hold a full-time job simultaneously, and the longer elapsed time to complete the thesis should permit the student to plan more ambitious longitudinal projects. However, part-time degrees take longer, are somewhat harder work than the full-time doctorate, and are still very expensive.

Therefore, this chance to conduct your own research should not be spurned by doing something mediocre or worse. A doctoral degree such as a PhD is an excellent opportunity to dedicate three or more years to conducting a substantial research project. This is perhaps the only time in people's lives where such an extended period is possible for just one research project, which they can focus on exclusively and write about at comparative leisure. Academics rarely, if ever, get that experience again. It would be a wasted opportunity for new researchers if this time were not spent in conducting some high quality research, which could make a substantial knowledge contribution, add value to academic practice, and enhance their own skills for further development or a career.

Picking a supervisor

A small part of achieving the above is to pick an appropriate supervisor. The obvious standard advice is to select a supervisor, and a department and university, that match your intended research study in terms of focus and research expertise (Mangematin, 2000). This alignment of your ideas with the ongoing research conducted by a PhD supervisor is considered an important determinant of successful PhD admission and completion (van Rooij et al., 2021). It is certainly how funders like the ESRC begin to judge who to fund (NINEDTP, 2021). We agree. But only up to a point. Beware the expert in your area of interest who will not let you do what you want, or who will stop you moving the field forward in a way that might be seen as undermining their own prior research (or their pet theories!). Some experts are possessive, insistent on you using the same methods approaches as they do, regardless of your research interests. Some will constrain you just because they know little or nothing of methods approaches other than a small sub-set. But in social science research, you have to own the project. The supervisor is there to guide you gently, provide robust critique when needed and, most importantly, to provide craft tips drawn from their own experiences.

Naturally, potential doctoral researchers can have a wide variety of reasons for choosing to do a PhD (or similar). These may include interest in the topic, career progression, or even putting off paid work! But most are interested, at least partly, in a more advanced level of academic experience (than a Bachelors' or Masters' degree provides), and professional development as a researcher (Skakni, 2018). These motivations mean that the supervisor has to be a successful researcher themselves to perform the supervisory role fully. And the supervisor has to know about and have used a wider range of methods approaches successfully, so that they can help convey the important skills and experiences to their mentees (see Chapter 19). This match-up is reflected in the longstanding evidence that the main contributors to high impact "prestigious" peer-reviewed journals are PhD graduates from "prestigious" universities (Perry, 1994). This is, at least partly, because these universities tend to have more research active staff members available to supervise students in their own mould (although there will be other differences as well, including perhaps more undergraduate workload pressure in less research active universities).

Nevertheless, all other things being equal, we recommend choosing the most research active supervisory team you can find, almost regardless of institution. New researchers should expect to learn in an active research environment where they can advance their knowledge of conducting research. And such higher level academic participation means that PhD researchers will learn to think bigger in their selection of research topics on social issues, and so design PhD projects with findings that have relevance for policy and practice. Thinking bigger in the conception and design of a project means constructing a feasible, pragmatic research question, designing an innovative research plan, and conducting a robust study with ambitious ideas for marshalling or collecting data. This level of confidence and ambition is contrary to much general advice on "how to do your PhD".

For at least twenty years in the UK, as elsewhere, there has been an increased focus on the skills of supervisors, and the skills that the supervisors and HE training modules can impart to students (Park, 2005; Roberts Report, 2002). Again, we do not argue with this trend. But the "skills" often referred to are supervisory rather than research ones. There is a danger that all of the training in how to be supervisor, how to record your meetings, and the need for supervisory certification, will tend to de-emphasise the importance of actual research experience. And overshadow the necessity for supervisors able to do high quality research so that they can help their students to do the same.

The official lists of requirements for PhD supervisors tend to be quite long, and being research active appears only once (e.g. Taylor and Clegg, 2021). Of course, no one is born as an experienced supervisor or researcher. This is why we referred to supervisory *teams* above. Most universities now arrange for two (sometimes more) supervisors, and this is a good idea for continuity in the unexpected absence of one of them. It also means that new members of staff can be paired with more experienced ones. As an example, Nadia Siddiqui was once the PhD student of Stephen Gorard. Subsequently, her first supervision of her own doctoral students was with Stephen Gorard. She is now a very experienced and promoted researcher in her own right. She is also in demand as an external examiner for others, worldwide.

The work in this book

This book presents chapters summarising the work of 17 PhD or EdD researchers, supervised by the two of us (sometimes with our valued colleague Professor Beng Huat See). These doctorates took place during our time at Durham University, UK (although some earlier students completed their studies at the University of Birmingham, UK). These examples are just the latest in a longer line, and a selection from a larger set, stretching back to the late 1990s. Their projects, and others like them, clearly demonstrate that PhD research can be successful. They are based on large-scale rich studies, with suitable research designs, robust findings, and they have made or will make a substantial contribution to knowledge in their field.

The quality of research exemplified here is based on studying real issues, using appropriate research designs, high quality data, the simplest of analyses, and clarity in writing for meaningful and readable research outputs. The findings from these projects also illustrate the benefit of collecting a variety of data including numbers, experiences, perceptions, images, and observations (only some of which are outlined in these brief chapter summaries). Unfortunately, these inclusive characteristics are not always visible in much academic research, let alone in doctoral studies.

There is often too great an emphasis in research methods training, and in materials advising PhD researchers, on the use of grand theoretical conceptions, or on the reflexivity of the researcher. As can be seen, the chapters in this book are genuinely reflective about their PhD journeys, and they evaluate important theoretical ideas such as what "effectiveness" or "fairness" are, or whether resilience or morality are malleable characteristics of people. The studies are both empirically and theoretically strong. But none have wasted time and words discussing paradigms wars, and epistemological and ontological dispositions, or justifying their "positionality" as a researcher of a certain type (see Chapter 19).

All of these researchers have completed their thesis in around three years (or equivalent for part-time), or are well on track to do so. A few completed in substantially less time, and a few went slightly into a fourth year. These emerging researchers mostly had no research funding for fieldwork expenses or similar, and many had to complete their studies during the COVID-19 worldwide lockdown. They certainly did not have it easy. Several chapters explain how the authors overcame challenges such as limited resources and barriers to data access. For example, everyone doing fieldwork, or using secondary data, in England had to pass a disclosure and barring service (DBS) check. Those using sensitive data had to take official training and pass a test to use the ONS Secure Research Service.

In general though, our experience of supervision and mentoring suggests that high quality studies like these examples are the actually easiest to complete, because they generate substantial content for the write up. The new researchers who struggle the most to write up their studies are generally the ones who have the least to say. This leads to the deplorable habit, widespread among academics, of filling their writing spaces with what read like pompous and verbose utterances instead. And which are not really research at all. This is what we want to help others to avoid.

The book contains research from educational contexts in China, England, Finland, Hungary, Lebanon, the Maldives, the Netherlands, Turkey and Thailand, and work by authors from India, and Saudi Arabia (courageously researching in the educational context of the UK). It is impressive that the international scholars have written their theses in English, and we have preserved as far as possible their sometimes unique form of expression, even though this means that the writing style is not always strictly consistent with English academic writing practices. Several students were awarded scholarships from their home countries, and most of these were bonded to return home and use their new skills there. Some others, who were self-funding, received help with research costs from their colleges at Durham University. If you do not ask you will not get! The researchers from England were funded by the Economic and Social Research Council (ESRC). This prestigious funding covers the fees, some expenses, and usually pays a stipend, all of which are invaluable.

Most of the authors here have published from their PhD research, some before their *viva*, and others soon after. A few have already produced a book or research monograph based on their doctorate, and others are arranging to do so at present. They have also presented at national and international conferences, written blogs, sent evidence to government committees, and talked in teacher forums. Some have had their research featured in the press or on TV and radio. These are all excellent things to do to engage with the widest possible academic and user audience. As supervisors, we helped them in all of these endeavours, reading drafts, editing texts, suggesting outlets, and offering strong reassurance when some early versions were rejected or ignored. The latter happens to all of us.

However, none of these often very prestigious publications names either of us as authors. Our contributions were as supervisors, which is what we are employed for (and what the students paid their fees for). We are aware that traditions vary by discipline, but we generally abhor the practice of supervisors muscling in on their students' (Masters' or doctoral) own publications just because they helped with the research or the writing (Krauth et al., 2017; Xu, 2020). We think more should be made of ethical concerns about this intellectual piracy (Kwok, 2005; Macfarlane, 2017). One piece of practical advice for potential research students – find a supervisor who will not be desperate to use your outputs in order to shore up their own CV.

The structure of the book

Following the introduction chapter, this book is divided into three parts, each containing relevant chapters on linked educational themes. The book ends with a chapter in which we offer advice on what we have learnt from supervising these excellent doctoral projects. We present the implications for new researchers, emphasising the feasibility of high quality ambitious PhD studies that can make real-life knowledge contributions, and play an important role in the academic development of early career researchers. This book is a very welcome opportunity for us to present and acknowledge the work of our excellent PhD researchers, many of whom are now our academic colleagues around the world.

The three main parts of this book cover a wide range of projects. Part I consists of doctoral projects which investigated educational effectiveness by evaluating policies, analysing administrative data, and reassessing the value of statistical techniques.

Part I – All of the chapters in this section of the book concern how we assess the effectiveness of schools, teachers, and school leaders.

Chapter 2. Tom Perry's chapter presents a wide-ranging analysis of value-added estimates of school effectiveness. The focus is the use of Progress 8 scores in England, the official measure of school performance, and its forerunners. However, the implications are important for all systems using value-added scores. Value-added "progress" measures were introduced for all English schools in 2016 as measures of school performance despite prior research highlighting high levels of instability in value-added measures and concerns about the omission of contextual variables. This work uses the National Pupil Database to assess the impact of disregarding contextual factors, the stability of school scores across time and the consistency of value-added performance for different cohorts within schools at a given point in time. The analyses confirm concerns about intake biases, showing that value-added measures exhibit worrying levels of instability. The analysis goes further by examining whether instability across time stems from differences between cohorts and whether measures based on a single cohort can reflect whole school performance now or in the future. In combination, these analyses suggest a general problem of imprecision within value-added estimates and that the current policy use of value-added scores is unjustified. Published school performance measures are likely to be profoundly misleading. This project has had an impact on the field of school effectiveness more widely. This chapter discusses how the study idea was conceived and executed, and contributed to establishing the author in an academic career.

Chapter 3. This topic is continued in the chapter by Mark Ledger, on his ESRC-funded PhD, examining whether Progress 8 as an example of value-added measures is appropriate for use in judging schools by government, school inspectors, or parents. Schools' Progress 8 scores matter, and people's lives are affected by the results. The research gathers detailed information from schools on their characteristics and the kinds of factors that educational effectiveness is usually attributed to. It then uses this information to predict changes in schools' value-added scores over time, and asks school leaders to do the same. The scores are very volatile and whilst this could theoretically be explained by genuine changes in school performance, the evidence suggests that this is not the case. School-related factors (on teaching for example) account for a surprisingly low percentage of the variation in value-added scores. There is also evidence to suggest that errors in students' prior-attainment have the potential to impact upon schools' ratings. Of greater concern is the impact that school intakes have upon schools' ratings. Differences between students' socio-economic status have close associations with school "performance" figures that effectively punish schools with educationally disadvantaged cohorts. These characteristics of students are not under the control of schools. The chapter therefore concludes that Progress 8 does not provide a valid or trustworthy measure of school performance.

Chapter 4. The study by Ismail Aslantas is about one of the most controversial and important matters in current education policy worldwide: teacher performance evaluation. Teachers are widely considered one of the most significant school-related factors in enhancing students' academic achievement. One of the key concerns of decision-makers is to ensure that effective teachers are hired in classrooms and parents also want their children to be taught by good teachers. However, measuring the quality of teachers is a complex and not easily achievable task. While it is widely agreed that evaluating teacher performance is beneficial in enhancing teacher development and student outcomes, there is no single agreed method to do so. Teacher effectiveness can be measured in a range of ways, including classroom observation, survey, self-evaluation, portfolio, and student achievement growth analysis. In recent years, academics and decision-makers have focused on value-added modelling, attributing differences in student scores to the actions of the teacher. This study presents a large-scale systematic review of the evidence on teacher effectiveness, and an analysis of the stability of value-added estimates using a longitudinal administrative data set extending over three school years, 2014–2017, from secondary schools in Turkey. The findings suggest that teacher accountability policies based on value-added models are misguided and unfair. Some of the stability analysis results have been published in a peer-reviewed journal.

Chapter 5. Binwei Lu evaluated the effectiveness of Grammar schools in England. Previous research evaluating grammar school effectiveness has generally relied on snapshot or longitudinal regression models to deal with pre-existing differences between grammar school pupils and those in non-selective schools. Such designs are only based on correlations, and cannot demonstrate clear positive causal relationships between grammar school attendance and subsequent attainment. After accounting for the variables available for the analysis, pupils in different schools might still have distinct and unmeasured characteristics which threaten the validity of any conclusions drawn. This study addresses the limitations of previous research, by demonstrating the feasibility of a regression discontinuity design (RDD) approach. This is the first use of RDD to make a robust causal inference about the effectiveness of grammar schools in one local authority in England. Conducting this design with national data on grammar school selection would create the most powerful evidence available so far. To promote an effective and equitable education system for generations to come, those advocating the expansion of grammar schools should make the responsible decision to disclose all grammar school selection data for the purposes of research. The chapter includes sections on the important stages of data access and analysis that led to publication in some of the most prestigious academic journals, and assisted the author in gaining a post at one of China's top universities.

Chapter 6. Ismail Shafeeu's PhD study is a study on the effectiveness of school leadership in the Republic of Maldives. A recent policy in the Maldives insisted on a 60% pass rate for students in the secondary school completion examination. As an essential part of this policy, the Ministry of Education developed an action plan, in which principal leadership was claimed to be one of the key factors contributing to pupils' academic attainment. This new study looked at the impact of leadership on attainment, based on the full national population of teachers working in all public secondary schools in the Maldives (N = 6,047). A survey questionnaire, based on the Principal Instructional Management Scale was administered to gather data on principals' instructional leadership. This data was combined with documentary and population census data to assess the combination of school leadership to the pass rate. The chapter describes the adventure of conducting a national teacher survey, and extending the study by linking the primary survey data with existing official data. The study led to publications in prestigious US journals, and assisted the author in becoming a Dean of Research in his home university.

Part II – The chapters in the second section of the book illustrate different approaches to improving student outcomes at school or university, either in terms of attainment or wider outcomes such as critical thinking or mindfulness.

Chapter 7. Phanatdao Chantarasiri was concerned with improving outcomes for English language learners at universities in Thailand. In tertiary English classes in Thailand, every undergraduate student is required to take two to four Basic to Advanced English classes. This study focuses on Thai instructors of English for Academic Purposes and English-major student teachers who study three and a half years in a faculty of Education, with the hope that they will be the future of English teachers in Thailand. This chapter presents the findings from a randomised controlled trial of co-operative learning. Co-operative learning requires students working together in a small group to help support each other in order to maximise their own learning as well as the others to accomplish a shared goal. The design is a large-scale experimental trial (with a wait-list), and standardised testing of student progress. There is also a full parallel process evaluation that covers the fidelity of arrangements from initial training of teaching staff through implementation of the intervention to subsequent testing.

Chapter 8. Meechai Wongdaeng addressed the same challenge with a different intervention. This chapter discusses the challenges faced by the higher education system in Thailand where a recent policy was introduced, requiring all students to reach a pass level in an international standardised test of English language. The study included a systematic review of inter-vention effectiveness on meta-cognition (learning to learn), and an experi-mental evaluation of an intervention based on meta-cognition. The trial outcomes have been assessed for immediate and long-term impact. The chapter discusses the stages of developing the experimental design and conducting the study with a large number of students in universities in Thailand, and the problems and facilitators encountered.

Chapter 9. Caiwei Wu was concerned with improving critical thinking for secondary school students in China. Due to the perceived shortcomings of the exam-oriented education, more educators are paying attention to student-centred teaching methods, and students' reasoning ability, including critical thinking. This new study included a systematic review of dialogic teaching approaches, and followed this with a randomised control trial of Philosophy for Children in Chinese secondary schools. Philosophy for Children (P4C) is an educational approach that helps children question, reason, construct arguments, and collaborate with others. Previous research suggests that it might improve children's thinking, at least at primary schools in Anglophone countries. This approach to teaching is new to Chinese teachers and students who have traditionally relied on rote learning and dissemination of knowledge. Independent thinking and questioning are rarely encouraged. The chapter presents impact findings and describes how teachers received P4C training, how P4C classes were conducted, and some reflections on the PhD experience.

Chapter 10. Nada El-Soufi's PhD project conducted a systematic review of a critical thinking intervention followed by a large-scale randomised control trial of an intervention assessing the impact on English learning outcomes in the University of Lebanon.

Chapter 11. Sophie Anderson combined several systematic reviews, analyses of longitudinal data, and a planned mindfulness intervention to assess whether pupils' academic buoyancy (everyday resilience) in education is a malleable trait. The chapter considers whether an intervention can make a difference to pupils' ability to bounce back after a setback, so making a difference in their educational outcomes. This ESRC-funded PhD research project is a successful example of combining different research designs and innovative datasets, and so generating robust findings that contribute practical knowledge in the field of education.

Chapter 12. The PhD by Pian Shi is a comparative study of primary school pupils in China and England, assessing differences in pupil's attitudes to, and learning of, morality, social action, and citizenship. The study has an experimental design involving a large number of schools and children in both countries, assessing similarities and differences in pupil's attitudes towards issues like honesty, fairness, and responsibility. The study has used innovative techniques, such as games playing and vignettes, in judging these wider outcomes of family and schooling. The chapter discusses how the project was conceived, designed and scaled up for large-scale recruitment in two very different countries.

Part III – The chapters in the final substantive section of the book all concern education policies and their evaluation.

Chapter 13. Rebecca Morris based her PhD research on a multi-method approach, including parent questionnaires and interviews and documentary analysis of admissions criteria, in the context of Free Schools in England. The Free Schools policy in England led to the opening of new autonomous state-funded schools. This study used national data from the Schools Census to present the proportions of socio-economically disadvantaged children attending the first three waves of these schools. The analysis compares the Free School intakes with other local schools and local authority data to establish whether the schools are taking an equal share of disadvantaged children in relation to their nearby competitors. Differences emerge between the different waves of schools with those that opened in 2011 generally underrepresenting disadvantaged children. In the second and third waves the picture is more mixed. New schools have diverse admissions criteria, which they can set themselves. The majority of secondary Free Schools appear to be adhering to the 2012 Admissions Code legislation. However, Free Schools with a faith designation or an alternative or specialist curri-culum appear particularly likely to have proportionally fewer disadvantaged children than might be expected based on their location. This chapter dis-cusses how the study was conceived and executed, and how it led to gov-ernment and media concern, and assisted entry to an academic career.

Chapter 14. Haifaa Alabbad analysed the patterns of attendance and exclusion in schools in England using the National Pupil Database. The Department for Education have taken schools and parents to court for not enforcing complete attendance at school, saying that absence must not be condoned, and pointing out the damage it causes to later attainment and participation. The issue is a worldwide one. Based on a large systematic review of interventions to reduce absence, interviews with schools and families, and an analysis of absences, exclusions and attainment for all pupils in England, this study provides a caution against over-interpreting the correlation between pupil absence from school and subsequent lower attainment. The best predictor of pupil absence in any key stage is not their background characteristics, their school, or their prior pattern of absence. It is their prior attainment. Put simply, pupils who are already doing badly at school may be simply withdrawing further, so producing more missed sessions, rather than the missed sessions causing the later lower attainment. The DfE also conflates very different types of absence. There are pupils who have chronic illness. Long-term absence from school for them could easily lead to lower qualifications in future years, but the pupils are not to be blamed for this. There are pupils whose home life means that school is not the highest priority every morning – such as those with a caring role for younger siblings, for example. Then there are pupils who are suspended or excluded from school, those "bunking off", and those who usually attend regularly but have taken a holiday in term-time. None of these situations is desirable, but each has different practical solutions.

Chapter 15. Pallavi Banerjee's chapter describes an evaluation of science, technology, engineering, and mathematics (STEM) widening participation interventions, and their impact on the attainment and participation of disadvantaged pupils in schools. STEM skills are considered valuable for economic growth. However, the number of young people pursuing STEM trajectories has long been a cause for concern in the UK and elsewhere. Many STEM enrichment and enhancement activities have been funded by the UK government, and private and charitable organisations, to raise pupils' interest in these subjects. This study measured the impact of these activities in supporting pupil understanding of maths by tracking the proportion of young people obtaining a "good" grade in standardised national tests such as GCSEs. Attainment is of course only one possible outcome of education but certainly a very important one because students are more likely to continue studying subjects in which they score higher. This makes maths attainment even more important as it is a pre-requisite for admission to STEM degree courses. This longitudinal, quasi-experimental design makes use of the National Pupil Database to assess the impact of these schemes on the maths attainment of participating schools. Following up 300 intervention schools for five years the study shows the intervention group did not do any better than the comparator. The chapter suggests directions for research and recommendations for practice, and the lessons learned on this PhD journey.

Chapter 16. Yiyi Tan conducted an evaluation of the contextual indicators used in the selection process for highly competitive Chinese universities. The PhD is based on multiple existing large-scale datasets of HE, population and attainment figures. The study evaluates the usefulness of these datasets for assessing inequalities in education, and looks in particular at the geographic stratification of admission to highly selective universities, ethnic disparities and provincial differences in HE participation, and what can be done about these. The chapter illustrates the power of existing data even when working in countries not renowned for the completeness of or ease of access to their official data. Disadvantaged groups need their situation explored and exposed using the new political arithmetic (a technique common to so many of the accounts in this book).

Chapter 17. Rita Hordosy studied large-scale datasets on school leavers and graduates in Europe, which are intended for use in educational policy planning, institutional decision-making and informing students. Many current national and institutional education policies address the issue of raising participation amongst young people and enhancing employability after leaving school or university, but what sort of information are these policies built on? This study compares national information systems from the last three decades across Europe that gather information on school leavers' and graduates' pathways after compulsory education. Using documentary data collected systematically the study describes the main focus, the research design and the sampling frame of the school leavers' and graduates' information systems, arriving at several different typologies. It then compares how stakeholders in England, Finland, and the Netherlands know what happens to the leavers from schools and universities. The research provides insight into the discrepancies of data production and its use, with recommendations for improvements. The chapter also presents accounts of the PhD journey from Hungary which led to successful career development in the UK.

Chapter 18. Caner Erkan took on the topical worldwide issue of how research evidence is, or is not, used in practice. This PhD involves a large-scale systematic review on the use of evidence by teachers, and how best to route new evidence into use. One of the most promising approaches was then trialled in a pilot trial to assess changes in teachers' attitudes to and use of evidence after participating in a tailored workshop, with support, to promote teachers understanding of research knowledge. Making evidence available is of no consequence in itself, and merely providing workshops or training is little better. To get widespread uptake of research evidence requires follow up and audit of the potential users. The chapter includes details on conducting a PhD project on an issue of such topical relevance in education policy worldwide, using multiple research designs.

References

Evans, S., Amaro, C., Herbert, R., Blossom, J., and Roberts, M. (2018). "Are you gonna publish that?" Peer-reviewed publication outcomes of doctoral dissertations in psychology. *PloS One*, 13(2), p. e0192219.

Higher Education Statistics Agency (HESA). (2018/19). Student numbers and characteristics. https://www.hesa.ac.uk/news/16-01-2020/sb255-higher-education-student-statistics/numbers

Krauth, N., Bowman, C., and Fraser, Z. (2017). The exegesis and co-authorship: Collaboration between supervisors and research students. *TEXT*, 21(Special 44), pp. 1–14.

Kwok, L. (2005). The white bull effect: Abusive co-authorship and publication parasitism. *Journal of Medical Ethics*, 31, pp. 554–556. doi: 10.1136/jme.2004 .010553

Macfarlane, B. (2017). The ethics of multiple authorship: Power, performativity and the gift economy. *Studies in Higher Education*, 42(7), pp. 1194–1210.

Mangematin, V. (2000). PhD job market: Professional trajectories and incentives during the PhD. *Research Policy*, 29(6), pp. 741–756.

NINEDTP. (2021). Supervision responsibility web pages. Available at https://www.ninedtp.ac.uk/supervisor-home/

Park, C. (2005). New variant PhD: The changing nature of the doctorate in the UK. *Journal of Higher Education Policy and Management*, 27(2), pp. 189–207.

Perry, G. (1994). Ranking MS and Ph.D. graduate programs in agricultural economics. *Applied Economic Perspectives and Policy*, 16(2), pp. 333–340.

Quality Assurance Agency QAA. (2020). Characteristics statement: Doctoral degree. https://www.qaa.ac.uk/docs/qaa/quality-code/doctoral-degree-characteristics-statement-2020.pdf

Roberts Report. (2002). *Set for success: The supply of people with science, engineering and technology skills*. London: UK Government Department of Trade and Industry and Department of Education and Skills

Skakni, I. (2018). Reasons, motives and motivations for completing a PhD: A typology of doctoral studies as a quest. *Studies in Graduate and Postdoctoral Education*, 9(2), pp. 197–212. doi: 10.1108/SGPE-D-18-00004

Smaldone, A., Heitkemper, E., Jackman, K., Joanne Woo, K., and Kelson, J. (2019). Dissemination of PhD dissertation research by dissertation format: A retrospective cohort study. *Journal of Nursing Scholarship*, 51(5), pp. 599–607.

Taylor, S., and Clegg, K. (2021). Towards a framework for the recognition of good supervisory practice. In *The Future of Doctoral Research* (pp. 224–238). Abingdon: Routledge.

Universities UK. (2019). *Higher Education facts and figures 2019*. Universities UK. https://www.universitiesuk.ac.uk/facts-and-stats/data-and-analysis/Documents/higher-education-facts-and-figures-2019.pdf van Rooij, E., Fokkens-Bruinsma, M., and Jansen, E. (2021). Factors that influence PhD candidates' success: The importance of PhD project characteristics. *Studies in Continuing Education*, 43(1), pp. 48–67.

Xu, L. (2020). Moving between fantasies, fallacies and realities: Students' perceptions of supervisors' roles in doctoral publishing. *Teaching in Higher Education*, pp. 1–15. doi: 0.1080/13562517.2020.1832065.

PART I

Educational Effectiveness

Part I consists of PhD projects which investigated educational effectiveness by evaluating policies, analysing administrative data, and reassessing the value of statistical techniques.

Educational effectiveness

There are chapters covering:

- The stability and usefulness of value-added measures of school performance
- To what extent official school performance measures represent actual school processes
- An exploration of how to judge teacher effectiveness
- An evaluation of the effectiveness of selective schools
- Whether leadership makes a different to student outcomes

The results here are largely negative. This makes the results extremely valuable as a body. They show how hard it is to assess the differential contribution of schools to their students' performance outcomes, using value-added measures (Chapter 2). They raise the doubt that official performance measures are measuring anything meaningful at all (Chapter 3). This, of course, makes it impossible to judge whether individual teachers in schools are being differentially effective (Chapter 4). As a society, we may want to know all of these things, but we cannot. Or at least we cannot be using the kinds of techniques assessed here, and used worldwide. The Regression Discontinuity Design may offer a workable alternative approach to school performance, but there is no evidence that selective school systems produce superior outcomes than mixed ability ones (Chapter 5). If we cannot say whether any school produces markedly better results for equivalent students, we are also unlikely to discover any evidence that school leaders make a difference to attainment outcomes (Chapter 6). Papers from all of these PhDs have been published in peer-reviewed journals.

CHAPTER 2

School value-added measures: Undertaking policy- and practice-relevant methodological research

Thomas Perry

Finding a PhD topic

Why do a PhD? One needs a pretty good reason to study and research something for up to four years full-time, with little or no salary, and without the guarantee of a job at the end of it. Looking back at it, I can form a (mostly) coherent *post hoc* rationalisation of the journey I have taken and how it leads to my current academic role and research interests. In reality, my PhD and post-PhD journey was far bumpier, rambling and uncertain than was comfortable. One thing I am confident of though was that a PhD was the right choice for me; it was an excellent "base camp" from which to build and develop as an academic and educator, and I did some important things right. Above all, I managed to maintain a good degree of ambition, purpose and curiosity throughout (with only the occasional wobble).

My university education was a BSc and MSc in economics at Leicester. Following these, despite encouragement from tutors to take up a PhD, I decided against the idea. I remember reading a textbook on the economics of education, one on game theory, another on behavioural economics – interesting stuff, but I could not find a topic that clicked for me. What I was sure of was the value of education so I decided to train as a teacher. A year of training and a few years of teaching down the line, I was sitting in staff meeting and we were poring over our latest school results, including some value-added (VA) scores. I knew VA scores were based on econometric-style models, and felt I understood the gist of how they worked. I was also aware that the "contextualised" value-added (CVA) measures had been scrapped. CVA, as well as taking into account pupil prior attainment (like all VA measures), also adjusted for socio-economic disadvantage and other factors that influence education performance but are out of a school's control. The school at which I worked at the time was in a deprived area of Birmingham, with low rates of attainment at entry, high rates of pupil mobility, and with many children having English as an additional language. A new measure

DOI: 10.4324/9781003201366-3

ignoring such contextual differences felt like a significant development and probably an unjust one too.

Wanting to know more and wondering if I could find some research on the topic, I had a rummage around on Google, and stumbled across Professor Stephen Gorard's paper, *Serious Doubts About School Effectiveness* (Gorard, 2010), in which he makes a powerful case that VA measures are practically meaningless, damaging and should be abandoned. I was not sure what to make of it, but I had an excellent problem statement for a potential PhD and a strong desire to know more. I had also found a topic which brought together my interests, my education and was something that I thought was important and timely. So I got in touch with Professor Gorard, put together a proposal and – on winning an ESRC studentship – the decision to embark on a PhD was made.

Foundations

My thesis examines the validity of school value-added measures and the validity of arguments for their interpretation and use (Perry, 2016a). Below, I describe what I did and what I found. However, what tends to be missed off in a thesis write up is an account of all the blind alleys, tangents, training, and study that took place, particularly in the first 12 to 18 months. So before discussing my PhD thesis, I am going to say a few words about the foundational first year or so of my PhD studies. As an ESRC student, I had to undertake some further training. I am of the view that the foundation for every strong, ambitious PhD project is a topic with personal and academic value, and ideally policy and/or practice relevance too. Moreover, we should not understate the importance of the foundational work – via concerted study, training, and preliminary research – needed to develop clear, feasible, and incisive research questions, and research plans designed to do the best possible job of answering them.

It was not until the second year that my methods and precise focus really took shape. I had a topic (value-added), and a few potentially original angles involving new data and analyses. In particular, I had a question about whether we might replace school value-added measures with regression discontinuity (RD) measures. RD measures use the school year cut-off between August 31st and September 1st to estimate the effect of an additional year of school. The idea is that pupils born in England on the 31st of August are only one day older but have had an extra year of schooling compared to their peers born 1st September. Therefore, it is possible to estimate the unbiased impact of this additional year. Because this measures the causal impact of the school, it is ostensibly far more robust than the value-added approach which identifies and uses the difference between pupils' actual scores and expectations based on (statistically) "like-for-like" students in other schools.

I had written a proposal which involved collecting quite a lot of pupil tracking data from schools to look at RD measures, but this was vague and, within weeks of starting, I had decided that RD measures were unlikely to work as a replacement for value-added as a within-school measure or an official measure of school effectiveness. I had decided that my original plans for data collection would be time consuming and not achieve much and that I did not have the data I needed to examine some of the questions that were emerging from the literature. Very little of what someone might see in my final thesis had (or could have) crystalised until I had got to grips with rather a lot of literature and had gained a working knowledge of research methods. Even with the best proposal and supervisory advice, few people start a PhD being familiar with a large body of literature, so in the early stages this needs to be worked at (how can you contribute to a "conversation" in the literature when you know so little about who everyone is and what has been said?). In hindsight, on day one all I really had was a topic and an ambition to know more, and it took a few months for me to realise that what I had planned in my proposal needed to be rethought and reworked.

The process of rebuilding my research plans was an iterative one which developed side-by-side with my growing understanding of literature in and around my topic and of research methods. I learnt what data was available, how I might analyse it, what had already been well researched in the literature and what questions remained. I told myself that I wanted to know "everything there is to know" about "measuring school performance". Having this broad test of relevance reflected my ambition to know as much as I could about my area as well as a desire to find the best possible focus for the empirical portion of my research. In my first 12+ months, I was also very conscious of the value of developing broad and advanced research methods and skills (in which I include writing, speaking and so on). I think that being ambitious in a PhD is partly about having an ambitious research programme, but it is also about having high and broad aims for development as a researcher. With value-added being fundamentally an econometric research method, methodological reading was especially important. This led me to read a chapter/paper every morning for most of my first year from a large pile of research methods textbooks and papers. My topic also had a strong political and practical angle, so I also got stuck into books and papers on education policy. The Education Secretary had decided that it was "wrong in principle" (Department for Education, 2010, p. 68) to have a measure that took student background into account, whereas as far as I could see, it was wrong not to!

Design and methods

Assessing the validity of value-added measures is far harder and more complex than one might think. Pupil outcomes are influenced by a range of "school factors" (such as how good the teaching is) and "non-school factors" (such as differences in the pupil intake). The latter are very important. "Raw" attainment measures such as average examination scores at age 16 reveal almost nothing about school effectiveness, but quite a lot about the characteristics of the school intake. The largest non-school factor is pupils' prior attainment (performance at the end of primary school before coming to a secondary school). There are also many substantial and persistent associations with contextual factors, such as economic disadvantage and English language status.

Faced with this problem of separating school and non-school factors, all VA and CVA measures work on the same eliminative logic of statistically controlling for non-school factors. The most basic assumption is that statistical "models appropriately control for pre-existing differences so that [value-added] estimates reflect the effects of the teacher or school being evaluated and not the effects of prior schools, prior teachers or other pre-existing differences" (Marsh et al., 2011, p. 283). Once the influence of non-school factors is eliminated, one is left with differences in pupil performance that might be attributed to the school. But how valid is this assumption? And how would we know if it was not true? Key threats to validity such as the confounding effects of unobserved variables and measurement error are, by their nature, difficult to rule out. Many non-school factors which influence learning go unmeasured (Dearden et al., 2011) and may even be unmeasurable in practice. This means that it is very difficult to know the true causes of the differences captured in value-added evidence and, crucially, to what extent these differences are causally attributable to schools.

To investigate, I used three large datasets in four linked analyses. I can only present a brief summary of each in this chapter.

School performance data

In England, details of school performance and characteristics for all state-funded schools are published annually in "performance tables" by the Department for Education (DfE). It is possible to match schools across years of data using unique school reference numbers.

National pupil database

The DfE collects pupil-level data which combines data on pupil and school characteristics with examination results from key stage examination years. It is possible to apply for pupil-level data through application to the DfE (and now Office for National Statistics) who encourage use of the data for appropriate research or school improvement purposes. The NPD is a very large dataset and has performance data going back to 1996, which have been matched with School Census data since 2002.

Making good progress

The NPD contained performance data for pupils at National Curriculum end of Key Stage years (KS1–5, corresponding to ages 7, 11, 14, 16, and 18 respectively). The thesis, however, required data for year groups who were between these years. During initial searches for existing data to meet this need, a DfE study known as "Making Good Progress" (MGP) was identified and access requested. The MGP study looked at how pupils progressed during Key Stages 2 and 3, collecting teacher-assessed performance data for all cohorts within this age range for three study years. The MGP dataset is large with data for 148,135 pupils spanning 342 schools, 10 local authorities, 6 consecutive school year groups (UK years 3 to 9) across 3 years and is "broadly representative" of pupils in years 3 to 9 nationally (Department for Education, 2011, p. 6).

Results

The first analysis examines sources of observable bias and error, primarily using the official English value-added measure. As discussed above, an important policy issue was the decision to move from a CVA measure to a VA measure. I wanted to know whether there were significant biases in the official value-added measures linked to non-school factors such as the proportion of disadvantaged pupils in the school.

Figure 2.1 shows a series of scatter plots of the relationship between the official school VA measure and several non-school factors. FSM stands for free school meals – a measure of family low income – and CLA betokens children living in state care. The solid red line is a fitted trend line, estimated using ordinary least squares. The dashed horizontal line represents 12 points above and below the neutral value-added score of 1,000 on the "Best 8" attainment measure, equivalent to approximately 2 GCSE grade changes across the Best 8 GCSE scores for all pupils at the school. These results portray a serious source of inequity in the English accountability system. The results showed that of the 3,017 mainstream, maintained schools included in the analysis, over one third (1,116) would change their KS4 performance score by 1 or more grade per pupil if a contextualised VA measure

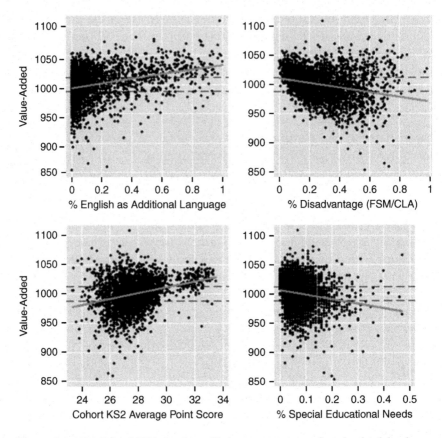

Figure 2.1 2014 School KS2–4 value-added scores against selected school level contextual variables

was used. Just over 10% of schools (310) would see results change by two or more GCSE grades or more per pupil.

For example, schools with more pupils eligible for free school meals, living in care, or with special educational needs (SEN), will tend to have lower value-added scores. And schools with higher attaining intakes tend to have higher value-added scores. This is so even though VA is meant to create scores independent of absolute level of attainment (and pupil background).

I conducted several sub-analyses including examining the level of missing data in the NPD and the influence of measurement error. These were important issues identified in previous research. In my original plans, assessing missing data and measurement error were positioned as roughly of equal importance to the overall thesis and analysis. In practice, their significance for the thesis was markedly different. For missing data, I found that overall rates were relatively low, but this was very difficult to assess given the practice of using default value such as the mean or the modal status (Evans, 2008). Official rates were low but that this was potentially a significant underestimate.

When it comes to the influence of measurement error, the findings were far more significant and led to a dedicated paper (Perry, 2019). This investigation started from a curious finding in the literature that I wanted to understand better: that VA measures were highly correlated with "raw" measures of final attainment (Gorard, 2006). Some correlation was to be expected, as higher performing schools would have both higher VA and higher attainment. But after controlling for prior attainment, the association ought to be far weaker. Also, I had found an association between school value-added and average prior attainment – where selective grammar schools for example had very high attaining students on entry also had much higher value-added. My (incorrect) assumption was that these two results were due to inadequate controls for prior attainment at pupil-level. Perhaps the relationship between prior and final attainment had been poorly specified? But this wasn't the case. When I looked at the pupil-level value-added, there was no relationship between VA and prior attainment (as one would hope). But when the school average was calculated and the same relationship was examined at school-level, these correlations suddenly appeared. This can be seen in Table 2.1.

What this table shows is that, despite (successful) control of prior attainment at *pupil-level* in the VA and CVA models, the *school-level* results

Table 2.1 Correlations between KS2–4 value-added measures, and raw scores for attainment at KS2 and KS4, 2004–2016

Year	Type of VA	KS2 correlation with VA	KS4 correlation with VA
2004	KS2–4 VA	.50	.85
2005	KS2–4 CVA	.01	.52
2006	KS2–4 CVA	.03	.43
2007	KS2–4 CVA	.00	.42
2008	KS2–4 CVA	.01	.29
2009	KS2–4 CVA	.01	.27
2010	KS2–4 CVA	.00	.27
2011	Best 8 VA	.17	.75
2012	Best 8 VA	.13	.76
2013	Best 8 VA	.15	.77
2014	Best 8 VA	.29	.75
2015	Best 8 VA	.38	.79
2016	Progress 8	.31	.74

for many VA measures are still highly correlated with prior attainment (which is the quintessential "non-school" factor) and a selective, grammar school effect pops up. What was going on? I must admit that I was quite stumped at the time and spent about a month poring over econometrics textbooks and the literature. This investigation led me to the prime suspect – measurement error in the prior attainment scores, coupled with a statistical issue known as "attenuation bias" which produces so-called "phantom" compositional effects (Perry, 2019). I asked myself how I might test this and decided to create a simulation where I introduce measurement error into the calculations and observed their effects. A carefully constructed simulation demonstrated – completely at odds with the common view that random pupil-level errors will cancel out at school-level (Reynolds et al., 2011) – that realistic levels of measurement error in prior attainment scores translated to appreciable school-level VA biases. Moreover, the "medium" level of error (based on expectations from research into examination reliability) produced a phantom grammar school "effect", uncannily similar to the ostensible grammar school effect identified in this study and by others.

In summary:

- School VA scores in England are not wholly independent of prior attainment at school-level.
- Failure to include contextual variables in the more recent VA measures has resulted in a number of substantial and systematic biases related to intake characteristics.
- There are several specific problems within the NPD that pose serious threats to the validity of school value-added measures. These relate to both measures of attainment and other contextual variables.
- Even random measurement error will translate to substantial school-level errors. This is especially the case for KS2–4 value-added and is likely to apply to VA measures more generally.

The second analysis involved comparison of a value-added measure with three variations of a regression discontinuity measure, also intended to assess school performance. As both VA and RD measures should be measuring school performance, a high correlation is an indication of the validity of each (convergent validity). The RD analysis also provided one of only a few estimates of absolute (rather than relative) school effects in the literature, by separating out age effects from school effects. Table 2.2 gives the age effect (per month) and the annual school effect for seven consecutive age groups (Years 3 to 9). Figures for other years of data are very similar and appear in Perry (2016b).

Table 2.2 Added year effects by national curriculum (NC) year at school, 2009–2010

National Curriculum year	Constant	Age effect per month	Annual progress
3	17.4	0.15	-
4	20.2	0.17	2.76
5	23.1	0.19	2.88
6	26.9	0.16	3.82
7	29.5	0.19	2.60
8	32.4	0.15	2.94
9	35.2	0.18	2.75

As well as showing the ability of regression discontinuity to calculate (overall) absolute school effects, the results are interesting in their own right. The average progress made in a year of schooling across the whole sample was approximately 3 National Curriculum points. This is in line with the design of the NC where 3 points are expected per year. Note, however, that in year 6, when national examinations are taken, progress exceeds this while progress in other NC years tends to be lower.

The overall school effect can be expressed as a percentage of the total progress: The mean annual rate of progress since the previous year is listed for each year. The overall mean age effect (per month) is approximately 0.17. This means that each year will see pupils making 2.04 points (12 × 0.17) of progress due to maturity alone. In this sense then, 2.04/3.00 (68%) of the observed improvement from year-to-year by pupils across this sample is due to pupil maturity and only 32% can be attributed to the impact of attending school.

Coming to the main question addressed in this study – I compared a CVA measure with two versions of a RD measure and what I called a "longitudinal" regression discontinuity (LRD) design that used two consecutive years of data to estimate a gain score for the pupils in question with the age effect subtracted. I found that CVA and LRD measures had high to very high correlations. The RD designs generally yield moderate correlations with the CVA measure but in some cases correlations were as low as 0.28.

In summary:

- Progress is heavily patterned by year group in the English system. Year 6 results (as used in KS1–2 VA and KS2–4), for example, are considerably higher than other years.
- Value-added is successfully capturing (but not attributing) differences in progress between pupils, at least to the extent to which the underlying measure of performance can accurately capture these.

- The standard regression discontinuity design is *not* suitable for comparing the effectiveness of different schools on an individual basis.
- The regression discontinuity design shows considerable promise as a way of monitoring or comparing systems or large groups of schools.

The third analysis addressed the temporal stability of the English value-added measure and the stability of estimated CVA performance for given MGP cohorts over time (see above). This study is made up two main parts. The first was a replication of Gorard et al. (2012) and Leckie and Goldstein (2011) using more up-to-date data (Table 2.3).

The stability of primary school VA scores is around 0.6, 0.46, and 0.35 for scores 1, 2, and 3 years apart, respectively. This level of instability in primary-level value-added scores means either that value-added is not providing a valid measure or that effectiveness is not a stable property of primary schools (Marks, 2015). It must be remembered that these correlations would need to be squared to create an "effect" size. Only just over a third of variation in schools' VA (0.6×0.6) can be associated with their scores just a year later. The figures for secondary schools are similar but slightly better. This kind of finding has now been confirmed over time, across different systems and using numerous datasets and is squarely at odds with the use of school value-added for high-stakes accountability. Use of VA does not make sense if it not both meaningful and a relatively permanent characteristic of schools.

In summary:

- School value-added scores have moderate to very low stability over time. Correlations drop very quickly when looking at performance 1, 2, and 3 years apart.
- Instability is not strongly linked with initial poor performance. It is a general characteristic of the value-added scores across the performance range.

The fourth analysis examined the issue of consistency within value-added measures, using the MGP dataset. If the performance of different age cohorts

Table 2.3 Pairwise correlations over time in primary school value-added measures

	1 year earlier	2 years earlier	3 years earlier
2014	0.61	0.46	0.35
2013	0.60	0.45	–
2012	0.59	–	–

Number of schools ranges annually from 13.473 to 14,454.

within a single school at a given point in time have a low correlation, this would suggest that the school VA measure is only reflective of the single cohort that has just completed the end of key stage examinations (and has now left the school). It would not be a school characteristic as such.

The correlations between cohorts at the same primary schools were generally very low to moderately low (Table 2.4). This means that knowing the CVA performance of Year 6 (11-year-olds) in a primary school relative to similar pupils in other schools reveals very little about the performance of Year 3 or Year 4. Even the correlation of consecutive years' performance of around 0.5 is not high. The CVA performances of Year 6 explains just 25% of the variance in Year 5 performances. It seems that VA scores, whatever they may represent, are not measures of whole school effectiveness. The figures for secondary schools are again similar but again slightly better.

These results provide a bleak picture of consistency in cohort performances within schools. These differences are sufficiently large to be a highly plausible driver of the year-to-year instability in the official VA measures demonstrated in Table 2.3, as different cohorts pass through the school. However, the instability of performance for cohorts across time now suggests that instability is a more general problem with the measures themselves.

I went on to look at consistency at pupil-level within cohorts as well. These analyses revealed huge variation in pupil performance underlying any given VA score. The mean VA score used for the official measures – completely at odds to the stated intentions of the measure – "masks" the performance of individual pupils under the average figure. In Perry (2016a, 2016b) I argue for the mean to be replaced with bands giving the proportion of pupils at several levels of value-added to make this variation clear rather than disguise it with an average figure.

Table 2.4 Pairwise correlations of cohort CVA scores, primary schools, 2008–2010

Year of data	National Curriculum year	Correlation with 1 year lower	Correlation with 2 years lower	Correlation with 3 years lower
2008	6	0.28	0.13	0.13
2009	6	0.49	0.27	0.19
2010	6	0.50	0.24	0.31
2008	5	0.46	0.29	–
2009	5	0.52	0.39	–
2010	5	0.59	0.40	–
2008	4	0.44	–	–
2009	4	0.48	–	–
2010	4	0.51	–	–

In summary:

- Consistency of VA scores over time, and between cohorts, in the same schools is rather low.
- School value-added scores mask very large differences in pupil performance within schools.

Implications and impact

Throughout the literature review chapters and substantive empirical studies of the thesis, I wrestled with the question of whether school value-added measures were valid and fair. In doing so, I created original and up-to-date results around direct (biases and error) and indirect (instability and inconsistency) threats to validity. At best, one can conclude that value-added scores contain an appreciable amount of error and bias, and so need to be interpreted with great caution alongside other sources of evidence. At worst, value-added scores may be so dwarfed by error and bias that, in the vast majority of cases, the scores will be highly misleading and any significant action taken as a result of value-added evidence will be ill-advised and potentially damaging. The truth may be somewhere between these positions. Value-added certainly cannot be characterised as a robust measure of school performance. Perhaps most importantly, the easy assumption by school effectiveness advocates that errors in the data are random and so will tend to cancel out has been shown to be false.

My overall conclusion however on validity was that "it depends". A central conclusion of the thesis is that validity is often best considered in relation to interpretation and use of a measure rather than just being considered as a property of a specific measure (Messick, 1987; Kane, 2013). This position draws on thinking in validity theory stressing the importance of considering validity (and validation) in far broader terms than the technical validity of specific measures (Newton and Shaw, 2014). I wrote a whole section on validity as interpretation and use where I identified a full range of factors affecting interpretation of validity at every stage of the production and use of VA measures, relating to: data quality; specification and modelling; output and presentation; use context and users; interpretation; uses, actions, and consequences. I also discussed users (policy-makers, teachers and school leaders, researchers) and different purposes to which the measures could be put. I feel there was and is huge scope for improvement in which value-added measures are used by policy-makers and within accountability systems, in how these are presented, and in how they are used by the inspectorate, school leaders and parents.

I devoted considerable time and effort in the years following the publication of my thesis and associated papers to contribution in public debates. This work led to my work being cited widely and internationally including by UNESCO, the Young Lives International Study, FFT Education Datalab and featured in national news media, including Schools Week, numerous blogs, and on BBC Radio 4, for which I was interviewed as an expert on school performance measures. I also took up in 2018 programme leadership of the educational leadership masters programmes at the University of Birmingham, which I had been teaching on since the second year of my PhD (2013). While less visible than some of the more public routes to sharing my research and understanding of VA, the conversations I had with educational leaders and students were some of the most rewarding and valuable.

I remain disappointed that the DfE is yet to make any of the simple changes required to make the English "Progress" measures fairer, and more accurate (Perry, 2018). The English accountability system therefore continues with a headline performance measure that is knowingly disadvantageous to schools with a disproportionate number of pupils whose characteristics are associated with lower performance such as those classified as being in poverty, and advantageous to schools with higher attaining intakes, such as selective grammar schools. It is a system that masks large within-cohort, -school, and -subject variation in performance; and that fails to communicate to (any of) its users the serious limitations of the measures.

Looking back

I started my PhD journey not knowing where my research might take me, and whether I would pursue an academic career or return to school teaching. What really grabbed me about value-added measures was the connection of methodology (in particular relating to secondary analysis), questions of social justice (relating to inequitable measures), effectiveness (trying to improve education), and evidence-informed policy and practice. These all still lie at the heart of my interests. Looking back, I wish I had done more fieldwork and a systematic review as part of my PhD, I had to learn those skills afterwards. But these things aside, my PhD laid solid foundations for my academic career, and – even if I had decided against pursuing a career involving research – it was a hugely rewarding and formative experience.

References

Dearden, L., Miranda, A., and Rabe-Hesketh, S. (2011). Measuring school value added with administrative data: The problem of missing variables. *Fiscal Studies*, 32(2), pp. 263–278.

Department for Education. (2010). The importance of teaching: The schools white paper.

Department for Education. (2011). How do pupils progress during key stages 2 and 3? Research Report DFE-RR096. Education Standards Analysis and Research Division, Department for Education .... DFE-RR-REPORT-TEMPLATE-FRONT-JL (publishing.service.gov.uk).

Evans, H. (2008). Value-added in English schools. *Education Finance and Policy*. Available at: Microsoft Word - VAMinEnglishSchools_HEvens.doc (psu.edu).

Gorard, S. (2006). Value-added is of little value. *Journal of Education Policy*, 21(2), pp. 235–243.

Gorard, S. (2010). Serious doubts about school effectiveness. *British Educational Research Journal*, 36(5), pp. 745–766.

Gorard, S., Hordosy, R., and Siddiqui, N. (2012). How unstable are "school effects" assessed by a value-added technique? *International Education Studies*, 6(1), pp. 1–9.

Kane, M.T. (2013). Validating the interpretations and uses of test scores. *Journal of Educational Measurement*, 50(1), pp. 1–73.

Leckie, G., and Goldstein, H. (2011). Understanding uncertainty in school league tables. *Fiscal studies*, 32(2), pp. 207–224.

Marks, G.N. (2015). The size, stability, and consistency of school effects: Evidence from Victoria. *School Effectiveness and School Improvement*, 26(3), pp. 397–414.

Marsh, H.W., Nagengast, B., Fletcher, J., and Televantou, I. (2011). Assessing educational effectiveness: Policy implications from diverse areas of research. *Fiscal Studies*, 32(2), pp. 279–295.

Messick, S. (1987). Validity. *ETS Research Report Series*, 1987(2), p. i-208.

Newton, P., and Shaw, S. (2014). *Validity in Educational and Psychological Assessment*. London: Sage.

Perry, T. (2016a). *The Validity, Interpretation and Use of School Value-Added Measures*. Edgbaston, UK: University of Birmingham.

Perry, T. (2016b). Inter-method reliability of school effectiveness measures: A comparison of value-added and regression discontinuity estimates. *School Effectiveness and School Improvement*, 28(1), pp. 22–38.

Perry, T. (2018). School progress measures are a missed opportunity for a fairer and more informative approach. Available at: https://blog.bham.ac.uk/socialsciencesbirmingham/2018/05/25/school-progress-measures-are-a-missed-opportunity-for-a-fairer-and-more-informative-approach/

Perry, T. (2019). "Phantom" compositional effects in English school value-added measures: The consequences of random baseline measurement error. *Research Papers in Education*, 34(2), pp. 239–262.

Reynolds, D., Chapman, C., Kelly, A., Muijs, D., and Sammons, P. (2011). Educational effectiveness: The development of the discipline, the critiques, the defence, and the present debate. *Effective Education*, 3(2), pp. 109–127.

CHAPTER 3

Is Progress 8 a valid and reliable measure of school effectiveness?

Mark Ledger

Introduction

Progress 8 is the Department for Education's headline indicator of secondary school performance in England (DfE, 2020). It is used as a measure of the progress that students make from the beginning of Key Stage 3 (age 11–12) to the end of Key Stage 4 (age 16–17), and is assumed to reflect the contribution that educational stakeholders make to students' learning. The results inform funding decisions and are intended to guide parents in selecting the best school for their child. They are utilised during Office for Standards in Education (OFSTED) inspections and schools' formative assessments, and have provided the basis for evaluating the equity of state-education. Schools' scores therefore matter and people's lives are affected by the results. However, both the validity and reliability of this type of value-added model have been questioned and the debates about their fairness remain unresolved (Morris et al., 2018).

One of the major problems for value-added models is that while raw-attainment scores for each school are reasonably stable over time, the value-added scores based on them are more volatile (Dumay et al., 2014). This instability does not prove that there is a problem with the measures, but it is how construct irrelevant variance would manifest (Perry, 2016).

This thesis addresses these concerns by scrutinising Progress 8 using four different research approaches. More specifically, it investigates whether the differences between schools' annual performance ratings and the change in schools' ratings over time can be explained by the kinds of factors that educational effectiveness is usually attributed to and, perhaps more importantly, whether these factors are under the control of schools. It also tests whether school leaders' expert knowledge of their institutions allows them to predict any annual changes in their schools' performance figures.

DOI: 10.4324/9781003201366-4

Background

What all stakeholders in education want is a fair measure of school performance. School effects, though, are not a readily-observable or manifest quality of schools (Gorard, 2011). In fact, attaining a valid and reliable measure of the contribution that schools make to their students' learning is more difficult than one might expect (Dumay et al., 2014). Whilst school effectiveness can be conceptualised in a multitude of different ways, the dominant approach in England and many other countries has been to use test scores as an indicator of students' cognitive development (Creemers and Kyriakides, 2008). However, it has long been acknowledged that comparing the raw performance of each school is insufficient as these figures are heavily biased by the initial ability and characteristics of schools' intakes (Goldstein and Woodhouse, 2000). It is therefore unfair to judge schools on their output alone, as their students can often have vastly different starting points (Raudenbush, 2004). This of course does not mean that schools are not differentially effective but indicates that we need a measure of school effectiveness that is capable of fairly differentiating between differences in pupil intake and genuine school effects.

Value-added models were developed to address this need. Although a variety of models exist, featuring increasingly sophisticated predictions, they all rely upon the same fundamental principles (Teddlie and Reynolds, 2000). Rather than measuring students' raw attainment, these models judge success by the progress that students make whilst attending a school (Lubienski and Lubienski, 2006). Data on all pupils in the relevant school population is used to predict how well students should perform in later assessments (Gorard, 2010). The difference between this estimate and the student's actual result is then used to judge how much progress the individual has made in comparison to similar individuals from other schools (Fitz-Gibbon, 1997). A positive residual indicates that the pupil has made more than the average amount of progress for their starting point, whilst a negative score shows that the pupil has made less progress than expected. A residual of zero indicates that the child's progression is in line with that of similar students from other schools. The results of these individual assessments are then averaged at school-level to provide an estimate of how effective the school is in comparison to other institutions. In theory, by comparing the performance of students with that of comparable pupils, this process removes the effect of differential pupil intake to schools, making value-added assessments a fairer and more valid measure of school performance (Rutter et al., 1979; Sandoval-Hernandez, 2008).

Value-added assessments of school performance therefore seem like a good idea. However, the validity of the method is not universally accepted

(Hoyle and Robinson, 2003). Much of the debate stems from the fact that schools' influence is envisaged as a latent property that is revealed by the calculation itself (Gorard et al., 2013). Once all extraneous influences have ostensibly been accounted for, it is presumed that any differences between the predicted and actual attainment of students are causally attributable to schools and thus that the scores represent the true contribution that each institution has made to its students' learning (Marsh et al., 2011).

It is important to recognise that whilst all value-added models rely heavily upon this assumption, it will never truly be the case (Coe and Fitz-Gibbon, 1998). Accurately modelling the impact of all of the extraneous influences upon students' learning is a practical impossibility (Meyer, 1997) and the problem cannot be negated with technical solutions (Creemers et al., 2010; Visscher, 2001). All value-added estimates will therefore contain any genuine educational effect and an error component of unknown size (Gorard, 2010). They are only approximations to school contributions (Fitz-Gibbon, 1997). A key question addressed in this thesis is therefore whether it is justified to treat these differences as an effect, or as inaccuracies because the main threats to validity, such as omitted variable bias and measurement error are difficult to rule out. Important influences are often neglected (Dearden et al., 2011) and some factors may even be unmeasurable in a practical context (Tymms, 1996). All of this uncertainty makes it difficult to be certain which mechanisms are responsible for the differences in schools' ratings and crucially whether these are under the control of schools. This thesis focusses on the Progress 8 measure and its role in the English secondary school accountability system. The problem, however, is common to all value-added models.

The empirical basis for the thesis

What is noticeable about research in this area, whether leading to support for or critique of value added is that it is conducted *post hoc* with existing datasets using non-experimental designs. It is a kind of increasingly sophisticated "dredging" for results. Such an important issue and current policy requires a better research base than that. The empirical sections of the thesis therefore set out to evaluate Progress 8 from new perspectives, with the researcher's and others' expectations set out clearly before any data was collected. The prospective element removes the temptation to re-interpret relationships after the results have been collated and provides a more convincing form of evidence.

The underlying assumption is that, if school effects are genuine, then one would expect leaders to be able to predict accurately an appreciable proportion of the value-added scores that schools receive, both at specific moments in time and over time. They would do this based on appraisal of their school's policies and practices, and any changes they know of since their last value-added score. Internal assessments of students' attainment could likewise be draw upon. I make this assertion because school leaders are a key authority for their schools. They are instrumental in developing their school's mission, structure, policies, culture, resources and strategies for improvement (Leithwood et al., 1998). It is therefore reasonable to presume that these individuals will have a detailed knowledge of the factors that differential school effectiveness is normally attributed to both in policy and research. If Progress 8 provides a valid and reliable measure of school performance, then knowledge of such factors and how they might have changed should help leaders to anticipate their schools' ratings. Even after we take into account that value-added ratings are a relative construct and that the precise Key Stage 4 attainment level required to achieve a particular ratings will vary slightly each year, it stands to reason that if the measure has any pragmatic value, those with the most informed opinion should be able to foresee, at the very least, any dramatic changes in their school "effect". Is this true?

Similarly, if school effects are causally attributable to schools, then we should find appreciable correlations between schools' ostensible value-added scores and indicators of effectiveness in their policy and practice. Since the late 1960s effectiveness researchers have tried to explain why some students and/or schools perform better than others. A common approach has been to identify factors that correlate with students' raw-attainment and to integrate these into conceptual models of educational effectiveness. My study adapted one of these frameworks "The Dynamic Model of Educational Effectiveness" (Creemers and Kyriakides, 2008), and used it to identify the factors that could have the greatest impact upon schools' Progress 8 results. These formed the basis of a questionnaire for school leaders.

Participation in Progress 8 is mandatory for all state-funded mainstream secondary schools in England. In 2018, a total of 3,659 schools fell into this category (EduBase, 2018). However, after restricting the sampling frame to exclude pupil referral units and schools that do not educate students from the beginning of Key Stage 3 to the end of Key Stage 4, the population for my study became 2,991 schools. The research used a convenience sample of 192 schools from this population. More specifically, all of the schools in the sampling frame were identified to using Edubase. Each was contacted via email requesting that they take part in the study. Non-responses were followed up with a second invitation. The researcher also visited all schools within a 50 mile radius of Durham to provide a more thorough outline of the project and to encourage participation.

An obvious limitation of this approach is that convenience samples are vulnerable to selection bias, and so differences between the achieved sample of schools and the population they are intended to represent. In this project however the primary objective was not to describe the distribution of a variable within the population. The principal concerns were to establish whether these school leaders could anticipate changes in their school performance ratings and whether correlates from educational effectiveness research could predict variation in the measures. The priority was therefore to ensure that a wide range of Progress 8 scores, estimations and practices were represented. This necessitated a large sample, which the adopted sampling procedures made possible.

Leaders' predictions of their upcoming value-added ratings for 2018, their appraisals of schools' policies and practices, any information about school intakes and examination entry practices, and their descriptions of school factors relevant to theories of educational effectiveness, were collected using electronic questionnaires, issued and returned between March 2018 and July 2018. Schools' value-added scores and data on the 2017 and 2018 cohorts for each school were accessed through DfE school-level performance datasets. See the thesis for fuller details of the instrument(s) used, and the complete dataset (Ledger, 2021).

Key findings

Can leaders predict their VA scores?

Based on responses from 182 schools, I computed the average deviation between school leaders' estimates of their upcoming 2018 value-added scores, and their schools' subsequent Progress 8 scores. Any deviation was expressed both in absolute terms and relative to size of schools' Progress 8 scores, with the relative error being defined as the difference between schools' official Progress 8 ratings and leaders' predictions, divided by the official Progress 8 score of the school. These figures establish how far school leaders' estimates were from the schools' actual performance ratings. A high degree of consistency between actual and predicted scores would be viewed as tentative evidence of Progress 8's validity, whereas large discrepancies would be treated as a cause for concern. The leaders would have known of, and were explicitly asked about, any changes in the school that could affect value-added scores. Small to moderate deviations, however, might be expected.

Sizeable prediction errors were common (mean absolute error = 0.19, standard deviation = 0.15, maximum error = 0.66), with many dwarfing the size of the schools' value-added residuals (mean relative error = 1.89, standard deviation = 5.39; maximum relative error = 43.00). Nearly 40% of leaders were unable to specify whether their schools' rating would improve, remain the same or decline in their next evaluation. Given the level of information that school leaders have at their disposal, this is not a high success rate. The unpredictability of Progress 8 ratings by experts suggests that they may not provide an accurate and reliable measure of school performance.

I calculated the correlation between school leaders' predictions and schools' Progress 8 scores, to establish whether higher than average predictions were associated with higher than average scores (R). This also yielded the proportion of the variation in Progress 8 scores that school leaders anticipated (R-squared).

As anticipated schools' performance ratings were volatile over time. In fact, the association observed between consecutive Progress 8 ratings (R = 0.78) was comparable but slightly lower than the correlation between consecutive Best 8 value added ratings in prior studies (Gorard et al., 2013; Leckie and Goldstein, 2009). This level of association means that even one year apart only 60% of the variation in schools' scores was consistent. Were this level of association to continue, schools' scores would be largely unrelated after only a few years. The same correlation between scores, for example, would result in 36% of the variation in ratings being consistent over two years, 22% over three, 13% over four and less than 8% after five years. This is concerning as parents have been actively encouraged to select their child's secondary school based on value-added ratings that were calculated six years before their child would sit their Key Stage 4 examinations. After such a prolonged period, however, it is doubtful that the earlier ratings, when the child was aged 11, would tell them anything about the education their child will receive. Progress 8 scores are not a good method for selecting the best secondary school for one's child.

If a high proportion of the variation in school effectiveness ratings were genuine, it is reasonable to expect that school leaders would have been able to anticipate changes in their schools' scores. The evidence in my study however demonstrated that the foresight of school leaders was limited. Whilst there was a reasonable correlation between school leaders' estimates of their school's Progress 8 scores and their school's official value-added ratings (R = 0.82), school leaders were not able to predict the new scores much better than merely using the known 2017 ratings. The high correlation between school leaders' estimates and the schools' previous performance ratings (R = 0.86) suggests that most of their ability to predict scores came directly from their knowledge of the 2017 results and/or them having access to the 2017 national attainment averages. Some leaders stated as much in their response.

It also is worth acknowledging though that even if reported correlations are interpreted in the best possible light and it is assumed that the inability of school leaders' to predict their schools' ratings is hindered only by the changes in the performance of other schools (the zero-sum problem), this would still be concerning. This is because the ratings would only allow school leaders to respond to the evaluations in a retrospective manner, and to act based on the performance of students that have already left their school. This raises the question of whether a relative measure of between-school performance is the best choice of performance indicator, even if it worked. An absolute measure such a regression discontinuity or a within-school measure may have greater utility.

A multiple-regression model was created, with schools' Progress 8 scores (2018) as the dependent variable, and the schools' former (2017) and predicted ratings (2018) entered as independent variables. These variables were entered in stages, so that the relationship between schools' Progress 8 ratings of 2017 and 2018 could be assessed, followed by the net impact of school leaders' predictions. Educational stakeholders would have access to schools' 2017 ratings, and the worth of leaders' predictions must therefore be judged in relation to the variation that the 2017 scores could explain. It was also expected that school leaders' insight would account for additional variation that the preceding ratings could not. The more unique information that school leaders' provide, the more useful the information they provide. The result showed that leaders are generally not able to predict a new set of scores for their school any better than just using the previous year's scores.

Testing the educational effectiveness model

A further series of regression models were created, involving 125 schools, to identify school factors that predict Progress 8 scores or changes in Progress 8 scores, and to help assess whether these factors are under the control of the school or not. The important consideration was the proportion of variation explained by factors that are within and outside of schools' control. Since all extraneous sources of bias have ostensibly been removed by the value-added calculation, all of the remaining useful variables should in theory be under schools' control.

Several forms of regression were used to evaluate whether this was the case. The first was a linear-regression model evaluating the relationship between each independent variable by itself and schools' Progress 8 scores, without controlling for external influences. The second was a forward-regression model which evaluated the collective influence of the 12 most useful predictive variables. And the third was a hierarchical model that evaluated the combined influence of the most predictive factors, using the underlying structure of the data, although all of the data was aggregated to the school-level before it was entered into the model.

An important contribution from this new study was that the models also assessed the influence of examination-entry differences (how much schools were "punished" for failing to fill Attainment 8 slots). Whilst it is recognised that the subject entry "buckets" and weightings were designed to incentivise schools' to provide all students with an academically-orientated programme of study, it was argued that if Progress 8 scores are intended to report upon the quality of schools' provisions, then the consequences of curricular deviations should not overwhelm the influence of instructional practices and policies. Otherwise Progress 8 would be mostly a model of curricular adherence.

The results suggest that non-school factors had a high and distorting level of influence on schools' value-added scores. Whether looking at the 2018 value-added scores, or changes in value-added from 2017 to 2018, two categories of extraneous variable had a close and persistent associations with schools' performance ratings. These were differences in school intakes, and differences in schools' examination entry practices. This was true whether simple linear, forward entry or hierarchical modelling were used.

Differences in school intakes, such as pupil SES, accounted for 44% of the variation in 2018 Progress 8 scores. This suggests that Progress 8 ratings provide an extremely biased appraisal of school performance that advantages schools with particular intakes. These intake variables also helped to explain the changes in schools' performance over time, though the effect recorded within this study was more modest (5% of variance was explained by changes in the three most influential intake characteristics).

Examination entry variables were also correlated with "performance". The more Attainment 8 slots that students filled the higher their school's performance rating was likely to be. The effect was sizeable, however, even after differences in schools' intake, instructional practices and policies had been taken into account. Differences in exam entry between schools accounted for over 20% of the variance in changes in schools' ratings from 2017 to 2018. These variables may play too great a role in the determination of schools' Progress 8 scores, especially when one considers the percentage of variance accounted for by other non-school factors.

These two groups of extraneous variables accounted for more variance, on average and collectively, than the operationalised aspects of schools' provisions. In fact, in the same hierarchical models, only 4% to 8% of the variation in schools' results, and 3% of the variation in schools' results over time, could be explained by school leaders' expert knowledge of the schools' instructional practices. Schools' policies were no more predictive; these explained a negligible amount of the variation in schools' results and just 3% of variation in results over time.

Though a substantial portion of the variation in schools' ratings remained unexplained and might therefore be attributed to school-related or to extraneous variables (although there is no way of knowing which), this is a concerning finding which suggests that the bias within Progress 8 measures has the capacity to overwhelm any genuine differences in schools' effectiveness.

In-depth analysis

Nine schools agreed to complete the very long version of the questionnaire that asked them about every aspect of the theoretical model of educational effectiveness. These were analysed in the same ways as the larger number of schools (above), but this time with a greater range of variables – including variations in the focus, timing and differentiation of school-related factors. The results showed that school-related factors could account for a higher percentage of variance when additional dimensions of the constructs were considered. The quality of teachers' instructional behaviour, for example, was of importance as it explained more of the variation in schools' performance that the frequency of specific actions and/or activities. The substantive findings of the analysis were, however, no different from above. Intake and examination variables still accounted for a higher percentage of variance, on average, than school-related variables.

The propagation of errors

I also ran a simulation with the full dataset to assess the implications of there being inaccuracies in students' Key Stage 2 and Key Stage 4 data. More specifically, the DfE national attainment averages were used to evaluate how a 10% measurement error in students' Key Stage 2 fine-levels would impact upon students' progression scores. The magnitude of these inaccuracies was then compared to the error that would occur if students' Attainment 8 score were over-stated by 10%. As far as I know, the relative effect of the two types of error has not been explored before.

The results showed that any errors within students' Key Stage 2 data tend to translate into larger discrepancies in the Attainment 8 estimates, both in absolute terms and relative to the original Key Stage 4 value. Were a student with an actual Key Stage 2 prior-attainment level of 5.2 to receive a fine-level rating of 5.7, for example, this would manifest as a 19.5 point error in the students' Attainment 8 estimate, which amounts to a 35.5% over-statement of their true Attainment 8 score.

One explanation for the discrepancy is the fact that students with favourable starting points will often pull further ahead during their education, and *vice versa* (Ready, 2013). It makes sense that the difference between the mean attainments of two dissimilar groups of students would expand between Key Stage 2 and Key Stage 4, making the consequences of misjudging a student's initial performance level graver than misjudging their final attainment by the same amount. The effect also occurred in the opposite direction, when students' earlier attainment was underestimated. Since these errors are outside of schools control, the potential for them to impact upon schools' performance ratings is substantial (see Perry, 2019).

Conclusion

The thesis therefore concludes that Progress 8 does not provide a valid or trustworthy measure of school performance. The scores are very volatile and whilst this could theoretically be explained by genuine changes in school performance, the evidence suggests that this is not the case. Of greatest concern is the impact that school intake appears to have upon schools' ratings. These factors, most noticeably differences between students' attendance and socio-economic status, have close associations with school performance that effectively punish schools with educationally disadvantaged cohorts. There is also evidence to suggest that errors in students' prior-attainment have the potential to impact upon schools' ratings and that schools' examination entry practices have too great a sway over the results. What is more, school-related factors (on teaching for example) accounted for a surprisingly low percentage of the variation in the scores, and whilst sceptical readers may attribute part of this to the authors' methodological decisions, it is notable that school leaders were no more successful in explaining the results.

What does this mean for policy?

The evidence summarised here suggests that the DfE's use of Progress 8, and indeed any value-added models, should be reconsidered. The measure is not valid or reliable enough to be used to make high-stakes decisions. The ratings are too biased to provide a fair measure of schools' contributions and too unstable to provide parents with dependable information about the effect attending one school over another.

Particular objection is taken to the decision to ignore differences in pupils' demographic and socioeconomic characteristics. This is profoundly unfair. Whilst most people would agree that schools bear some of the responsibility for addressing the inequities within society, failing to acknowledge external influences and their effect upon students' achievement essentially credits or blames schools for the educational affluence of the populations that they serve. Many researchers have therefore asserted that uncontextualised value-added models, such as Progress 8, are likely to reward and punish the wrong schools, and the new results support this idea.

The inaccurate classification of schools also has the capacity to undermine the national accountability system and any effect that it has upon students' learning. Furthermore, when used in high-stakes situations value-added models may discourage schools from admitting particular types of pupil, or encourage them to find ways of excluding weaker students from examinations. Indeed, since the introduction of Progress 8 there has been a notable rise in pupil exclusions (DfE, 2018), which has been partially attributed to schools attempting to game the accountability system (Leckie and Goldstein, 2019). It is likewise important to remember that schools' progression scores also reflect upon teachers. So, if disadvantaged schools are more likely to receive negative ratings, there is an incentive for effective teachers to relocate to advantaged schools where their efforts and skillsets are more likely to be recognised. Both of these side effects would exacerbate existing social inequalities.

References

Coe, R., and Fitz-Gibbon, C. (1998). School effectiveness research: Criticisms and recommendations. *Oxford Review of Education*, 24(4), pp. 421–438. doi: 10.1080/0305498980240401

Creemers, B., and Kyriakides, L. (2008). *The Dynamics of Educational Effectiveness: A Contribution to Policy, Practice and Theory in Contemporary Schools*. Oxford: Routledge.

Creemers, B., Kyriakides, L., and Sammons, P. (2010). *Methodological Advances in Educational Effectiveness Research*. Routledge.

Dearden, L., Miranda, A., and Rabe-Hesketh, S. (2011). Measuring school value added with administrative data: The problem of missing variables. *Fiscal Studies*, 32(2), pp. 263–278. doi: 10.1111/j.1475-5890.2011.00136.x

DfE (2018). *Permanent and Fixed Period Exclusions in England: 2016 to 2017*. London: Department for Education. Retrieved from https://www.gov.uk/government/statistics/permanent-and-fixed-period-exclusions-in-england-2016-to-2017

DfE (2020, February). *Secondary Accountability Measures Guide for Maintained Secondary Schools, Academies and Free Schools*. London: Department for Education. Retrieved from https://assets.publishing.service.gov.uk/government/uploads/system/uploads/attachment_data/file/872997/Secondary_account-ability_measures_guidance_February_2020_3.pdf

Dumay, X., Coe, R., and Anumendem, D. (2014). Stability over time of different methods of estimating school performance. *School Effectiveness and School Improvement*, 25(1), pp. 64–82. doi: 10.1080/09243453.2012.759599

EduBase (2018). NPD Key Stage 4 performance tables – England (revised version) [Dataset]. Accessed through https://get-information-schools.service.gov.uk/Downloads

Fitz-Gibbon, C. (1997). *The Value Added National Project: Final Report: Feasibility Studies for a National System of Value-added Indicators*. SCAA.

https://assets.publishing.service.gov.uk/government/uploads/system/uploads/attachment_data/file/605795/0297_CarolTaylorFitz-Gabbon__Feasibility_Study_Nat_System_VA_Indicators.pdf

Goldstein, H., and Woodhouse, G. (2000). School effectiveness research and educational policy. *Oxford Review of Education*, 26(3–4), pp. 353–363. doi: 10.1080/3054980020001873

Gorard, S. (2010). Serious doubts about school effectiveness. *British Educational Research Journal*, 36(5), pp. 745–766. doi: 10.1080/01411920903144251

Gorard, S. (2011). Now you see it, now you don't: School effectiveness as conjuring? *Research in Education*, 86(1), pp. 39–45. doi: 10.7227/RIE.86.4

Gorard, S., Hordosy, R., and Siddiqui, N. (2013). How unstable are "school effects" assessed by a value-added technique? *International Education Studies*, 6(1), pp. 1–9. doi: 10.5539/ies.v6n1p1

Hoyle, R., and Robinson, J. (2003). League tables and school effectiveness: A mathematical model. *Proceedings of the Royal Society of London B*, 270, pp. 113–199. doi: 10.1098/rspb.2002.2223

Leckie, G., and Goldstein, H. (2009). The limitations of using school league tables to inform school choice. *Journal of the Royal Statistical Society*, 172(4), pp. 835–851. doi: 10.1111/j.1467-985X.2009.00597.x

Leckie, G., and Goldstein, H. (2019). The importance of adjusting for pupil background in school value-added models: A study of Progress 8 and school accountability in England. *British Educational Research Journal*, 45(3), pp. 518–538. doi: 10.1002/berj.3511

Ledger, M. (2021). *Is Progress 8 a valid and reliable measure of school effectiveness?* Unpublished PhD thesis. School of Education, Leazes road, Durham: Durham University.

Leithwood, K., Leonard, L., and Sharratt, L. (1998). Conditions forstering organizational learning in schools. *Educational Administration Quarterly*, 34(2), pp. 243–276. doi: 10.1177/0013161X98034002005

Lubienski, S., and Lubienski, C. (2006). School sector and academic achievement: A multi-level analysis of NAEP mathematics data. *American Educational Research Journal*, 43(4), pp. 651–698. doi: 10.3102/00028312043004651

Marsh, H., Nagengast, B., Fletcher, J., and Televantou, I. (2011). Assessing educational effectiveness: Policy implications from diverse areas of research. *Fiscal Studies*, 32(2), pp. 279–295. doi: 10.1111/j.1475-5890.2011.00137.x

Meyer, R. (1997). Value-added indicators of school performance: A primer. *Economics of Education Review*, 16(3), pp. 283–301. doi: 10.1016/S0272-7757(96)00081-7

Morris, T., Davies, N., Dorling, D., Richmond, R., and Smith, G.D. (2018). Testing the validity of value-added measures of educational progress with genetic data. *British Educational Research Journal*, 44(5), pp. 725–747. doi: 10.1002/berj.3466

Perry, T. (2016). *The validity, interpretation and use of value-added measures.* Unpublished PhD thesis. Edgbaston, Birmingham: University of Birmingham.

Perry, T. (2019). "Phantom" compositional effects in English school value-added measures: The consequences of random baseline measurement error. *Research Papers in Education*, 34(2), pp. 239–262. doi: 10.1080/02671522.2018.1424926

Raudenbush, S. (2004). What are value-added models estimating and what does this imply for statistical practice? *Journal of Educational and Behavioral Statistics*, 29(1), pp. 121–129. doi: 10.3102/10769986029001121

Ready, D. (2013). Associations between student achievement and student learning implications for value-added school accountability models. *Educational Policy*, 27(1), pp. 92–120. doi: 10.1177/0895904811429289

Rutter, M., Maughan, B., Mortimore, P., and Ouston, J. (1979). *Fifteen Thousand Hours: Secondary Schools and their Effects on Children*. Harvard University Press, USA: Open Books Publishing Ltd.

Sandoval-Hernandez, A. (2008). School effectiveness research: A review of criticisms and some proposals to address them. *Educate*, Special Issue, pp. 31–44.

Teddlie, C., and Reynolds, D. (2000). *The International Handbook of School Effectiveness Research*. Farmer Press.

Tymms, P. (1996). Theories, models and simulations: School effectiveness at an impasse. In J. Gray, D. Reynolds, C. Fitz-Gibbon, and D. Jesson (eds.), *Merging Traditions: The Future of Research on School Effectiveness and School Improvement* (pp. 121–135). Cassell.

Visscher, A.J. (2001). Public school performance indicators: Problems and recommendations. *Studies in Educational Evaluation*, 27(3), pp. 199–214. doi: 10.1016/S0191-491X(01)00026-8

The stability problem in using value-added measurements for teacher performance evaluation

Ismail Aslantas

Introduction

Teachers are judged on their performance in various ways, which can have implications for a number of outcomes such as teachers' career, salaries, and motivation to stay (or not) in the profession. There are good reasons for monitoring teachers' performance. However, there is lack of consensus on the best way to capture teachers' performance, and how fair it is to judge them in relation to the students they teach, or the school where they work. This PhD adds to current debates by examining the stability of value-added models (VAMs) in estimating teacher effectiveness, when obtained under different data analysis methods, using contextual predictors such as observable student, teacher/classroom and school characteristics, or not, and varying the number of prior test scores. The study began with a systematic review of international evidence on the stability of VAMs, followed by an analysis of data for 1,027 teachers linked to 35,435 Grade 8 students (age 14) in one province in Turkey to test the stability of value-added estimates under various conditions. Integrating the results of this secondary data analysis with the systematic review provided an opportunity to make a strong comparison of the findings of the studies and to see the bigger picture.

Background

Teachers matter in the development of children, and for perhaps as long as schools have existed, governments have been concerned about the quality of teachers. Attempts have been made to identify what makes an effective teacher (Darling-Hammond, 2015; Rivkin et al., 2005). While most people think they know what an effective teacher would looks like, actually trying to measure these qualities is not easy nor straightforward (Darling-Hammond, 2000; Gorard, 2013; McCaffrey et al., 2003). Some common methods to judge teacher performance are classroom observations, student evaluation,

DOI: 10.4324/9781003201366-5

peer feedback, and use of portfolios. One approach that is increasingly being used in many countries is the value-added approach, where teachers are assessed in terms of the amount of progress their students make in standardised tests or assessments (Coe et al., 2014; Kane and Cantrell, 2010; Kane et al., 2015; See, 2020). Value-added approaches are portrayed as a more objective measure because the progress children made can be attributed to the teacher and this progress can be objectively measured. In a number of countries such teacher evaluation outcomes have been used for making high stake decisions regarding teacher promotion, salary increases, and even continuation of service. Teachers are rewarded or penalised based on these value-added measures.

Over the years different VAMs have been developed, utilising existing education datasets in statistical models. In such models, teachers' performance is estimated by using their students' test scores in a subject and grade. The impact of a teacher on student outcomes is estimated as the difference between what the students are expected to achieve and what they actually achieve (Kersting et al., 2013; Sander et al., 1997). Since VAMs are also used for making decisions about a teacher, such as promotion, transfer, dismissal, and wage increases, the reliability and validity of such models are of paramount importance. Despite increasing concerns about the reliability and validity of VAMs (Brown et al., 2010; Garrett and Steinberg, 2015; Glazerman et al., 2010; Rothstein, 2007; Stacy et al., 2018), policymakers' continue to use VAMs in accountability systems (McCaffrey et al., 2004; Swanson, 2009). Is this justified? Figure 4.1.

Conducting the systematic review

Findings the studies

When the related literature was initially examined, I realised that stability studies were carried out from three main perspectives. Therefore, in this systematic review, the stability of the estimates referred to the stableness of the estimates due to (a) the predictors used in the estimations, (b) the number of test scores used, and (c) the analysis methods applied. Existing literature on the stability of VAMs estimates was retrieved based on these three perspectives. To conduct the systematic review study, I followed the stages suggested by Torgerson (2003). To ensure that the search process was systematic and organised, I used a modified form of the Preferred Reporting Items for Systematic Reviews and Meta-Analyses (PRISMA) (Moher et al., 2009) flow diagram.

To identify appropriate databases to search, I contacted experts in the field and staff at the university library, and decided on a total of 17 electronic databases from 6 major providers. Other outputs were obtained from my

Figure 4.1 What does an effective teacher look like?

personal contacts with research centres, foundations, and researchers who have worked on teacher performance evaluation based on VAMs. I contacted well-known researchers in this area via e-mails and "ResearchGate.net" to identify isolated published and/or unpublished studies related to the review topic. I also manually searched reference lists of well-known studies to identify studies that may not have been picked up in the electronic databases using a snowballing approach. Google and Google Scholar were thoroughly searched for grey literature. Full details of the methods used in this chapter appear in my thesis.

I formulated appropriate search strings that are relevant to how stable teacher effectiveness estimates are measured by VAMs. The keywords included "teacher performance", "student performance", "value-added model" and "stability". I scanned some well-known studies to identify synonyms and alternatives. These search terms were then applied to databases and providers. Applying these search terms to the databases, a total of 1,439 articles were identified initially. I merged the results in EndNote X8 reference management software. This identified 492 duplicated results. A further 175 duplicated cases were identified by me during the screening phases. All duplicates were removed, leaving 772 unique pieces.

The next and most time-consuming stage in the review process was to screen the studies by applying a set of pre-agreed inclusion and exclusion criteria and removing irrelevant pieces. I did this in two steps. First, I excluded all pieces that were not written in English, relevant to education, set in K-12 or equivalent settings, primary or empirical research, and/or related to teacher evaluation. I did this by looking at the titles and abstracts. This removed a further 309 studies (and I kept those I labelled "not sure yet"). Next, I read the text of the remaining 463 pieces, using the same criteria as above, and adding 5 more. The other screening criteria were whether the report included:

- Statement of stability of estimates
- Student test or gains scores as dependent variables
- Observable student, teacher and school characteristics (e.g., sex, ethnicity, teaching experience, school type) as predictors
- The contribution of predictors to estimates
- The number of test scores used

I screened 473 remained studies (10 further studies were identified from alerts) and determined that 423 of these did not meet the criteria, leaving 50 for synthesis. To help ensure that relevant pieces were not mistakenly removed, a second reviewer was engaged to review a random sample of around 10% of the literature in the review list (70 papers). The percentage agreement between raters was 95% and the inter-rater reliability was 0.75.

Data extraction and quality appraisal

Quality appraisal is crucial for systematic reviews (El Soufi and See, 2019), because it helps to clarify the relationship between the differences in the strength of evidence of research and the differences between the results of these studies. It also helps for the interpretation of the findings (Bettany-Saltikov and McSherry, 2016), otherwise bundling weak and robust evidence in the same pot with equal weighting can lead to invalid or misleading conclusions. I used the "sieve" appraisal tool designed by Gorard (2014), which is a practical and easy to way evaluate the quality of individual studies. It takes into account the research design and factors that affect the validity of the study such as sample quality, scale, and attrition (Table 4.1).

Each study was judged in relation to the research design (whether the research design is an RCT with random allocation of cases), scale (sample size per comparison group), level of attrition (the incompleteness of data), data quality (how securely outcomes are measured), and given a padlock or security rating from 0 🔒 (no useful evidence) to 4 🔒 (most trustworthy). For more information on using the "sieve", see Gorard (2018).

For this review, I was interested in studies about the stability of VAMs and so those that were comparative or correlational in design were suitable for fulfil the aim of the research. If these were also large scale with low attrition, and allowed random student-teacher allocation they would be rated 4 🔒. The number of studies with each rating appears in Table 4.2 (studies with 0 rating are ignored here).

At the same time as the quality appraisal, the key data from each piece as extracted and recorded in a spreadsheet. This included key information about the individual studies in accordance with the purpose of the review,

Table 4.1 A "sieve" to assist in the estimation of trustworthiness of any research study

Design	Scale	Completeness of data	Data quality	Rating
Strong design for research question	Large number of cases per comparison group	Minimal missing data, no evidence of impact on findings	Standardised, independent, pre-specified, accurate	4 🔒
Good design for research question	Medium number of cases per comparison group	Some missing data, possible impact on findings	Standardised, independent, not pre-specified, some errors	3 🔒
Weak design for research question	Small number of cases per comparison group	Moderate missing data, likely impact on findings	Not standardised, independent, or pre-specified, some errors	2 🔒
Very weak design for research question	Very small number of cases per comparison group	High level of missing data, clear impact on findings	Weak measures, high level of error, too many outcomes	1 🔒
No consideration of design	A trivial scale of the study, or number is unclear	Huge amount of missing data, or not reported	Very weak measures, or accuracy not addressed	0 🔒

Table 4.2 A summary of study ratings

Rating	Number of studies found
4 🔒	13
3 🔒	33
2 🔒	2
1 🔒	2
Total	50

such as the author(s) names, date of the publication and title, type of research design used, country of study, number of participants, method of assigning teachers to students, scale, completeness of data used, study setting, dependent variable(s), data analysis method(s), stability of estimates due to the number of test scores, stability of estimates due to the predictors, and stability of estimates due to analysis method(s).

Summary of review findings

Twenty-five studies considered the use of different predictors to test the contribution of the predictors, of which four were rated 4 🔒, eighteen 3 🔒, two 2 🔒, and one was rated 1 🔒. In summary, the strongest studies show that students' previous achievement is the best predictor of teacher effectiveness, and that the inclusion of other variables adds little to the predictive power of teacher performance assessment models.

Fifteen studies were retrieved regarding the contribution of using additional prior attainment measures in teacher value-added effectiveness estimates. Out of 15 studies, one was rated with 4 🔒, thirteen 3 🔒, and one 1 🔒. There is no strong evidence that using additional prior test scores, over and above the most recent, increases the stability of teacher effectiveness estimates.

There were 21 studies that evaluated the stability of VAMs in estimating teacher effectiveness when using different methods of data analysis. Nine studies were rated 4 🔒, ten 3 🔒, one 2 🔒, and one 1 🔒. Different methods of analysis can produce greatly different estimates. The overall findings suggest that teacher performance estimates based on students' achievement growth varied substantially depending upon the preferred model and would result in very different conclusions about the teachers. There is no way of deciding that any single data analysis method is superior to any other method. The variability in the results, though, again casts doubt on the feasibility of using VAMs in practice.

Conducting the secondary data analysis

The dataset

This element of the research is a retrospective study to estimate the contribution of contextual predictors at student, school, and teacher/classroom-level, students' prior test score(s), and the choice of data analyses method, to teacher effectiveness estimates.

Value-added estimates require at least one previous year's test score along with the outcome score of the same student. I decided to base this study in secondary schools in a large province in Turkey where such student level datasets were available. The target student population was those who can be tracked academically from Grade 6 through to 8 (years 7 to 9). The student data was obtained from a project, named Step by Step Achievement (SBSA), which has been run by the Samsun Provincial Directorate of National Education (2014). All SBSA exam scores over the years, including students' background information, their school and class information (including teacher name) were stored electronically in the provincial directorate's electronic systems.

Having received permission, I downloaded the longitudinal test scores (spanning 3 years) of all students registered on the system (35,435 students in total) and then merged them with other student-level data, including names, unique school number, classroom information, sex, and their language learner status.

The next step was to link the student and teacher data. Although the names of the teachers associated with the students were available in the system, as I was given restricted access to the system, the teacher names were not accessible for me at this stage. However, this information was then provided via email in an excel spreadsheet.

In order to assess the stability of value-added teacher performance estimates, it is essential that student data can be linked to teacher data longitudinally (Clotfelter et al., 2006; Goldhaber, 2007). Since the electronic storage system did not contain teacher-level data, the teacher information was requested from the schools where they worked through the provincial directorate. Unfortunately, not many school directorates were willing to share the requested teacher information with me (and none of the private schools shared their teacher information). Therefore, I was able to use less than half of the data available in the administrative dataset for the analyses of this study.

The number of teachers in each teaching subject involved in this research (mathematics, Turkish, science, revolution history, and English) range from 174 to 232, and these were linked to 35,435 students in 8th grade. The school directorates provided the following information about a total of 1,027 teachers with names, sex, number of years of teaching experience, number of years teaching in the current school, appointment field, major degree subject, and their highest level of qualification and field. After obtaining this information, I merged teachers' background information with the student-level variables.

Finally, school-level data was obtained from the Ministry of National Education's official website (Ministry of National Education MoNE, 2017). A list of all secondary schools was downloaded from the website of Samsun Provincial Directory of National Education (Samsun Provincial Directorate of National Education, 2017). Only schools with matching data were retained. School-level data included school type (private or state-funded), school category (general, regional boarding or vocational secondary school), location of school (urban, suburban or rural), and school service scores. To maintain confidentiality, participants' identities were removed from the merged dataset and identification numbers were assigned to each student, teacher, school, and school location. The resulting sample sizes appear in Table 4.3.

Table 4.3 Study sample sizes

Subject	Students	Teachers	Schools
Mathematics	7,543	230	145
Turkish	7,594	232	150
Science	7,116	204	137
Revolution history	6,638	174	131
English	6,544	187	132
Total	35,435	1,027	695

To obtain teacher effectiveness estimates, student attainment in Grade 8 was regressed on the same student's prior attainment and other predictors. Individual student residual scores obtained from the final model (the difference between predicted and actual attainment level) were aggregated at the teacher level, and tentatively attributed to a teacher's individual value-added effectiveness score. Multiple linear regression analysis with forward entry of variables was used to determine the contribution of contextual predictors to these teachers' value-added estimates. Forward-selection helped to assess whether adding new predictor(s) causes a noticeable improvement in the model, compared to the previous step. The aim was to create the best-predicting regression model but including as few predictors as possible. Variables that did not add to the quality of the prediction were omitted. The contribution of contextual predictors to teachers' value-added estimates was assessed hierarchically – student characteristics (including prior attainment), followed by school characteristics, and then teacher/classroom characteristics.

The resulting teacher "effectiveness" scores from the final model were then compared over two years (with different students), between the same teachers teaching in different classrooms, or using different types of multiple regression, and with two (rather than one) years of prior attainment. When comparing teachers' scores for students with more than prior score, or in more than one classroom, only 151 could be linked to 2,526 students. Each version of the teacher effectiveness scores was correlated with others using Pearson's R.

Over two years of data, the correlations suggest that there is no meaningful positive relationship between teachers' current and previous effectiveness estimates for any subject areas (Table 4.4). The R values are very low, meaning that there is no clear link between a teacher's score in one year compared to the next. Whatever they represent, these "effectiveness" estimates are not a constant characteristic of teacher. In fact, the correlations for each teaching subject are negative, meaning that an effective teacher in one year tens to become ineffective in the next, and vice versa. This provides no

Table 4.4 Correlation between teachers' current and previous value-added effectiveness scores

Mathematics	−0.03
Turkish	−0.13
Science	0
Revolution history	−0.13
English	−0.02

empirical or ethical basis for rewarding, promoting or criticising a teacher for their purported "effectiveness" scores.

VAMs used for teacher evaluation attempt to isolate a particular teacher's effects on their students' learning from all other factors outside of the teacher's control. A teacher teaching the same subject in different classrooms in the same school year would be expected to have a similar effectiveness score in each classroom in a given year, if the VAM approach were valid. I calculated the percentage of teachers who stayed in the same effectiveness category when teaching different classes.

A total of 510 teachers were identified that taught in multiple classes for this analyse. As some teachers were assigned more than two classrooms, those classrooms were converted to pairs; for instance, where a teacher was assigned to three classes, three pairs of classrooms were created, such as class A and B, class A and C, and class B and C. Thereby 939 pairs of classrooms were identified for this comparative analyses. As seen in Table 4.5, none of the models used generated truly consistent results between paired classrooms. However modelled, a clear majority of teachers appeared to be differently effective when teaching in different classrooms. Whatever the models are measuring, it does not seem to be a consistent characteristic of teachers. This reinforces the finding in Table 4.4 (over time).

Only a small number of teachers (fewer than 40 per subject) had students with scores from two years earlier. For this subset, it was clear that using the extra year of results made little difference to their teacher effectiveness scores.

The final analysis investigated the consistency of teacher value-added effectiveness estimates derived from three common value-added approaches – the

Table 4.5 Percentage of teachers in the same effectiveness category for different classes

Subject	Residual gain	OLS	HLM
Maths	38	27	13
Turkish	30	28	10
Science	35	35	20
Revolution history	43	38	19
English	36	31	20

Table 4.6 Correlation between OLS, residual gain, and hierarchical linear modelling results

	Residual gain score	HLM score
Maths OLS score	0.83	0.95
Turkish OLS score	0.87	0.96
Science OLS score	0.87	0.95
Revolution history OLS score	0.90	0.91
English OLS score	0.86	0.95

residual gain model, ordinary least squares (OLS) multiple regression, and a two-level hierarchical linear model (HLM). Each estimate used the students' 8th grade test scores in the relevant teaching subject as the outcome variable. Students' prior attainment was used as a single predictor in residual gain. The contextual variables such as sex, ethnicity, teaching experience, and school type, were also used in the OLS-based and HLM models. The OLS estimates were correlated with the two other estimates (Table 4.6). All of the correlations were strong. OLS and HLM largely yielded the same or very similar results. The residual gain results differed slightly more, but this was presumably because they alone did not include contextual factors.

Synthesising the findings and their implications

Overall, the picture is not promising for the use of VAMs to assess teacher performance.

There is no evidence that any specific data analysis method is superior to other methods regarding the ability to consistently estimate teachers' effectiveness under a variety of conditions. However, based on a high consistency between models, internal consistency, transparency, and functionality, the results of the study indicated that the simple OLS-based multiple regression model should be preferred over the more complex residual gain and hierarchical linear models.

The existing literature reports mixed results about the contribution of using additional year(s) of data to estimate teacher effectiveness. Some studies (Goldhaber and Hansen, 2010, 2013; McCaffrey et al., 2009; Potamites et al., 2009; Stacy et al., 2018) suggested that there are advantages to including additional lagged test scores to improve the stability of value-added estimates, while others (Ehlert et al., 2014; Johnson et al., 2015; Kersting et al., 2013) revealed it to be of little benefit. The secondary data analysis here supports researchers in the literature review who report a very limited contribution from using extra years of data.

Consistent with the findings of the systematic review, the secondary data analysis revealed that the strongest student-related factor in explaining variation in student's current test scores in each teaching subject is their most recent prior attainment (Aslantas, 2020). The new results also showed that approximately half of the variance in the pupils' latest test score was explained by their nearest prior test results, alone. It is clear, and already reasonably well-established that student achievement mostly depends on the performance of the student in early education. This suggests that the focus of education and policy investment should be on the earlier years.

Contrary to the findings of Aaronson et al. (2007), Bessolo (2013), McCaffrey et al. (2009), and the MET Project (Kane and Cantrell, 2010), which found positive correlations between teachers' performance estimates from year to year, this analysis found no meaningful stability in teachers' current and previous effectiveness scores. In fact, the Pearson correlation coefficients were negative for all teaching subjects, which means that there actually is a (weak) negative relationship between teachers' current and previous scores. If these estimates are really a measure of teacher effectiveness they are too volatile to be of any practical use. Therefore, performance results achieved through VAMs should not be relied upon, especially for high-stakes personnel decisions. Promoting or punishing employees based on unreliable results is unfair to both teachers and other professionals (and institutions, such as schools).

To recap, the findings from this study provide no evidence that value-added estimates of teacher performance are useful in measuring teacher effectiveness. They do not produce reliable and consistent results and thus risk misclassifying teachers. They should not be used for making high stake decisions regarding teachers' promotion, dismissal, or bonuses. An alternative must be sought.

References

Aaronson, D., Barrow, L., and Sander, W. (2007). Teacher and student achievement in the Chicago public high schools. *Journal of Labor Economics*, 25(1), pp. 95–135.

Aslantas, I. (2020). Impact of contextual predictors on value-added teacher effectiveness estimates. *Education Sciences*, 10(12), p. 390.

Bessolo, J. (2013). *The stability of teacher effects on student math and reading achievement over time: A study of one midsize district*. EdD thesis. University of Kansas. Available at: https://kuscholarworks.ku.edu/bitstream/handle/1808/15129/Bessolo_ku_0099D_12677_DATA_1.pdf?sequence=1. Accessed on 1 July 2019.

Bettany-Saltikov, J., and McSherry, R. (2016). *How to Do a Systematic Literature Review in Nursing: A Step-by-Step Guide*, 2nd ed. Maidenhead: McGraw-Hill/Open University Press.

Brown, H., Chudowsky, N., and Koenig, J. (eds.). (2010). *Getting Value Out of Value-Added: Report of a Workshop*. Washington, DC: National Academies Press.

Clotfelter, C.T., Ladd, H., and Vigdor, J.L. (2006). Teacher-student matching and the assessment of teacher effectiveness. *The Journal of Human Resources*, 41(4), pp. 778–820.

Coe, R., Aloisi, C., Higgins, S., and Major, L.E. (2014). *What Makes Great Teaching? Review of the Underpinning Research*. London: Sutton Trust.

Darling-Hammond, L. (2000). Teacher quality and student achievement: A review of state policy. *Education Policy Analysis Archives*, 8(1), pp. 1–44.

Darling-Hammond, L. (2015). Can value added add value to teacher evaluation? *Educational Researcher*, 44(2), pp. 132–137.

Ehlert, M., Koedel, C., Parsons, E., and Podgursky, M.J. (2014). The sensitivity of value-added estimates to specification adjustments: Evidence from school- and teacher-level models in Missouri. *Statistics and Public Policy*, 1(1), pp. 19–27.

El Soufi, N., and See, B.H. (2019). Does explicit teaching of critical thinking improve critical thinking skills of English language learners in higher education? A critical review of causal evidence. *Studies in Educational Evaluation*, 60, pp. 140–162.

Garrett, R., and Steinberg, M.P. (2015). Examining teacher effectiveness using classroom observation scores: Evidence from the randomization of teachers to students. *Educational Evaluation and Policy Analysis*, 37, pp. 224–242.

Glazerman, S., Loeb, S., Goldhaber, D., Raudenbush, S., and Whitehurst, G. (2010). *Evaluating Teachers: The Important Role of Value-Added*. Washington, DC: The Brookings Institution.

Goldhaber, D. (2007). Everyone's doing it, but what does teacher testing tell us about teacher effectiveness? *Journal of Human Resources*, 42(4), pp. 765–794.

Goldhaber, D., and Hansen, M. (2010). *Assessing the Potential of Using Value-Added Estimates of Teacher Job Performance for Making Tenure Decisions*. Washington, DC: National Center for Analysis of Longitudinal Data in Education Research.

Goldhaber, D., and Hansen, M. (2013). Is it just a bad class? Assessing the long-term stability of estimated teacher performance. *Economica*, 80, pp. 589–612.

Gorard, S. (2013). What difference do teachers make? A consideration of the wider outcomes of schooling. *Irish Educational Studies*, 32(1), pp. 69–82.

Gorard, S. (2014). A proposal for judging the trustworthiness of research findings. *Radical Statistics*, 110, pp. 47–59.

Gorard, S. (2018). *Education Policy: Evidence of equity and effectiveness*. Bristol: Policy Press.

Johnson, M.T., Lipscomb, S., and Gill, B. (2015). Sensitivity of teacher value-added estimates to student and peer control variables. *Journal of Research on Educational Effectiveness*, 8(1), pp. 60–83.

Kane, T.J., and Cantrell, S.M. (2010). *Learning about teaching: Initial findings from the Measures of Effective Teaching Project.* MET Project Research Paper. Seattle, WA: Bill & Melinda Gates Foundation.

Kane, T.J., Kerr, K.A., and Pianta, R.C. (2015). *Designing Teacher Evaluation Systems: New Guidance from the Measures of Effective Teaching Project.* San Francisco, CA: Jossey-Bass, A Wiley Brand.

Kersting, N.B., Chen, M.-K., and Stigler, J.W. (2013). Value-added teacher estimates as part of teacher evaluations: Exploring the effects of data and model specifications on the stability of teacher value-added scores. *Education Policy Analysis Archives*, 21(7), pp. 1–39.

McCaffrey, D.F., Lockwood, J.R., Koretz, D.M., and Hamilton, L.S. (2003). *Evaluating Value-Added Models for Teacher Accountability.* Santa Monica, CA: The RAND Corporation.

McCaffrey, D.F., Lockwood, J.R., Koretz, D.M., Louis, T.A., and Hamilton, L. (2004). Models for value-added modeling of teacher effects. *Journal of Educational and Behavioral Statistics*, 29(1), pp. 67–101.

McCaffrey, D.F., Sass, T.R., Lockwood, J.R., and Mihaly, K. (2009). The intertemporal variability of teacher effect estimates. *Education Finance and Policy*, 4(4), pp. 572–606.

Ministry of National Education (MoNE). (2017). *Schools and other institutions.* Available at: https://mebbis.meb.gov.tr/KurumListesi.aspx. Accessed on 11 November 2017.

Moher, D., Liberati, A., Tetzlaff, J., and Altman D.G. (2009). Preferred reporting items for systematic reviews and meta-analyses: The PRISMA statement. *BMJ*, 339, p. b2535.

Potamites, L., Booker, K., Chaplin, D., and Isenberg, E. (2009). *Measuring School and Teacher Effectiveness in the EPIC Charter School Consortium-Year 2.* Washington, DC: USA: Mathematica Policy Research.

Rivkin, S.G., Hanushek, E.A., and Kain, J.F. (2005). Teachers, schools, and academic achievement. *Econometrica*, 73(2), pp. 417–458.

Rothstein, J. (2007). *Do value-added models add value? Tracking, fixed effects, and causal inference.* Working Papers 1036. Princeton, NJ: Center for Economic Policy Studies, Princeton University.

Samsun Provincial Directorate of National Education. (2014). *Step by step achievement project.* Available at: https://samsun.meb.gov.tr/meb_iys_dosyalar/2015_01/15053803_adimadimbaariprojesdzeltlen2.pdf. Accessed on 10 November 2017.

Samsun Provincial Directorate of National Education. (2017). *The list of institutions.* Available at: https://mebbis.meb.gov.tr/KurumListesi.aspx. Accessed on 11 November 2017.

Sander, W.L., Saxton, A.M., and Horn, S.P. (1997). The Tennessee Value-Added Assessment System: A quantitative, outcomes-based approach to educational assessment. In J. Millman (ed.), *Grading Teachers, Grading Schools. Is Student Achievement a Valid Evaluation Measures?* (pp. 137–162). Thousand Oaks, CA: Corwin Press.

See, B.H. (2020). Challenges in using research evidence in improving teaching quality. *BERA Research Intelligence*, 144, pp. 20–21.

Stacy, B., Guarino, C., and Wooldridge, J. (2018). Does the precision and stability of value-added estimates of teacher performance depend on the types of students they serve? *Economics of Education Review*, 64, pp. 50–74.

Swanson, P.L. (2009). *A quantitative study of school characteristics that impact student achievement on state assessments and those assessments' associations to ACT scores in Tennessee.* EdD thesis. East Tennessee State University. Available at: https://dc.etsu.edu/cgi/viewcontent.cgi?article=3189&context=etd. Accessed on 22 May 2019.

Torgerson, C. (2003). *Systematic Reviews.* London: Continuum.

CHAPTER 5

Does academic selection promote effectiveness and equity? Evaluating a classic topic using a new approach

Binwei Lu

Introduction

This doctoral project focuses on the effectiveness and equity of academic selection in England, using the National Pupil Database (NPD), Higher Education Statistics Agency (HESA) data, and a local dataset providing the results of the grammar schools' selection test. The study looked at pupils' access to grammar schools, their outcomes, and the relationship with pupils' family background.

The action of selecting pupils based on early-age academic ability, and then providing divergent educational routes depending on the selection results, is usually referred to as academic selection. Selective placement in schools and colleges is a long-established practice worldwide. It is based on the belief that academic selection raises overall educational standards while also providing better educational opportunities for economically disadvantaged but able students. However, detractors argue that the selective system is no more effective than a comprehensive one of all-ability schools, and may reinforce the link between family origins and future destinations. In most Anglophone countries, the potential harm from early-age academic selection has led to a more comprehensive system of secondary education. However, between-school separation remains a widespread practice around the world. Among the 72 participants in The Programme of International Student Assessment (PISA), 15 countries (including Germany and Singapore) still select pupils into tracks before the age of 15 (OECD, 2015). The long-lasting debate on the role of early-age academic selection in social effectiveness and equity implies the importance of an accurate evaluation of its real influence.

In England, secondary education in the 1940s was selective (Kerckhoff et al., 1998). Under the fully-selective system, grammar schools were intended for academically-oriented pupils, providing the primary route to Higher Education (HE) institutions, then taking only around 5% of the age

DOI: 10.4324/9781003201366-6

cohort. The remaining secondary modern and technical schools usually taught a more restricted academic curriculum, or practical subjects equipping pupils with the basic literacy and numeracy skills necessary for other occupations (Morris and Perry, 2017). Since the 1960s, most schools have been converted to mixed-ability schools. However, 163 grammar schools remain in England, and they educate about 5% of the pupils in the English state-funded system today (Bolton, 2017). Despite their small number, grammar schools receive considerable political and public attention because of their link to effectiveness and equity, which are not only political buzzwords in England, but significant global issues (Gorard and Siddiqui, 2018).

Academic effectiveness is one of the most important aspects of education systems. Since grammar schools usually have high rankings in school league tables, some commentators perceive this as effectiveness and promote their existence and expansion of. Regarded by some in government as better at raising academic standards than other state-funded schools, grammar schools in England have prompted political attempts at expansion (Department for Education DfE, 2016; The Conservative Party, 2017). These attempts are political because the balance of evidence on the actual effectiveness of grammar schools suggests that they do not work. Schools with better test scores than others usually also have more advantaged intakes with higher prior attainment anyway (Gorard and See, 2013).

Since children cannot be randomly allocated to schools in order to test the impact of each route on their life chances, most existing research uses statistical models and control for pre-existing differences between grammar school pupils and those in non-selective schools. However, this reliance on passive designs does not really permit causal inference. The results only reveal correlations between grammar school attendance and academic performance. These estimations become biased whenever influential baseline variables between pupil groups are neglected, unavailable, or unmeasurable (Gorard, 2010). Thus, when differences between students emerge in their subsequent attainment, it is unclear whether these are due to the school attended, or imperfections in the modelling process, or indeed anything else. This casts doubt on any estimated grammar school "effect".

While performance standards are a major concern for governments, outcome distribution across different social groups is also a critical issue. Educational equity is emphasised internationally, and it has become a core issue in the international development agenda proposed by the United Nations. Grammar schools are meant to improve social mobility according to the advocates of grammar schools. This is because grammar schools select pupils by ability alone, rather than by other family background characteristics such as social status and income. However, the underrepresentation of disadvantaged pupils in grammar schools suggests that grammar schools might not only be academically selective, but socially selective as well. Therefore, the assumption behind grammar schools' role in helping the poor also needs further assessment.

This study focuses on potential impacts of grammar schools, and evaluates whether expanding or closing them would lead to a more effective and equitable education system in England. While the analysis only focuses on grammar schools in England, this study is relevant to the practices of selection and differentiation around the world.

Summary of methods used

Most of the data used in this study came from the National Pupil Database (NPD), which includes official annual performance, school, and family background data for all pupils in England, collected by the DfE. The study is based on the 2010/2011 cohort of Key Stage 2 (KS2, age 11). Among the 612,027 pupil records for this year group, there are 186,461 pupils in 36 selective local authorities (LAs). The analysis first shows how the difficulty of grammar school selection varies across LAs. This process includes 160,070 valid cases and excludes 26,391 (14%) cases with missing KS2 attainment data. The analysis also pays attention to several subgroups, such as pupils eligible for free school meals (FSM), pupils with special educational needs (SEN), and pupils speaking English as an additional language (EAL).

These data are analysed descriptively and used in a variety of predictive models. The models include ordinary least square (OLS) linear regression, using student background and prior attainment as predictors, along with school information including whether the student attended a grammar school. These models are used to assess who goes to grammar schools, and whether attendance benefits their KS4 scores. A binary logistic regression model using the same predictors is applied to assess the impact of grammar school attendance on admission to university.

Unlike traditional regression models passively accounting for pre-existing differences between groups, the regression discontinuity design (RDD) approach is considered the best alternative to a randomised control trial (RCT). The basis of an RDD is that participants are allocated to either the treatment or the control group according to the cut-off point on a continuous assignment variable. Only those who reach the cut-off point receive the treatment. If participants' assignment variables could not be manipulated with precision, their chances of just making it or just missing it can be regarded as locally random (Lee and Lemieux, 2009). As the values of the assignment variable are similar among participants in the neighbourhood of the cut-off point, a comparison of the outcome variable between the treatment and control group can attribute any discontinuity at the cut-off point to the treatment (Lee and Lemieux, 2009). This process provides perfect a counterfactual and solves the problem of pre-existing differences between the treatment and control group.

It would have been preferable to have had the 11+ grammar school entry results for this same for all students who sat the test. It is not clear why this data (suitably anonymised) is not available to researchers in the same way as KS2 and KS4 results are. I had to make an analysis for the RDD of an 11+ file kindly provided by a local group of parents. This 11+ file has 7,917 valid cases of local pupils who sat the 11+ in this LA in 2011 (2011/2012 KS2 cohort). The 11+ file is then linked to the NPD data of the same 2011/2012 KS2 cohort for the 2016/2017 GCSE results. However, since the 11+ data is anonymous, the 11+ file and the NPD data extract are matched through family backgrounds and KS2 attainment. In order to make one-to-one unique matches between the two files, duplicate cases with same combinations of background information had to be deleted. This process excluded 52% (4,119) of the total cases in the 11+ file. While this process might threaten the representativeness of the sample, it is the best available option due to the limited information in the 11+ file. After data clearing, 2,541 cases in the mainstream state-funded schools were kept for the RDD analysis.

In this study, the treatment effect of interest is the effectiveness of grammar schools compared with other non-selective mainstream state secondary schools. The outcome variable used as the indicator of school effectiveness is the capped GCSE point score. As the total test score on the 11+ is the major factor deciding pupils' eligibility to attend grammar schools, it is centred at the lowest passing score and set as the assignment variable (point 0 is the cut-off point).

Full details of the datasets and their analyses appear in the thesis (Lu, 2020).

Summary of key findings

Attendance at schools across local authority boundaries

Judging by the characteristics of pupils who move to another local authority (LA) for secondary education of any kind, and those who do not, crossing LA boundaries has become a shortcut for more affluent families to manoeuvre within the school, which may be less of an option for disadvantaged families (Table 5.1). White pupils, those with special educational needs (SEN), and especially those living in poverty (eligible for free school meals) are less likely to attend a school in a different LA to their home. Those with higher primary school grades are slightly more likely to cross LA boundaries, and Asian origin and especially Black pupils are much more likely to. These

Table 5.1 Characteristics of pupils moving across LAs and staying within home LAs

	Moving LA	*Staying in home LA*	*Gap*
KS2 mark	142	126	+0.06
FSM %	11.9	17.1	−0.18
SEN %	7.7	10.8	−0.17
White pupils %	63.4	76.4	−0.09
Asian pupils %	11.9	8.8	+0.15
Black pupils %	7.2	3.2	+0.38

differences are then reflected in the stratified student intakes to grammar schools.

The varied proportion of available grammar school places in each selective LA also leads to an imbalance in grammar school opportunities. The attainment threshold for grammar school selection varies across LAss, depending on how many places are available. Some LAs allow pupils from the bottom national quartile for KS2 performance to attend grammar schools. Others only enrol pupils with well above-average performance. This leads to dissimilar student compositions between grammar schools across LAs. The inequality of opportunity between LAs means that sending children to another LA could influence their chances of getting into grammar schools. For all of the secondary school pupils in selective LAs, only 9% of them moved outsides their home LAs for secondary education. However, the corresponding proportion in grammar schools is considerably higher, over 25%. Consistent with the high proportion of relocated pupils in grammar schools, pupils moving across LAs are usually more likely to attend grammar schools than those who stay within the home LA, even after accounting for prior attainment (Figure 5.1).

Who goes to grammar school?

Regardless of location, grammar school intakes are patterned by pupil background characteristics. Early-age inequality in the average achievement between different social groups is substantial. Therefore, what appears to be selection for grammar school by attainment at age 11 is indirectly associated with selection by family background. And even after accounting for early-age attainment, grammar schools are still not equally accessible for different social groups. For pupils with equivalent KS2 attainment, ethnic minorities usually have more access than white pupils, but pupils from poorer areas, those eligible for FSM, and those who have SEN, tend to have fewer opportunities to attend grammar schools. See full details of this analysis in Lu (2018).

Although grammar schools select by "ability", the lower rate of disadvantaged pupils attending grammar schools even after accounting for

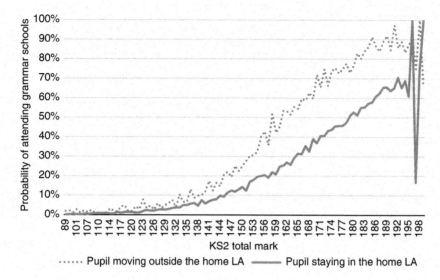

Figure 5.1 The probability of attending grammar school for pupils moving across LAs, by KS2 scores

prior attainment, means that the selection fails to offer equal opportunities for pupils with equivalent performance. This implies that the selection system does not achieve the principle of unbiased merit-based equity. Moreover, the status quo of the layered attainment between social groups means that if secondary schools are allowed to select by ability, they are actually selecting pupils from more advantaged backgrounds. This does not help pupils with greater needs, and may in fact impede their chances. Therefore, the grammar school selection system has failed to help needs-based equity.

Grammar school effectiveness in improving academic outcomes

OLS linear regression models, based on 149,072 pupils, reveal little or no benefit from attending a grammar school, in terms of Key Stage 4 (age 16) attainment. Table 5.2 lists all of the predictors, based on school intakes, that are taken into account before considering any impact from grammar school attendance. Key predictors of KS4 attainment are poverty (IDACI, FSM), SEN status (very few pupils with SEN attend grammar schools), and prior attainment score at KS2.

In the first model, not using whether a pupil was in a grammar school or not, the model had an R squared of 0.59. This means that the model explains around 59% of the variance in KS4 outcomes. The second model includes

Table 5.2 OLS linear regression models predicting capped GCSE grades

Predictor	Without knowledge of attending grammar	With knowledge of attending grammar
Girl (vs boy)	2.30	2.30
Age in year (months)	−0.11	−0.11
IDACI score	−5.78	−5.82
FSM-eligible (vs not)	−2.62	−2.62
SEN (vs not)	−1.90	−1.90
EAL (vs not)	2.80	2.81
Asian (vs white)	1.13	1.12
Black (vs white	1.95	1.97
Other ethnicity (vs white)	0.96	0.97
KS2 total mark, English and maths	0.23	0.23
Mean KS2 total mark for school	0.08	0.07
Mean FSM proportion for school	−0.05	−0.05
Attend grammar School (vs not)	–	0.31

whether a pupil was in a grammar school or not. The R squared was again 0.59. Once we know the prior attainment and background characteristics of pupils, knowledge of whether they were at a grammar school or not makes no difference to the quality of the prediction. Looked at this way, there is no grammar school "effect".

Adding knowledge of whether a pupil was in a grammar school or not does lead to a slight adjustment of some predictor coefficients. Most, like FSM-eligibility or KS attainment remain the same. A few, like EAL and ethnicity change slightly, giving grammar school attendance a kind of proxy value of 0.31. I call it a proxy value because a child's language or ethnicity are set long before they attend grammar school or not. If the 0.31 represented a true "effect" it would be small (just under one third of a GCSE grade), which is very small when considering that it is cumulative over five years.

An alternative way of looking at the situation is using the RDD. The example here is based on partial data from only one selective LA (unlike the OLS analysis based on national data). This small demonstration is therefore intended to explore feasibility of the method rather than provide a definitive answer.

Figure 5.2 plots the 11+ selection test results on the x axis, standardised based on an average score threshold for grammar school attendance (0). The y axis plots the KS4 outcomes. Each circle represents a number of pupils (fewer low scoring pupils take the 11+, for example). The clear circles denote

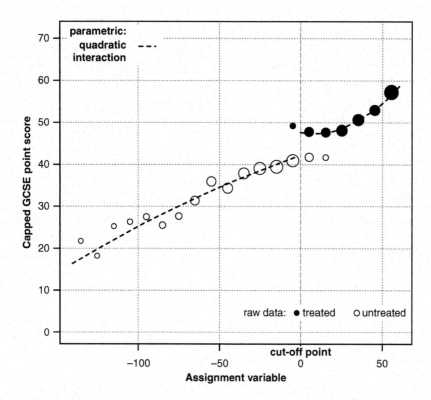

Figure 5.2 The grammar school effect in the RDD parametric approach

non-attendance and the black circles denote attendance at a grammar school. It is clear that pupils who do better at the 11+ tend to do better also at KS4. Ignoring the threshold point for the moment, there is relatively straight regression line. This suggests that, for most pupils, there is no advantage in attending grammar school, and no disadvantage in not doing so. Near the threshold, however, the small number pupils just obtaining the necessary 11+ marks to attend grammar school seem to have better KS4 outcomes than the small number just missing the threshold score. There is some evidence of a discontinuity.

This gain can be estimated at around 4.5 point scores for capped GCSEs, equivalent to half a grade per GCSE subject, and about 10% of the average attainment of pupils below the cut-off point. The results thus imply a benefit from attending grammar schools for the borderline pupils in this participating LA.

The RDD section of this study is in accordance with the only previous RDD research on the grammar school effect in England, which revealed that the treatment effect on the Year 9 test score was 7% of the average performance of pupils just below the cut-off point (Clark, 2010). The results of the RDD in this study are also within the range of the national pattern of possible grammar school advantage presented by Coe et al. (2008). Nevertheless, the results with such a small sample only show that this approach is feasible. The problems in obtaining the data and then matching the 11+ results to the NPD (above) mean that this element of the study is largely for demonstration.

The effectiveness of selective LAs

While attending grammar schools may be associated with a small positive impact on KS4 attainment for their borderline pupils, the presence of these academically selective schools does not improve the overall performance standards of the local area. After accounting for pupil-level and school-level characteristics, in models based on 481,681 pupils, there is no obvious difference in effectiveness between selective and non-selective LAs. As above, once pupil background and prior attainment is accounted for, knowledge of being in selective LA or not, or the type of school attended in a selective LA, does not improve the OLS models. The R squared for both models is 0.56.

In fact the coefficients suggest that going to school in a selective LA is actually a slight disadvantage, amounting to −0.1 in terms of capped GCSE scores (Table 5.3). While grammar school pupils perform slightly better than equivalent pupils in comprehensive LAs (coefficient of 0.15), pupils in selective LAs who failed to get into grammar school perform worse than those

Table 5.3 OLS models predicting capped GCSE grades in selective and non-selective LAs

Predictor	LA type	School type
Girl (vs boy)	2.43	2.43
Age in year (months)	−0.11	−0.11
IDACI score	−6.53	−6.56
FSM-eligible (vs not)	−2.71	−2.71
SEN (vs not)	−1.79	−1.79
EAL (vs not)	3.29	3.29
Asian (vs white)	1.20	1.20
Black (vs white	1.67	1.68
Other ethnicity (vs white)	0.95	0.95
KS2 total mark, English and maths	0.23	0.23
Mean KS2 total mark for school	0.08	0.07
Mean FSM proportion for school	−0.03	−0.03
In selective LA (vs not)	−0.10	
Attend grammar school (vs not)	–	0.15
Attend non-selective school in selective area (vs not)	–	−0.13

in comprehensive LAs (0.13). Thus, these two contrary effects, if this is indeed what they are, lead to a zero-sum situation.

Grammar school attendance and participation in HE

Grammar school attendance may or may not slightly increase KS attainment for borderline pupils' at KS4, but it is clear that grammar schools convey no advantage in gaining admission to higher education (HE). Based on 117,506 cases, a logistic regression model to predict HE admission or not suggests that grammar school attendance makes no difference. Around 43.5% of students attended university in this cohort, making the base value for the model 56.5. Adding predictors based on student background, prior attainment at KS2, and school-level factors, the model predicted 66.2% of the outcomes correctly. This is an increase of 9.7 percentage points (22% of the outstanding variation) on 56.5%. The predictors used are the first model in Table 5.4. Adding knowledge of whether a student was from a grammar school or not, in the second model, did not increase the accuracy of the prediction (still 66.2%).

Table 5.4 Logistic regression models predicting HE participation

Predictor	Without knowledge of attending grammar	With knowledge of attending grammar
Girl (vs boy)	1.37	1.37
Age in year (months)	0.99	0.99
IDACI score	0.48	0.48
FSM-eligible (vs not)	0.79	0.79
SEN School Action (vs no SEN)	0.98	0.98
SEN School Action Plus (vs no SEN)	1.01	1.01
SEN Statement (vs no SEN)	1.07	1.07
EAL (vs not)	1.43	1.43
Asian (vs white)	1.82	1.82
Black (vs white)	2.35	2.35
Chinese (vs white)	2.87	2.87
Mixed (vs white)	0.97	0.97
Unclassified (vs white)	1.31	1.31
Other ethnicity (vs white)	1.57	1.57
KS2 total mark, English and maths	1.02	1.02
Mean KS2 total mark for school	1.02	1.02
Mean FSM proportion for school	0.99	0.99
Attend grammar School (vs not)	–	1.02

The odds ratio for grammar schools is 1.018 after accounting for baseline variables at KS2, demonstrating that grammar school pupils are only 2% more likely to attend HE than equivalent pupils in non-selective schools. The odds ratio even dropped to 0.82 when pupil's KS4 attainment were included, suggesting that grammar school pupils are substantially less likely to go to university than their peers with equivalent KS4 qualifications.

Furthermore, for pupils with similar backgrounds and attainment, attending grammar schools is associated with a lower rate of attending the Russell Group universities (considered the most prestigious in the UK). This may be a sign that grammar schools do not provide effective extra help which is beneficial to HE participation, or it may be a consequence of widening participation initiatives intended to increase HE participation rates for disadvantaged pupil groups (Department for Education DfE, 2017).

Conclusions and reflections

To conclude, this study found no good evidence that grammar schools are more effective nationally than non-selective mainstream state-funded schools in terms of academic performance. There is no advantage from grammar school attendance for HE participation or attendance at university. Selective local authorities do not get better academic results, as a whole, than non-selective ones. This all means that even if grammar schools were considered more effective than non-selective ones, there is no gain to the system. Any gain is matched by a reduction in attainment scores in all other schools in that area. The idea that grammar schools and the academically selective system raise national academic standards is unrealistic.

The pattern of effectiveness therefore does not support any expansion of grammar schools. However, the negative consequences for social equity of a selective system argue strongly for not expanding and even removing them. The layered early-age attainment between social groups, compounded by the imperfect selection process, reveals that grammar school selection is not fair, even when prior attainment is taken into account. Meanwhile, the unbalanced opportunity to attend grammar schools and the small advantage associated with grammar school attendance (as well as the potential negative influence on pupils who failed to get into grammar schools) amplify the attainment gap between pupils from high and low socioeconomic status groups through the mechanism of selection and differentiation. Thus, the system has failed to comply with the principle of equity, in terms of either merit-based or needs-based standards.

Overall, the analysis in this study finds no substantial advantage associated with early-age academic selection in England. This conclusion is consistent with international evidence that selection during compulsory education is usually associated with a lower level of equity, and may also reduce performance standards (e.g. Hanushek and Wößmann, 2006). The findings here are not only relevant to grammar schools in England, but to the widespread global practice of separating pupils at an early-age based on academic ability.

Academic selection in England is a classic topic and it has attracted researchers' attention for decades. However, this large-scale work addresses the classic theme in a novel way. Using national datasets in the UK, the evidence in this study covered entire year groups in England. As the study applies population rather than sample data, there is no need to consider threats such as generalisability of the conclusion. These factors make the study robust. Additionally, the study also uses the innovative RDD approach, and it is the first attempt at using this strong design to evaluate the current effectiveness of grammar schools in England. Conducting this design with national data on grammar school selection would solve the problems in previous studies that used passive designs to control for pre-existing differences between grammar school pupils and others. The strength and novelty of this study has been recognised through my publications in academic journals, such as the *British Educational Research Journal* (Lu, 2019), *Educational Review* (Lu, 2018), and the *Cambridge Journal of Education* (Lu, 2021). The research findings have been covered widely by the media, including the Times, Independent, Daily Mail, TES, and Forbes. The thesis was awarded a judge commendation in the 2021 BERA doctoral thesis award.

Given that I knew nothing about grammar schools, or indeed about the UK education system at all, before starting, this study clearly demonstrates that a doctoral project can be both topical and have real-life impact. A doctoral thesis might be the most ideal research project a researcher can realise in their academic life, because it is less prone to time pressure or funders' preference than is usual. It would be a great shame to make any unnecessary compromise in research design or ambition. As early-career researchers, doctoral students should be confident that their studies will make a real difference, believing that education systems can be more than a microcosm of the larger society replicating broader social problems, and that reforms within schools enacted prior to fundamental social change are indeed a realistic possibility (Gorard and Smith, 2010).

References

Bolton, P. (2017). *Grammar school statistics*. Retrieved from http://researchbriefings. parliament.uk/ResearchBriefing/Summary/SN01398#fullreport

Clark, D. (2010). Selective schools and academic achievement. *The B.E. Journal of Economic Analysis & Policy*, 10(1), pp. 1–40.

Coe, R., Jones, K., Searle, J., Kokotsaki, D., Kosnin, A., and Skinner, P. (2008). *Evidence on the effects of selective educational systems: A report for the Sutton Trust.* Retrieved from https://www.suttontrust.com/wp-content/uploads/2 008/10/SuttonTrustFullReportFinal-1.pdf

Department for Education (DfE). (2016). *Schools that work for everyone: Government consultation.* Retrieved from https://consult.education.gov.uk/ school-frameworks/schools-that-work-for-everyone/supporting_documents/ SCHOOLS%20THAT%20WORK%20FOR%20EVERYONE%20%2 0FINAL.PDF

Department for Education (DfE). (2017). *Widening participation in higher education, England, 2014/15 age cohort.* Retrieved from https://assets.publishing. service.gov.uk/government/uploads/system/uploads/attachment_data/file/6351 03/SFR39-2017-MainText.pdf

Gorard, S. (2010). Serious doubts about school effectiveness. *British Educational Research Journal,* 36(5), pp. 745–766. doi: 10.1080/01411920903144251

Gorard, S., and See, B.H. (2013). *Overcoming Disadvantage in Education.* Abingdon: Routledge.

Gorard, S., and Smith, E. (2010). *Equity in Education: An International Comparison of Pupil Perspectives.* London: Palgrave Macmillan UK.

Gorard, S., and Siddiqui, N. (2018). Grammar schools in England: A new analysis of social segregation and academic outcomes. *British Journal of Sociology of Education,* 39(7), pp. 909–924. doi: 10.1080/01425692.201 8.1443432

Hanushek, E., and Wößmann, L. (2006). Does educational tracking affect performance and inequality? Differences-in-differences evidence across countries. *The Economic Journal,* 116(510), pp. C63–C76. doi: 10.1111/j.1468-02 97.2006.01076.x

Kerckhoff, A., Fogelman, K., Crook, D., and Reeder, D. (1998). *Going Comprehensive in England and Wales: A Study of Uneven Change.* London: Routledge.

Lee, D., and Lemieux, T. (2009). Regression discontinuity designs in economics. Retrieved from https://www.nber.org/papers/w14723.pdf

Lu, B. (2018). Selection on attainment? Local authorities, pupil backgrounds, attainment and grammar school opportunities. *Educational Review.* doi: 10.1 080/00131911.2018.1483893

Lu, B. (2019). How can we evaluate the effectiveness of grammar schools in England? A regression discontinuity approach. *British Educational Research Journal.* doi: 10.1002/berj.3581

Lu, B. (2020). *The effectiveness and equity of grammar schools in England.* PhD thesis. School of Education, Leaze's Road, Durham, UK: Durham University.

Lu, B. (2021). Does attending academically selective schools increase higher education participation rates? *Cambridge Journal of Education,* 1–23. doi: 10.1080/0305764X.2020.1863914

Morris, R., and Perry, T. (2017). Reframing the English grammar schools debate. *Educational Review,* 69(1), pp. 1–24.

OECD. (2015). *Universal basic skills: What countries stand to gain.* Retrieved from http://www.oecd.org/edu/universal-basic-skills-9789264234833-en.htm

The Conservative Party. (2017). *Forward Together, Our Plan for a Stronger Britain and Prosperous Future: The Conservative and Unionist Party Manifesto 2017.* London: St. Ives PLC.

CHAPTER **6**

Does instructional leadership make schools more effective? Evidence from the Maldives

Ismail Shafeeu

Introduction

This PhD study looked at the link between instructional leadership in schools and student attainment in the Maldives. The Ministry of Education introduced a policy stating that 60% of students should pass the secondary school completion examination, in each school (Ministry of Education, 2009). They developed an action plan and attainment targets for each secondary school. Official letters were sent to principals telling them to achieve these goals.

The Ministry also announced that they were changing the role of principals from school administrators to that of *instructional leaders*. It was intended that principals would take a more active role in the instructional process of the school. The ministry introduced a new post called the *school administrator* who would manage the day-to-day administrative tasks of the school so that principals could increase their involvement in instructional activities. These structural changes were carried out based on the assumption that strong instructional leadership could help to raise pupils' attainment outcomes.

However, many educators were critical of the unintended outcomes that might be associated with this policy. It was predicted that, to demonstrate success, academically weak students might be excluded from taking part in the secondary school completion examination. By doing this, the Ministry of Education could claim that they have achieved the desired outcome of this policy (Shafeeu et al., 2011). It is evident that the implementation of this policy put significant pressure on principals to achieve the targets assigned by the Ministry of Education. A key question, therefore, is whether the type of leadership provided by principals could make a difference in promoting students' attainment in the secondary school completion examination.

     DOI: 10.4324/9781003201366-7

The study

Research in educational leadership and management is important for educational improvement. However, Gorard (2005) stated that the field of educational leadership research is inward-looking and somewhat unwilling to investigate the real effect of leadership on students' attainment. This new study was therefore designed to examine the relationship between the principals' instructional leadership and students' attainment in the Maldives. There are four main research questions, discussed in turn:

1. What is the level of the principal's instructional leadership practices in Maldives schools?
2. What is the level of effective school correlates in Maldives schools?
3. What is the relationship between the principal's instructional leadership and effective school correlates?
4. To what extent does instructional leadership contribute to differences in pupils' academic attainment?

To address the first two research questions of the study a cross-sectional survey of teachers was conducted in all public secondary schools in the Maldives, asking about the level of principals' instructional leadership and the existence of effective school characteristics. The main reason for using all cases is to obtain accurate results that provide a more robust response to the research questions that are considered in this study (Gorard, 2001). This provides a "snapshot" of the entire population at a given time (Levin, 2006; Sobol, 2004). The survey had items on principals' instructional leadership based on Hallinger's (1990) Instructional Management Rating Scale (PIMRS), and on staff perceptions of effective school characteristics adapted from the work of Evers and Bacon (1994), which was based on the effective school characteristics identified by Lezotte (1991).

PIMRS assesses three broad dimensions of instructional leadership – defining the school mission, managing the instructional programme, and promoting a positive learning climate. Since its introduction, PIMRS has been used in more than 330 studies across the globe, making it one of the most widely used measure of principals' instructional leadership over the past 30 years (Hallinger, 2015). Effective school characteristics (Lezotte and Snyder, 2011) can be summarised as the school having:

- Clear and Focused Mission
- Frequent Monitoring of Student Progress
- Safe and Orderly Environment
- Instructional Leadership

- Frequent Monitoring of Student Progress
- High Expectations for Success
- Positive Home-School Relations

Apart from the capital city, each island generally has one school. The questionnaires were sent by ferry to 180 islands, sealed in labelled waterproof plastic bags. During May, the sea was particularly rough, and only 165 schools were able to return the completed questionnaires. Additional work with the assistance of research assistance resulted in returns from the remaining 20 schools, in June 2016. As I could not travel to all the islands, I devised a standard operating procedure (SOP) for distribution and collection of the survey questionnaires in each school. I obtained approval from the Ministry of Education for survey to be conducted in government-run schools. Questionnaires were printed and sent to appointed atoll-level coordinators, who sent them to appointed research assistants from each school, for distribution among the schoolteachers.

Following a pilot survey involving five schools (450 teachers), the construction and coherence of the questionnaire was assessed using Principal Component Analysis (Rattray and Jones, 2007), and Cronbach alpha coefficients. The main survey involved all 185 offering secondary schooling in the Maldives. Questionnaires were sent to 6,047 teachers, and returned by 4,922, with an overall response rate of 81%.

3. What is the relationship between the principal's instructional leadership and effective school correlates?

A correlational approach was used to address the third question, and check whether there is any relationship between teachers' reports of their principals' instructional leadership and the existence of effective school characteristics. The aggregated mean score for instructional leadership and effective school correlates are used in a Pearson correlation analysis. Linear regression modelling is employed to check whether the existence of effective school characteristics can be predicted from the principal's instructional leadership. Instructional leadership is considered one of the characteristics of an effective school (Lezotte, 1991). Therefore, to avoid any possibility of misleading correlation due to a shared item between the two measures, the instructional leadership dimension is omitted from the effective school characteristics. I also considered teachers' demographic information (such as sex and qualifications) to see if they were linked to how teachers rated their school's instructional leadership and effective school characteristics.

4. To what extent does instructional leadership contribute to differences in pupils' academic attainment?

The fourth research question considers the extent to which instructional leadership contributes to school effectiveness by improving pupils' academic attainment in the secondary school completion examination. I used secondary student attainment in 2016 as an indicator of school effectiveness. Students are required to do six Cambridge O-level subjects and Islamic studies and Dhivehi language in the local SSC examination. This cohort completed their national assessment at primary level in 2009. At the time, this was the only cohort that had records of their prior primary attainment available in the Ministry of Education, and I needed to link students' attainment at both primary and secondary level. The Ministry of Education definition of success is five or more passes in the secondary school completion examinations, and this was used to create a binary variable based on the criteria of the 60% pass policy (Ministry of Education, 2009). Students who did not meet this criterion are considered as a "fail".

Records of the students' primary school attainment indicated that 5,413 students took part in the 2009 national assessment. However, during the data linking process, it was found that only 4,202 took part in the secondary school completion examination. This indicated that for some reason, over 22% of the students did not take the secondary school completion examination. These students may have been prevented from taking part in the examination at school level due to their lower attainment. By doing this, the school would have a better chance of achieving the goal of the 60% pass policy. No specific reason was identified for dropout rates in different school zones (because of the distances, the islands are organised into eight zones). And there is no indication that student' dropout rate has any relationship with income and educational level of the school zone (correlations of −0.01 and 0.05 respectively).

No individual data was available on students' background characteristics such as family income and the educational level of parents. Instead, the income and educational level of the community for each school, are used as proxy data to provide context for student attainment. The National Bureau of Statistics provided the data on employment and the percentage of the population with secondary education on each island. Data from the National Human Development Report (NHDR) of the Maldives 2014 included the percentage of the population with at least secondary education and the estimated income level of the eight school zones. The zonal income data reported in the NHDR is primarily based on the second Household Income and Expenditure Survey (HIES) conducted in the Maldives (Department of National Planning, 2014).

The above data are all used to create a logistic regression model to consider the contribution of principals' instructional leadership to student attainment once other factors, including prior attainment, are accounted for.

The key findings

Over two thirds of teachers expressed the view that principals demonstrated instructional leadership, and over 80% reported that they observed effective school characteristics in their school. The two sets of responses are strongly linked. The correlation between principals' instructional leadership and effective school characteristics is 0.72. The correlation between teachers' reports of their principals' instructional leadership and student attainment in the secondary school completion examination was 0.62. The correlation between teachers' reports of effective school characteristics and student attainment in the secondary school completion examination was 0.73. These results are summarised in Figure 6.1.

Findings similar to these are often used to claim that principals' instructional leadership has both a direct and an indirect effect on pupils' educational attainment. However, there is a strong indication that factors related to students such as prior attainment, age and gender are also associated with their attainment. Moreover, there is a substantial amount of evidence to indicate that factors related to the school community can influence students' academic progress in school (Coleman et al., 1966; Hirsch, 2007; Jencks et al., 1972; Schneider and Coleman, 2018). Without considering such factors, it would be misleading to use the above findings to suggest that principals' instructional leadership has a strong positive impact on school effectiveness, which, in turn, has a positive effect on students' attainment.

Therefore, binary logistic regression modelling is used to explore the potential impact of principals' instructional leadership in the context of

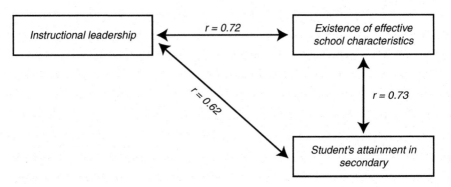

Figure 6.1 The relationship between instructional leadership, effective school characteristics and students' attainment

various factors that may also have an effect on students' attainment (research question 4). The predicted outcome was whether a student achieved a "pass" (passes in five subjects). Predictors included community, school, teacher and student factors, and principals' instructional leadership. The model presented here use all students including cases with missing data (assuming that students without outcomes did not pass). Further approaches to dealing with missing data appear in the full thesis (Shafeeu, 2019a), and further details of the study appear in my paper in the *International Journal of Leadership in Education* (Shafeeu, 2019b). All approaches to handling missing data lead to the same substantive conclusions.

Only 39.5% of all cases had a record of passing examination. The other 61.5% either failed or had no record of taking the examination. The baseline model for the logistic regression is therefore 61.5% accurate with no predictors. Adding the community factors (proxy area level indicators) only increases the accuracy of the model to 62% (1.3% of the outstanding unexplained 39.5 percentage points). The addition of five sets of independent variables (community factors, teachers' factors, school factors, students' factors and principals' instructional leadership) suggested that there was a substantial improvement to the model. Through the addition of the independent variables, the predictive ability of the model increased to 90.5%, see Table 6.1.

The variables representing community, teachers and schools do not add much to the accuracy of the model. This is unusual for socio-economic context, but is perhaps explained by the fact that the socioeconomic status (SES) data is not for individuals (unlike the prior attainment data, for example). It therefore makes little difference whether these factors are considered before or alongside principal leadership.

After context is accounted for, the best predictor is prior attainment along with other student-level measures. Almost all of the variation in outcomes that can be explained is explained by knowledge of the students themselves. This is quite usual for studies of school effectiveness. Almost no variation in student outcomes can be predicted by each school's score for principal instructional leadership.

Table 6.1 Percentage of student passes correctly predicted at each stage of the model

Input block	All cases (%)	Additional percentage correct
Baseline	61.5	–
Community factors	62.0	1.3
Teacher factors	62.2	0.5
School factors	62.7	1.3
Student factors	90.3	69.9
Principal leadership	90.4	0.3

Table 6.2 Coefficients (odds ratios) for the variables used in Table 6.1

Input block	*Variables*	*Odds (ExpB)*
Community factors	Island: Employment rate	1.00
	Island: Population with secondary education	0.99
	Zone: Income index	4.10
	Zone: Population with secondary education	1.04
Teacher factors	Experience (number of years worked)	1.10
	Percentage of trained teachers in schools	1.01
	Qualification: Percentage of undergraduates	1.01
	Qualification: Percentage of postgraduates	1.01
School factors	Existence of effective school characteristics	1.09
Student factors	Prior attainment at primary English	2.09
	Prior attainment at primary Mathematics	1.05
	Age in months	1.01
	Gender (female)	1.25
Principal leadership	Mean of principals' instructional leadership	1.08

Looking at the coefficients for the same model, it is clear that it is prior attainment in English (rather than maths) that is the key predictor of later general attainment (Table 6.2). Coming from a high-income zone is linked to better exam results, as is having a more experienced teacher, attending a school with reported effective school characteristics, and being female.

The fundamental purpose of the effective school movement and the underlying idea of instructional leadership is to promote educational attainment of students in schools. However, the findings of this study suggest that the most important factors for academic attainment are directly related to students' context factors and their school community.

Discussion

The mother tongue of most Maldivians is the native Dhivehi language. However, due to the adoption of an international curriculum, English language is used as the medium of instruction in schools. Therefore, students' ability to interact in the English language is vital for effective teaching and learning. The number of students passing in English Language at IGCSE in each school has a strong relationship with the number of students meeting the national requirement of five subject passes (correlation of 0.74).

There is considerable evidence to support the idea that language development is essential for learning (Berk, 2015; Brock and Rankin, 2008; Couchenour and Chrisman, 2013; Navas et al., 2017). Moreover, language development is known to have a strong influence on the cognitive development of students (Berk, 2015; Vygotskiĭ et al., 2012). In addition to this, students' ability to use language promotes self-esteem and confidence, which can have a positive effect on learning (Irvin et al., 2007; Ross et al., 2016). The general practice in the Maldives is that use of the English language is often limited to classroom activities, and there is little use of the English language in social interaction and in the community. This may have contributed to the lack of English language development of students, ultimately affecting their ability to understand what is being taught in English syllabus followed in schools.

The findings also revealed that girls are 38% more likely to gain passes in five or more subjects in the secondary school completion examination than boys. The international literature suggests that girls outperform boys in secondary school education (Crosnoe et al., 2008). This is also true in the Maldivian education system. As Gorard et al. (2001) have suggested, further research is required to discover the potential socioeconomic, classroom and individual factors that may contribute to this gender gap in the Maldives. However, the data used in this study suggests that over 58% of the dropout students in the years 2014 and 2015 are boys. It is likely that this dropout rate is due to an intervention from the school in order to (falsely and unfairly) increase the pass percentage of the school in the secondary school completion examination.

The results indicate that there is a strong relationship between the income of the school zone and the percentage of the population that are educated above secondary level (correlation of 0.76). Family SES, and parental support and involvement, are powerful predictors of student attainment (Battle and Pastrana, 2007; Fan and Chen, 2001; Gorard and See, 2009; See and Gorard, 2015). Students in schools in low-income zones are less likely to obtain the political, economic and social advantage that are crucial for school success. As a result, students' literacy and numeracy at primary level in the low-income zones are lower than those studying in more economically prosperous islands.

The most economically advantaged areas of the Maldives are the capital city, Malé, and islands where there is local tourism, and islands with or near local airports. Often, these islands have larger populations compared with the neighbouring islands. The larger populations provide better economic opportunities, and receive more attention from the government for political advantage. The combination of these factors may play an important role in schools on such islands, because they receive resources that are generally unavailable to schools in smaller island communities.

The findings indicate that principals' instructional leadership does not contribute directly to students' academic attainment in a differential way, and so is unlikely to help achieve the intended goal of the 60% pass policy. However, in 2017, the Ministry of Education announced the achievement of the national goal of 60% of passes in the secondary school completion examination. The minister reiterated this as a success of the current

Progressive Party of the Maldives (PPM) government in the 39th General Conference of UNESCO (UNESCO, 2017). How was this target met?

The 60% pass target

When the policy was implemented in 2008, the percentage of students passing was nearly 30%. When I received the secondary data on students' attainment in 2015, the percentage of students passing was reported as 46.2%. However, in 2016, 70% of students were reported as having achieved passes in five or more subjects (Figure 6.2).

The nature of this study and its findings compelled me to explore the possible reasons for this sudden rise in students' attainment during the last two years, especially given that the island community indicators and school context variables do not demonstrate any significant variation over the last two years. I identified the net enrolment of students in the final year of secondary education (grade 10) and the numbers of students enrolled in the examination. Nearly 92% of pupils sat five or more subjects in the secondary school completion examination, before the implementation of the 60% pass policy. However, from 2016, fewer students were allowed to sit five or more subjects. And without any formal policy change, instead of using the full enrolment of students, the Ministry of Education started using the number of students who sat more than five subjects to calculate the pass percentage of students at the national level. Calculation using this approach results in the pass percentage of students in five or more subjects in the secondary

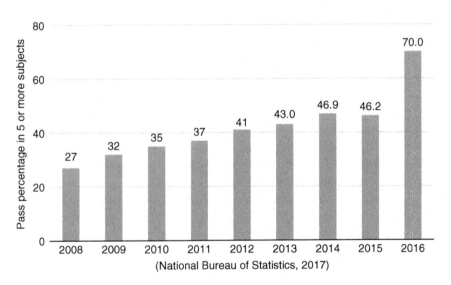

(National Bureau of Statistics, 2017)

Figure 6.2 Pass percentage of students in five or more subjects, 2008–2016

school completion examination appearing a 70% in 2016. Calculation based on this approach is shown below.

$$Pass \ per \ cent = \frac{Number \ of \ students \ passed \ in \ 5 \ subjects}{Number \ of \ students \ examined \ in \ 5 \ subjects} = \frac{2507}{3552}$$

$$= 70.6$$

In all previous years the full population of students were used as denominator to calculate the percentage of pass in the secondary school completion examination. Table 6.3 shows the actual pass percentages of students in five or more subjects using the previous approach. There has been an improvement over time, but the figure of 45.6% is nowhere near the 60% pass rate specified, let alone the 71% success rate claimed by the government.

Under the "no child left behind" policy, the Ministry of Education introduced several vocational training programmes such as *Dhasvaaru*, school TVET and polytechnic courses (Ministry of Education, 2016c). The quality of these courses is often questioned by the teachers and educators. Students who could not obtain the required number of passes in the secondary school completion examination were instructed to enrol in one of the these programmes. However, even with this change, the Ministry of Education was not able to achieve the goal of the 60% pass policy. Moreover, there is a concern that these programmes are used partly as a political tool to show that the government have succeeded in achieving the national educational goals.

Implications

The Maldives is the first country in the South Asian Association for Regional Cooperation (SAARC) region to achieve the Millennium Development Goals (MDG) of universal primary education. However, the quality of the education in the primary grades is not considered to be at a satisfactory level.

Table 6.3 Pass percentages of students in 2008 and 2016

	2008	2016
Grade 10 enrolment N	8,478	5,743
Students who sat the examination N	7,781	5,497
Students sitting 5+ subjects N	7,781	3,552
Students passing 5+ subjects N	2,233	2,507
Percentage of students passing 5+ subjects	28.7	45.6

Data taken from School Statistics 2008 and 2016 (Ministry of Education, 2008, 2016b)

In addition to this, English language ability of the pupils are of a great concern. This is known from the various national assessments conducted by the Ministry of Education. The national assessment conducted in 2009 suggested that less than 30% of the students were able to achieve the national pass levels in both Mathematics and English Language (Aturupane and Shojo, 2012). This shows that there is a need to improve the literacy and numeracy of students at primary level. The result of the national assessment also indicated that students' attainment in English Language is lower than their Mathematics attainment. Therefore, it is very likely that students' low ability in English Language may hinder their academic progress in school. If the Ministry of Education wants to increase the students' pass percentage at secondary level and improve school effectiveness in the Maldives, more importance should be given to preventing students failing at primary grades. Rather than obscure any weakness of primary education through adjusted figures and the introduction of *ad hoc* TVET programmes.

The findings also suggest that pupils' attainment is linked to socioeconomic background. Therefore, school principals can play a role in gathering information about individual student SES, and alert the authorities to various challenges that may be associated with lower SES and family background. These data can be used to formulate effective interventions to overcome disadvantage in education in Maldivian islands.

Since 2014, the Ministry of Education has provided in-service training to more than 150 school principals. These programmes are mainly conducted in the capital city Malé and in Malaysia (Ministry of Education, 2016c). The purpose of these programmes is to improve the principals' leadership in order to increase school effectiveness in the Maldives. However, the effectiveness of the training has not been evaluated. In addition to this, the training programmes are not designed to address the challenges faced by individual schools, especially in poorer zones. Both of these issues could be improved.

The literature on school leadership claims that school leadership can have an effect on students' attainment (Day et al., 2016; Leithwood et al., 2010). In this new study, teachers generally gave a high rating to their principals' instructional leadership and the existence of effective school correlates. However, the analysis conducted by using longitudinal data on students' attainment suggested that principals' instructional leadership does not play a substantial role in improving school effectiveness in the Maldives. The focus of attention in terms of improving student results needs to be elsewhere.

References

Aturupane, H., and Shojo, M. (2012). *Enhancing the quality of education in the Maldives: Challenges and prospects.* The World Bank.

Battle, J., and Pastrana, A. (2007). The relative importance of race and socio-economic status among hispanic and white students. *Hispanic Journal of Behavioral Sciences*, 29(1), pp. 35–49. doi: 10.1177/0739986306294783

Berk, L. (2015). *Child Development*. Pearson Australia.

Brock, A., and Rankin, C. (2008). *Communication, Language and Literacy from Birth to Five*. London: SAGE Publications.

Coleman, J.S., Campbell, E.Q., Hobson, C.J., McPartland, J., Mood, A.M., Weinfeld, F.D., and York, R.L., Equality of Educational Opportunity, US Printing Office, Washington, DC. (1966). *Equality of educational opportunity*. Washington: U.S. Government Printing Office.

Couchenour, D., and Chrisman, K. (2013). *Families, Schools and Communities: Together for Young Children*, 5th ed. California: Cengage Learning.

Crosnoe, R., Riegle-Crumb, C., Field, S., Frank, K., and Muller, C. (2008). Peer group contexts of girls' and boys' academic experiences. *Child Development*, 79(1), pp. 139–155.

Day, C., Gu, Q., and Sammons, P. (2016). The impact of leadership on student outcomes: How successful school leaders use transformational and instructional strategies to make a difference. *Educational Administration Quarterly*, 52(2), pp. 221–258. doi: 10.1177/0013161x15616863

Department of National Planning. (2014). *Household Income and Expenditure Survey 2010-2012*. Malé, Maldives: Ministry of Finance and Treasury.

Fan, X., and Chen, M. (2001). Parental involvement and students' academic achievement: A meta-analysis. *Educational Psychology Review*, 13(1), pp. 1–22. doi: 10.1023/a:1009048817385

Gorard, S. (2001). *Quantitative Methods in Educational Research. The Role of Numbers Made Easy*. London: Continuum.

Gorard, S. (2005). Current contexts for research in educational leadership and management. *Educational Management Administration & Leadership*, 33(2), pp. 155–164. doi: 10.1177/1741143205051050

Gorard, S., Rees, G., and Salisbury, J. (2001). Investigating the patterns of differential attainment of boys and girls at school. *British Educational Research Journal*, 27(2), pp. 125–139.

Gorard, S., and See, B.H. (2009). The impact of socio-economic status on participation and attainment in science. *Studies in Science Education*, 45(1), pp. 93–129. doi: 10.1080/03057260802681821

Hallinger, P. (1990). *Principal Instructional Management Rating Scale*. Sarasota, FL: Leading Development Associates.

Hallinger, P. (2015). *List of PIMRS studies 1983–2015*. Retrieved from http://philiphallinger.com/wp-content/uploads/2015/12/PIMRS-Reference-List-Updated-11-2015.pdf

Hallinger, P., and Heck, R.H. (1996). Reassessing the principal's role in school effectiveness: A review of empirical research, 1980–1995. *Educational Administration Quarterly*, 32(1), pp. 5–44.

Hirsch, D. (2007). *Experiences of poverty and educational disadvantage*. York: Joseph Rowntree Foundation. jrf.org.uk.

Irvin, J.L., Meltzer, J., and Dukes, M.S. (2007). *Taking Action on Adolescent Literacy: An Implementation Guide for School Leaders*. Alexandria, VA: Association for Supervision and Curriculum Development.

Jencks, C., Smith, M., Acland, H., Bane, M., Cohen, D., Gintis, H., ... and Michelson, S. (1972). *Inequality: A Reassessment of the Effect of Family and Schooling in American Schools*. New York: Basic Books.

Leithwood, K., Anderson, S., Mascall, B., and Strauss, T. (2010). School leaders' influences on student learning: The four paths. In T. Bush, L. Bell, and D. Middlewood (eds.), *The Principles of Educational Leadership and Management* (pp. 13–30). London: Sage.

Levin, K.A. (2006). Study design III: Cross-sectional studies. *Evidence Based Dentistry*, 7(1), pp. 24–25. doi: 10.1038/sj.ebd.6400375

Lezotte, L.W. (1991). *Correlates of Effective Schools: The First and Second Generation*. Okemos, MI: Effective Schools Products, Ltd.

Lezotte, L.W., and Snyder, K.M.K. (2011). *What Effective Schools Do: Re-envisioning the Correlates*. Bloomington, IN: Solution Tree Press.

Ministry of Education. (2008). *School Statistics 2008*. Malé, Maldives: Ministry of Education.

Ministry of Education. (2009). *Increasing GCE O' level pass percentage: Circular number 03/2009*. Malé, Maldives: Ministry of Education.

Ministry of Education. (2016b). *School Statistics 2016*. Malé, Maldives: Ministry of Education.

Ministry of Education. (2016c). *Thahuzeeb Muju'thamakah Tharubavee Thauleemu*. Malé, Maldives: Ministry of Education.

Navas, A.L., Ciboto, T., and Borges, J.P.A. (2017). Reading disorders and the role of speech-language pathologists. In F. Fernandes (ed.), *Advances in Speech-Language Pathology*. London: InTech Open.

Rattray, J., and Jones, M.C. (2007). Essential elements of questionnaire design and development. *Journal of Clinical Nursing*, 16(2), pp. 234–243.

Ross, M., Perkins, H., and Bodey, K. (2016). Academic motivation and information literacy self-efficacy: The importance of a simple desire to know. *Library & Information Science Research*, 38(1), pp. 2–9. doi: 10.1016/j.lisr.2016.01.002

Schneider, B., and Coleman, S.J. (2018). *Parents, Their Children, And Schools*. New York: Taylor & Francis.

See, B.H., and Gorard, S. (2015). The role of parents in young people's education – a critical review of the causal evidence. *Oxford Review of Education*, 41(3), pp. 346–366. doi: 10.1080/03054985.2015.1031648

Shafeeu, I. (2019a). *Relationship between principals' instructional leadership and school effectiveness. Does it make a difference? Evidence from the Maldives*. Doctoral thesis. United Kingdom: Durham University. Retrieved from http://etheses.dur.ac.uk/13134/

Shafeeu, I. (2019b). Instructional leadership: Does it make a difference? Evidence from the Maldives. *International Journal of Leadership in Education*. Routledge. doi: 10.1080/13603124.2019.1690697

Shafeeu, I., Shahma, A., Moosa, V., Musthafa, A., and Imran, M. (2011). Policy on increasing pass percentage in lower secondary examinations. *Strategic Policy Management in Education.* Faculty of Education, University of Malaya.

Sobol, J.J. (2004). Cross-sectional research design. In J.S. Albanese (ed.), *The Encyclopedia of Criminology and Criminal Justice.* Hoboken, NJ: John Wiley & Sons.

UNESCO. (2017). Records of the General Conference: 38th Session Proceedings. Paper presented at the 39th General Conference of the UNESCO, Paris.

Vygotskiĭ, L.S., Hanfmann, E., Vakar, G., and Kozulin, A. (2012). *Thought and Language.* Revised and Expanded Edition. USA: MIT Press.

Educational Improvement

Part II consists of PhD projects which investigated educational improvement through systematic reviews of evidence, experimental field trials, and use of large-scale datasets.

Educational improvement

There are chapters covering:

- Can co-operative learning and group-work help English language learners?
- Can we raise attainment through metacognition or learning to learn?
- Does Philosophy for Children work as a dialogic approach to teaching in China?
- Is critical thinking teachable?
- Is academic buoyancy (mindfulness) a useful concept for dealing with everyday setbacks in education?
- Are morality and moral awareness a cultural phenomenon?

The results here are mixed, showing how hard it is to identify beneficial programmes for education. It has been estimated that only around 10% to 15% of the most plausible-sounding educational ideas actually work when tested independently. Co-operative learning did not work for English language learners in Thailand (Chapter 8). But there is confirmed promise from the use of learning to learn techniques (Chapter 9), and primary school discussions in a philosophical style (Chapter 10). On the other hand, wider school outcomes such as critical thinking (Chapter 11) and buoyancy (Chapter 12) may be intrinsically harder to change and to show evidence of changing. Researching the morality of school-age children may be even harder again (Chapter 13). However, through novel methods, and combinations of randomised control trials, systematic reviews and primary data, all of these chapters move their fields forward in key ways.

DOI: 10.4324/9781003201366-8

Can co-operative learning and group-work help English language learners in Thailand?

Phanatdao Chantarasiri

Introduction

This PhD centres on an evaluation of an intervention to improve the learning of English by Thai students at university. The design is a randomised control trial and comparative study, in which 614 university students participated.

In an increasingly interconnected world, all knowledge can be spread widely, apparently without time and space barriers. The English language plays an important role as an international language, and a medium of communication between people with different languages and cultures. Around 1.35 billion out of approximately 7.8 billion people around the world speak English, making English probably the most-spoken language in the world (Lyons, 2021). Many transactions and processes in business, education, sciences or technology now require high proficiency in English. The high demand for literacy and proficiency in English has influenced numerous educational institutions to seek the ways to improve the English proficiency of their citizens.

In Thailand, English language is a compulsory foreign language described in the Basic Education Core Curriculum, and required for all grade levels. Actions taken by the Thai Ministry of Education to enhance the effectiveness of English language teaching and learning include:

- Increasing the numbers of hours of compulsory and elective English language classes
- Introducing online courses and language-learning applications
- Providing training programmes for Thai teachers of English language by English specialists to support and strengthen their English teaching skills (Fredrickson, 2016)
- And offering upgraded bilingual educational programme as an alternative to English language learning (Language Learning and Teaching Unit, 2017)

DOI: 10.4324/9781003201366-9

However, English language teaching in Thailand remains largely based on rote memorisation of vocabulary and grammar structures, mostly using text-based instructional materials. Teaching English in university classes is based on a teacher centred lecture format. Lecturing remains the dominant method of instruction in higher education classes throughout the world (McKeachie and Svinicki, 2011; Millis, 2012).

This traditional learning approach is linked to lack of motivation, low participation and even boredom among Thai students learning English. It seems that many Thai students do not move beyond learning of basic English grammar and are not able to communicate with foreigners in English even at a basic level. English learners have few opportunities to be exposed to and interact in the target language of study. Hence, many Thai students do not see the importance and use of learning English. Most of them only learn English language in the classroom for a few hours each week and use the Thai language in their daily life outside the classroom. With the traditional methods of rote memorisation, students will tend to remember the content of English lesson for a short period of time in order to pass the exam, and soon forget it. Many students also have difficulties applying what they have learned in real-life contexts.

The Education First English Proficiency Index (EF Education First, 2018) is based on the acquisition of English skills of students from secondary and tertiary level across five regions and over 400 cities around the world. According to this proficiency index, Thailand was a low proficiency country. In EF Education First (2020), based on the proficiency scores of 2.2 million non-native English speakers in 100 counties, Thailand was a "Very Low Proficiency" country, far behind many of its neighbouring countries and most of the world. English teaching and learning in Thailand is in a difficult and challenging situation.

In tertiary English classes in Thailand, every undergraduate student is required to take two to four Basic to Advanced English classes. However, this study focuses on Thai instructors of English language and English-major student teachers who study three and a half years in the faculty of Education, and do one-term teaching practicums in the local schools, with the hope that they will be the future of English teachers in Thailand.

Co-operative learning

One of the important wider educational reforms by the Ministry of Education has been to promote student-centred education (Ministry of Education, 2008, 2012). The Active Learning Approach is evidence-led, and suggested as one of the most productive approaches that can "provide [a] natural environment for learning the English language" (Trivedi, 2013).

Faust and Paulson (1998) proposed a number of active learning techniques and activities for applying in college classrooms, and co-operative learning strategies is one of the techniques for more complex tasks. Co-operative learning has become one of the dominant instructional practice around the world (Johnson and Johnson, 2009). Co-operative learning, especially Student Teams Achievement Divisions (STAD), has been extensively researched with apparently with successful results in term of English achievement (e.g. Anwer et al., 2018; Khan and Akhtar, 2017; Kurniawan et al., 2017; Mudofir, 2017; Munir et al., 2017; Syafiq and Rahmawati, 2017; Upa and Ridho, 2019).

Co-operative learning requires students working together in a small group to help support each other in order to maximise their own learning as well as the others to accomplish a shared goal. When students work co-operatively in their small group, they learn how to communicate, give and receive help, express their ideas and listen to other ideas and perspective, handle the differences and solve problems democratically (Gillies, 2007). In co-operative learning, "the success of one student helps other students to be success" (Slavin, 1982, p. 6) as opposed to traditional classroom where students compete for grades.

According Johnson and Johnson (2014), there are five basis elements for small-group learning to be co-operative – positive interdependence, individual accountability, face-to-face promotive interaction, social skills, and group skills. See my thesis for full descriptions of every element of co-operative learning.

Student Teams Achievement Divisions (STAD)

STAD is a co-operative learning model developed by Slavin (1986). In this model, students are assigned by teacher to a small heterogeneous group of four to five members, mixed according to sex, ethnicity, academic performance, and so on (Balfakih, 2003). The groups work together to achieve shared goals and complete given tasks. Everyone is responsible for their learning and also helps, motivates, and encourages other group members to learn. Therefore, the primary goals of the group are that everyone learns the material and makes sure that other group members also master the material (Khansir and Alipour, 2015).

The STAD model has five major components which are: class presentations, teams, quizzes, individual improvement scores, and team recognition (Slavin, 1986).

Class presentation. The teacher presents concepts and material in a class presentation which can be in the form of lecture, class discussion or presentation with audio-visual methods. Students need to pay attention to the class presentation to be able to do the later quizzes. Quiz scores are combined to create team scores.

Student teams consist of four to five heterogeneous members (as above). Teams offer peer support and encouragement for every student to try their best because every member is accounted for in the team success.

Individual quizzes are used to evaluate students' achievement of class content and material. Students take quizzes on their own without any assistance from other team members to help ensure that every student is responsible for learning the content and material.

Individual improvement scores are achievement goals for each student to work harder than they did before. Each student is provided with their "base" scores, the minimum scores to reach on each quiz. The individual improvement scores are each student's quiz scores that surpass their "base" score. In order to help their teams, students need to perform better than they did on previous quizzes.

Team recognition. Many forms of team recognition can be applied depending on different classes and context. However, teachers' appreciation of teams' cooperation and success is most significant (Slavin, 1986).

Armstrong and Palmer (1998) found that the STAD method was easy to implement especially in block schedule classes where the instruction period is long for each class. Furthermore, this model is recommended to be adapted in many subject areas such as mathematics, science, language arts, and foreign language. But especially in English language classes (Ghaith and Yaghi, 1998). Accordingly, Khan and Akhtar (2017) highly recommended that STAD to be applied to teach English grammar in English language classroom. For language learning classes, STAD is intended to help second language students obtain linguistic knowledge (Ghaith and Yaghi, 1998) by giving students chances to communicate and negotiate ideas with others in target language (Khansir and Alipour, 2015; Kurniawan et al., 2017). This can foster deeper understanding of material (Saniei and Ghadikolaei, 2015; Sunarti and Rachman, 2018) and offer positive impact on learning language skills (Kurniawan et al., 2017).

Summary of the methods used

Design

This research project employed a cluster-randomised controlled trial in order to determine the effects of implementing co-operative learning model, STAD, on English language achievement as compared to groups that employed the normal method of teaching, that is, "treatment as usual". To measure and evaluate the mean achievement scores in English language, a pre-test and post-test design was used. The pre- and post-tests were paper and pencil tests administered under exam conditions and proctored by participant instructors. The intervention carried out in the "English Structure for Teachers of English" module from Faculty of Education, Rajabhat University in Thailand – a higher education institution partly operated by the government.

With the historical foundation of teacher colleges, administration, university culture, ranking, and curriculums are different than other types of universities in Thailand. There are 38 Rajabhat Universities located around the country. For Faculty of Education under the Rajabhat University System, each major degree course use the same curriculum across the country.

The duration of the study was 16 weeks (one term) consisting of 16 face-to-face classes. Each class was three hours period for every week and took place at their universities. Unfortunately, because of the COVID-19 outbreak, the average number of classes students could possibly meet in their normal classroom condition was approximately 8 to 12.

Observation of classes and informal conversations with teachers and students, where it was possible, helped in assessing the challenges and strengths of implementing co-operative learning.

Participants

Since only cluster randomisation at university level was feasible, the experiment involved 614 students from 13 universities forming 13 clusters (Figure 7.1). A total of eight universities which agreed to participate in the intervention were randomly assigned to an experimental group and a control group, four universities in each group. The other five universities only agreed to complete the pre-test and post-test, and are described as a comparator group. The reason for including universities in a comparator group was to increase the sample size. There were 23 classes in total

The participants for this research include instructors of the module "English Structure for Teachers of English" and all of their students who enrolled in the module from 13 universities. The participating instructors were 13 Thai instructors of English language at university level from 13 Rajabhat Universities, in Thailand. The instructors were responsible for the module delivered, the teaching lessons and all classroom management.

The students participating in this study were first-year student teachers who were majoring in English from Faculty of Education, in 13 Rajabhat Universities in Thailand. There were 235 students in experimental, 145 in control, and 234 in the comparator groups. They all were non-native speakers of English and Thai language is their mother tongue. Their ages were approximately 17 to 18 years.

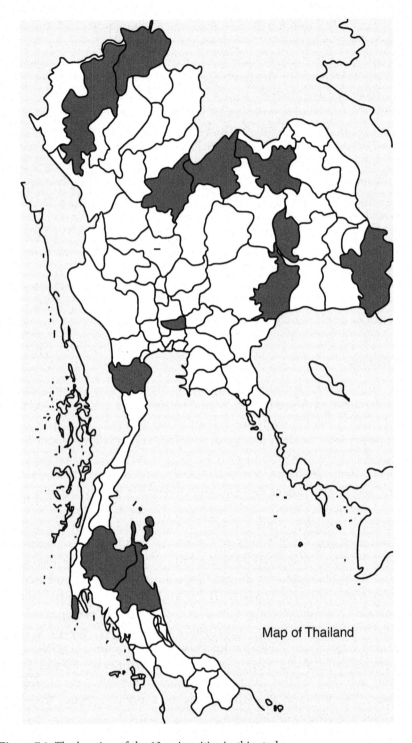

Map of Thailand

Figure 7.1 The location of the 13 universities in this study

Prior to the term start, the instructors in the intervention group were trained by the researcher in how to apply co-operative learning model in their English classes.

Outcome measures

To evaluate students' English language proficiency and to determine the effectiveness of implementing the co-operative learning model to enhance student teachers' achievement in English language, the Cambridge Assessment English "B1 Preliminary" was used as the main research instrument. B1 Preliminary for general and higher education is an English language exam at Level B1 of the Common European Framework of Reference for Languages or CEFR. This standardised test is considered as an intermediate-level qualification for those who have mastered the basics of English and have practical language skills for everyday use. According to Cambridge Assessment English, this test is suitable for older teens and people who have left school.

There are four sections in the B1 Preliminary test; reading, writing, listening, and speaking. The intervention is carried out in the "English Structure for Teachers of English" module. Speaking and writing are not the main focus of this module. For this reason, only listening and reading were adapted for use in the study. Two parallel versions of sample tests were downloaded from Cambridge Assessment English Website and used with permission from the developer for research purposes only.

In order to evaluate students' performance among these groups (experimental, control, and compare) and to determine whether students in any groups show improvement, the differences between pre- and post-intervention scores were used to create gain scores. Differences between groups in terms of gains scores were converted into standardised "effect" sizes, as in the difference between means divided by their overall standard deviation (Gorard, 2021).

Summary of key findings

Impact

Looking first at the intervention (co-operative learning) group and all others (both the randomised control and the natural comparator group), there is some evidence of a slight benefit from the intervention (Table 7.1). The comparator students were ahead, on average, in their test scores at the outset, and again after the intervention. Both groups had worse scores in the second test (it is not clear why). However, the score for the intervention group declined less.

Table 7.1 Comparison of gain score and effect size between experimental group and all comparator students (n = 499)

	N	Pre-test	SD	Post-test	SD	Gain score	SD	Effect size
Intervention	224	7.28	3.37	7.08	3.42	−0.20	3.09	+0.09
Comparators	275	8.05	3.45	7.53	3.67	−0.52	3.63	
Overall	499	7.70	3.43	7.33	3.57	−0.38	3.40	

Table 7.2 Comparison of gain score and effect size between experimental and comparison groups (n = 371)

	N	Pre-test	SD	Post-test	SD	Gain score	SD	Effect size
Intervention	224	7.28	3.37	7.08	3.42	−0.20	3.09	+0.32
Comparison	147	7.21	3.00	6.01	2.97	−1.20	3.16	
Overall	371	7.25	3.21	6.66	3.29	−0.60	3.15	

When considering the two different types of comparators separately, it is clear that the suggestion of benefit from the intervention comes solely from the non-randomised comparator group (Table 7.2). Here the groups are more balanced at the outset with the intervention fractionally ahead. Both groups have worse scores on the second test, but this is much more marked for the comparator group.

More importantly, this means that the randomised control group actually did better than the intervention group (ES = −0.13). At the outset, the intervention and control groups were not balanced, with the pre-test score of the control group already ahead (Table 7.3). The control group actually improved their pre-intervention scores (+0.26), whereas, as already noted, the scores for the intervention group declined (−0.20).

Overall, the results suggest that the intervention as implemented shows no benefit for students' English language achievement. There is no strong evidence of co-operative learning model, namely STAD, leading to improved student teachers' English language achievement, compared to not doing it. Any interpretations or conclusion draw from this study should be considered with caution.

Table 7.3 Comparison of gain score and effect size between experimental and control groups (n = 352)

	N	Pre-test	SD	Post-test	SD	Gain score	SD	Effect size
Experimental	224	7.28	3.37	7.08	3.42	−0.20	3.09	−0.13
Control	128	9.01	3.73	9.27	3.65	+0.26	3.97	
Overall	352	7.91	3.60	7.88	3.66	−0.03	3.44	

Fidelity of implementation

The COVID-19 pandemic and lockdown started in the term in which the intervention was conducted. The Thai Ministry of Education had ordered that all schools and universities had to be temporary closed. The beginning of term was postponed. All universities announced that all lessons needed to be switched to distance or on-line learning. This was a particular problem for implementing co-operative learning wherein students are required to work together closely in teams. Therefore, after discussing these issues and teaching and learning conditions with all instructors, the mutual agreement was that the intervention would start when the teaching was restarted in normal classroom environments. Or, at least, until the Ministry of Education eased some teaching and learning regulations. The universities participating in this study are located in different provinces and some are located in different regions. Some universities were located in high-risk areas for the infection. As a result, each university announced their own specific regulations depending on the situation in their areas.

Since the study was carried out during the COVID-19 pandemic, the intervention in each university was necessarily adapted to meet with university and state regulations under the circumstances. Even the numbers of classes varied depending on the location of the university and whether it was located in a high-risk area for disease outbreak. None of the universities involved in this study completed the whole 16 classes as planned; some were able to deliver only 8 classes. Furthermore, students in the experimental groups inevitably received different modes of teaching: face-to-face, online or hybrid due to the university regulations in each area.

For effective implementation, it is suggested that the co-operative learning instruction should be applied at least a term or more, for group members to build their relationships as well as work on their academic progress through their support and encouragement of each other both cognitively and socially (Johnson and Johnson, 2009, 2014; Jolliffe, 2007). Consequently, a trial of a one term intervention without COVID interruption could be conducted again, in order to investigate the effectiveness of co-operative learning instruction, and to confirm whether this current study findings were affected by the pandemic restrictions on teaching and learning.

Nevertheless, according to lesson observations in the experimental classes, all instructors had tried their best to deliver the lessons and follow the teaching steps, as they had been trained. The experimental instructors had adapted the co-operative lessons as they had been trained into their teaching, some of which was under restricted conditions. The use of co-operative learning is feasible. Instructors and students generally showed positive attitudes towards co-operative learning, and supported its activities.

There was no diffusion because of the cluster randomisation at university level. Each university was either randomised to experimental or control groups. Each university was located in a different province, and some are located in different regions. There was no evidence that control instructors had accessed or used instruction materials of co-operative learning which were used in experimental classes. Thus, it was very unlikely that students in different groups had discussed, shared or exchanged class materials or learning methods.

According to interviews with students, some did not fully participate in co-operative activities because they did not understand their value. Students who disliked cooperative learning indicated that their peers did not work for the teams as much as they expected. A common complaint from students was their friends' unwillingness to work together for their teams or do their shared parts of the work. This lowered others group members' motivation to learn as a group. The instructors also reported some students might prefer to work individually.

Brief reflections on the study

If the Thai Ministry of Education or any educational institution wish to apply co-operative learning and transform classrooms from traditional or so-called "passive" to more active learning classrooms, they will have to make effective policies that suit local contexts. Long-term, teacher education may be the most suitable place to start any shift in adjusting the classroom environment, activities, and materials to help enhance student achievement in the English language in Thailand. In the meantime, teachers/instructors would need to be trained better than currently, in order to be familiar and confident with co-operative learning and to ensure its proper and correct implementation. Of course, the findings of this study provide no evidence, yet, that co-operative learning is indeed the way to go, if improving test scores is the sole or main objective.

References

Anwer, M., Tatlah, I., and Butt, I. (2018). Effect of co-operative learning on students' achievement in English tenses. *Pakistan Journal of Education*, 35(2), pp. 37–52.

Balfakih, N. (2003). The effectiveness of student team-achievement division (STAD) for teaching high school chemistry in the United Arab Emirates. *International Journal of Science Education*, 25(5), pp. 605–624. doi: 10.1080/ 09500690110078879

EF Education First. (2018). *EF English Proficiency Index 2018*. https://www.ef. com/assetscdn/WIBIwq6RdJvcD9bc8RMd/legacy/__/~/media/centralefcom/ epi/downloads/full-reports/v8/ef-epi-2018-english.pdf

EF Education First. (2020). *EF English Proficiency Index 2020*. https://www.ef. com/assetscdn/WIBIwq6RdJvcD9bc8RMd/legacy/__/~/media/centralefcom/ epi/downloads/full-reports/v8/ef-epi-2018-english.pdf

Faust, J., and Paulson, D. (1998). Active learning in the college classroom. *Journal on Excellence in College Teaching*, 9(2), pp. 3–24.

Fredrickson, T. (2016, June 6). More English for Prathom students. *Bangkok Post*. https://www.bangkokpost.com/learning/easy/1003037/more-english-for-prathom-students

Ghaith, G., and Yaghi, H. (1998). Effect of co-operative learning on the acquisition of second language rules and mechanics. *System*, 26, pp. 223–234. doi: 10.1016/S0346-251X(98)00005-0

Gillies, R.M. (2007). *Co-operative Learning: Integrating Theory and Practice*. London: SAGE.

Gorard, S. (2021). *How to Make Sense of Statistics: Everything You Need to Know about Using Numbers in Social Science*. London: SAGE.

Johnson, D., and Johnson, R. (2009). An educational psychology success story: Social interdependence theory and co-operative learning. *Educational Researcher*, 38(5), pp. 365–379. doi: 10.3102/0013189x09339057

Johnson, D., and Johnson, R. (2014). Co-operative learning in 21st century. *Anales de Psicología*, 30(3), pp. 841–851. doi: 10.6018/analesps.30.3.201241

Jolliffe, W. (2007). Cooperative Learning in the Classroom: Putting it into Practice. London: Sage.

Khan, A., and Akhtar, M. (2017). Investigating the effectiveness of co-operative learning method on teaching of English grammar. *Bulletin of Education and Research*, 39(1), pp. 1–16.

Khansir, A., and Alipour, T. (2015). The impact of Students Team Achievement Divisions (STAD) on Iranian EFL learners' listening comprehension. *Theory and Practice in Language Studies*, 5(8), pp. 1710–1715.

Kurniawan, I., Mukhaiyar, and Rozimela, Y. (2017). The effect of Student Teams-Achievement Division (STAD) technique toward students' speaking skill and class participation. *Journal of English Education and Teaching (JEET)*, 1(1), pp. 35–47.

Language Learning and Teaching Unit. (2017). *Upgrading English Program Workshop*. Bureau of Academic Affirs and Educational Standards, Office of the Basic Education Commission.

Lyons, D. (2021). How many people speak English, and where is it spoken? *Babble Maganize*. https://www.babbel.com/en/magazine/how-many-people-speak-english-and-where-is-it-spoken

McKeachie, W., and Svinicki, M. (2011). *McKeachie's Teaching Tips: Strategies, Research, and Theory for College and Univeristy Teachers*, 13th ed. USA: Cengage Learning.

Millis, B. (2012). IDEA Paper No. 53: Active learning strategies in face-to-face courses. *The IDEA Center.* https://www.ideaedu.org/Portals/0/Uploads/Documents/IDEAPapers/IDEA Papers/PaperIDEA_53.pdf

Ministry of Education. (2008). *Administrators and child centered strategies.* http://www.moe.go.th/moe/th/cms_group/detail.php?NewsID=98&Key=aca_article

Ministry of Education. (2012). Student-centered education. *Ministry of Education News.* http://www.moe.go.th/moe/th/news/detail.php?NewsID=31786&Key=hotnews

Mudofir, I. (2017). STAD vs conventional and learning modality towards English fluency learning outcome. *International Journal of Social Science and Humanity,* 7(4), pp. 228–232.

Munir, S., Emzir, E., and Rahmat, A. (2017). The effect of teaching methods and learning styles on students' English achievement (an experimental study at Junior High School 1 Pasangkayu). *Journal of Education, Teaching and Learning,* 2(2), pp. 233–237.

Saniei, A., and Ghadikolaei, F. (2015). The contribution of Student Teams-Achievement Divisions (STAD) to teaching English collocations to intermediate learners. *International Journal of Language Learning and Applied Linguistics World (IJLLALW),* 8(2), pp. 125–133.

Slavin, R. (1982). Co-operative learning: Student teams. What research says to the teacher. National Education Association Professional Library, PO Box 509, West Haven, CT 06516.

Slavin, R. (1986). *Student Team Learning: An Overview and Practical Guide,* 2nd ed. National Education Association of the United States.

Sunarti, and Rachman, D. (2018). The effectiveness of flip classroom with Student Teams-Achievement Divisions (STAD) method to teach reading viewed from students' English learning interest. *Journal of Linguistic and English Teaching,* 3(2), pp. 183–194. doi: 10.24903/sj.v3i2.246

Syafiq, A., and Rahmawati, A. (2017). The effect of Student Team Achievement Division Co-operative Learning (STAD CL) in teaching the reading comprehension. *Jurnal Refleksi Edukatika,* 7(2), pp. 118–122.

Trivedi, K. (2013). Effectiveness of active learning approach in teaching English language of standard IX students. *Voice of Research,* 2(1), pp. 30–32.

Upa, R., and Ridho, M. (2019). Teaching translation through STAD (Students Team Achievement Division) Technique. *Jurnal Studi Guru Dan Pembelajaran,* 2(3), pp. 246–251. doi: 10.30605/jsgp.2.3.2019.48

CHAPTER 8

The role of metacognition in the learning of English as a foreign language

Meechai Wongdaeng

Introduction

The idea of metacognitive and self-regulatory development has been widely applied in various educational contexts, including English language education. A systematic review was conducted to examine the existing evidence on the impact of metacognitive interventions for English as a Foreign Language (EFL) learners. The results show promise of the approach in EFL contexts, but were inconclusive due to limitations of much research so far, in terms of design, sample size, attrition and other factors. This indicates the need for studies on the topic to pay higher attention to such key research elements. Based on the systematic review's findings, a cluster randomised control trial was conducted with a group of EFL learners in Southern Thai universities, faced with a new challenge of passing a standardised English test to satisfy their graduation requirement. More than 400 EFL students took part as either intervention or control participants while approximately 360 students were included as a further comparator group. The results show that the intervention group made more progress in English language than their non-intervention peers. The integrated in-depth process evaluation describes both the positive features and the drawbacks of the intervention. The chapter ends with some implications for policy and practice.

Background

English language education has been playing an influential role in education policy worldwide as the language is associated with improving personal employability and increasing a country's competitiveness (Hayes, 2010). English language has, therefore, been an integral part of the educational curriculum globally. In Thailand, English has continually received high re-cognition in education policy and curriculum development. The official establishment of the Association of the Southeast Asian Nations (ASEAN) as

DOI: 10.4324/9781003201366-10

a shared economic community in 2015 has elevated the significance of the English language further, because it was declared the official working language of the region. English language policies in Thailand have therefore been emphasized but improvement has not yet been seen in learning outcomes (Kaur et al., 2016).

The Exit English Examination policy was launched in 2016 across public universities in Thailand requiring students to pass an accepted standardised English test as another graduation requirement (Wudthayagorn, 2019). The policy's aim was to improve university students' English competence. Despite such an aim, the policy appears deficient in two aspects. It failed to consider the unanticipated effect which can occur for students in less privileged areas who might have already been disadvantaged. This is directly relevant to the target participants of the study who live in the southernmost provinces which are under heightened security measures which deter the economic and educational development (Prachathai, 2017). Also, the policy is not accompanied with a due mechanism to support smooth implementation. A good support system is important for a policy success (Trowler, 2003).

To support the learners in disadvantaged areas so that they can satisfy the new graduation requirement and have better opportunities for future career path, an effective learning intervention could be helpful. A rapid review of literature on effective ways to improve learning led to synthesis studies by Dignath and Büttner (2008), Education Endowment Foundation (EEF) (2018), Higgins et al. (2005) and Wang et al. (1990). All report the effectiveness of metacognitive development for improving learning. From a further review of EFL literature, the same kind of intervention has been widely applied in tertiary EFL research and high potential for improving English learning have been reported (e.g., Chou, 2017; Cross, 2011; Rahimirad and Shams, 2014).

Therefore, a metacognitive approach to second language teaching and learning is the focus of enquiry of this study and a model of metacognitive instruction has been developed, implemented, and assessed for its effectiveness.

The concept of metacognition is multifaceted and has been given multiple interpretations (Efklides, 2008). However, the fundamental core emphasised in most definitions are the knowledge and regulation of one's cognitive activities in learning processes (Livingston, 2003). "Metacognition" is commonly known as "thinking about thinking". Flavell (1976) defined it as "one's own knowledge concerning one's own cognitive processes and products or anything related to them" (p. 232). In educational terms, it is students' awareness of their own strengths and weaknesses as learners and their ability to use such awareness strategically to direct their learning (Quigley et al., 2018). The processes through which learners employ their self-awareness to monitor and direct their learning behaviours to achieve learning goals are also called self-regulation (Zimmerman, 2002).

To foster optimal benefits from metacognitive and self-regulatory development, instruction should be organised in a way that could guide the leaners about strategies to use, how to use and when and why to use them. In the Metacognitive Pedagogical Sequence (MPS) by Vandergrift (2004) which has been widely applied in EFL listening studies, seven stages were proposed to guide learners to plan their listening, monitor, and verify strategies in multiple listening attempts and evaluate their performance. In the present study, the Plan, Monitor, Evaluate, Retrieve (PMER) model was developed for metacognitive and self-regulatory instruction in second language listening.

The PMER model is informed by the principles of metacognition and self-regulation proposed by both cognitive development and language acquisition scholars. The first three processes in the model are the most common metacognitive strategies. The strategies for each process are largely influenced by Zimmerman (2000)'s model but have been adapted to cater for second language listening. The strategies are expressed in a mnemonic manner to aid memory. The model also includes pedagogical sequence, in line with Vandergrift and Goh (2012) to resonate with classroom practices. The role of retrieval practice is the key distinctive feature of the model. Moreover, the model realises the important role of metacognitive awareness as the fundamental element in each metacognitive process (Pintrich, 2002).

The research questions

This study addressed the following research questions:

- To what extent does metacognitive instruction have an impact on the listening and overall English achievement of EFL learners in southern Thai universities?
- To what extent does metacognitive instruction have an impact on metacognitive awareness for listening of English learners in southern Thai universities?
- In what manner is the impact of metacognitive instruction associated with differences in biographical variables such as gender, first language background and socio-economic backgrounds, and pre-existing proficiency levels?
- What are the teachers and students' perceptions of metacognitive instruction?

Due to shortage of space, only the headline findings are presented here for the first and the last questions. These involve two main elements – a systematic review and an evaluation.

Systematic review

The systematic review identifies, examines and synthesises relevant studies on the effectiveness of metacognitive interventions in tertiary EFL contexts. To minimise bias, prior criteria were developed for including and excluding studies. Research had to be about:

- Learners of English as a foreign language (EFL) in higher education
- Metacognitive interventions or systematic reviews or meta-analyses which review studies based on metacognitive interventions
- Studies must involve a comparison group for counterfactual evidence
- Language competence such as reading, listening and vocabulary is a primary or secondary outcome. Studies assessing satisfaction, perceptions, awareness alone will be excluded.

An electronic search was conducted with seven data sources (Table 8.1). The search string "metacogniti*" AND "English" AND "effect" OR "experimental" was used with some adaptations in some databases to miss out the fewest studies. A total of 2,942 studies were found.

The identified studies underwent deduplication and two screening stages first by titles and abstracts and second by full text screening. The screening criteria were applied, leading to 29 studies being retained for data extraction. A full PRISMA flowchart appears in the thesis.

The 29 included studies underwent quality appraisal based on criteria adapted from Gorard (2014)'s "Sieve" for research findings and the EEF (2019)'s classification of security of findings. Among the 29 studies, three received a security rating of 2 (on a scale of 0 of no consequence, to 4 the strongest that can be expected). These three are controlled trials with random allocation of students and use standardised and independent tests for measuring the outcomes. However, their sample size is small (but larger than most of the other studies).

Table 8.1 The databases searched, and the number of studies identified

Databases	N of Hits
Scopus	180
JSTOR	920
ScienceDirect (Elsevier)	1,315
Education Resource Information Centre (ERIC)	207
Web of Science	167
Google Scholar	146
ThaiJO	7
TOTAL	2,942

Seifoori (2016) focused on the speaking skills of 114 Iranian undergraduates. The results suggest that the intervention group outperforms the control group (ES 0.47) and that using both pre and online task planners have the highest benefits to the students.

Tavakoli and Koosha (2016) investigated reading comprehension among 100 Iranian students and was based on the CALLA model by Chamot and O'Malley (1994). The results clearly favoured the intervention group with an effect size of 1.50. The researchers emphasised guiding students when and how to employ strategies over the knowledge of strategies.

Abdelhafez (2006) focused on reading and listening comprehension of 80 Egyptian students. It also followed the procedure in the CALLA model and highlighted opportunities for guided and free practice. The results favour the invention group with an average effect size of 1.62.

Seventeen studies are classified with a rating of 1. These studies are based on controlled trials with an even smaller sample size compared to the previous group. Thirteen of them reported a positive impact from the intervention while four reported no effect. Eight studies targeted reading comprehension with six reporting positive effect and two no effect. Key factors associated with the improvement were reported to include:

- Developing metacognitive strategies helps learners to self-regulate (Msaddek, 2016; Razı and Çubukçu, 2014; Roohani and Asiabani, 2015).
- Strategic behaviours make reading easier (Roohani and Asiabani, 2015; Zenotz, 2012)
- Reflection skills aid the identification of contextual clues for comprehension and helps to monitor their reading processes (Teng and Reynolds, 2019; Tsai and Talley, 2014).

Possible reasons for no-effect were an online mode of learning which has less student interaction (Altay and Altay, 2017).

Within this group, four studies targeted listening comprehension. Three of them reported effectiveness and one showed no effect. The Metacognitive Pedagogical Sequence (MPS) proposed by Vandergrift (2004) was applied in all studies. Reasons attributed to the effectiveness are as follows:

- Awareness of the metacognitive strategies makes the students perceive to be more self-assured and feel less tension (Rahimirad and Shams, 2014).
- Conscious planning helps the students to apply strategies more appropriately (Bozorgian and Alamdari, 2017; Chou, 2017).
- Appropriate use of metacognitive strategies and top-down processing is the key to successful listening (Chou, 2017).

All nine studies of the remaining and weakest studies reported positive effects.

Overall, the results demonstrate a high potential for metacognitive interventions in language development among EFL learners. However, effectiveness remains inconclusive because almost all studies obtained their results from very small sample sizes, permitting chances for the results to be inflated (Coe, 2002). More robust studies on the topic are still needed. The key features from the thematic synthesis should be considered in any future research.

Randomised control trial

A randomised control trial (RCT) is one of the strongest research designs for establishing a causal link between an intervention and any effect (Gorard, 2013). Fourteen sets of students from two universities in the two southernmost provinces of Thailand were recruited. Six each were in faculties of education and political science. There were randomised in a stratified way to yield three of each in each arm of the trial. There were 6 clusters with 216 students in the intervention group and 6 clusters with 258 students in the control group. The other 2 sets of 441 students provided an additional non-randomised comparator (not receiving the intervention). This made the study the biggest trial on the topic, at the time this study was conducted.

Random allocation took place at cluster level, which can minimise contamination caused by the possible spillover between the intervention and control participants (Hutchison and Styles, 2010). However, individuals within the same cluster can have similar characteristics which may confuse the assessment of impact.

The intervention, based on the six-phase PMER model, was implemented by the teachers responsible for the classes in five sessions over the first semester of academic year 2020 while the researcher joined as a teacher in one cluster to allow comparison of the results. The first session was a presentation of different types of learning strategies and an introduction of metacognitive awareness. The second, third and fourth sessions focused on each metacognitive strategy, such as planning, monitoring, and evaluation and the fifth session was a combination of all skills. At the end of each session, there was a retrieval practice to promote recall and consolidation of what students have learnt. In addition, two independent practices were provided for each session, totalling ten practices overall. These practices were available online for students to learn at their own time outside the classroom.

Outcome measurement was based on tests adapted from the University English test which students have to take. A questionnaire based on the

Metacognitive Awareness Listening Questionnaire (MALQ) by Vandergrift et al. (2006) was used to assess metacognitive awareness which is the secondary outcome of the study. Moreover, the open-ended responses in the questionnaire, classroom observations and semi-structured interviews formed the process evaluation to assess how well the intervention went.

Summary of key findings

At the end of the trial, there was a small percentage of dropout/missing data. The complete results from 197 intervention students, 249 control students, and 360 comparison students were used in the following analyses.

Impact evaluation

The overall English scores at the outset, which reflect the pre-existing English proficiency of the intervention and the control group, appear quite similar, but the "effect" size of this difference is around +0.09, with the intervention group already ahead (Table 8.2). The score of the (non-randomised) comparator group is clearly lower than the intervention group ("effect" size of +1.05). At the end, the intervention group has clearly made more progress than both other groups.

Similarly, looking only at results for the listening section, the intervention group was already slightly ahead of the control ("effect" size of +0.13). Again, the score of the (non-randomised) comparator group is clearly lower ("effect" size of +0.97). And again, after the intervention, the intervention group has clearly made more progress than both other groups.

All of these initial differences are part of the justification for using gain scores for the headline findings, which look at progress rather than absolute attainment (Table 8.3).

The gain scores from pre- to post-intervention tests were computed from the above figures and converted to simple "effect" sizes (the difference

Table 8.2 Students' overall English test scores, pre and post-intervention

Groups	Pre-test mean	SD	Post-test mean	Post-test SD
Intervention	16.8	6.5	22.0	7.3
Control	16.2	6.9	15.2	8.4
Comparison	10.7	4.0	11.6	4.2
Overall intervention and control	16.4	6.7	18.2	8.6
Overall intervention and comparison	12.8	5.8	15.3	7.4

Table 8.3 Students' English listening test scores, pre and post-intervention

Groups	Pre-test mean	SD	Post-test mean	Post-test SD
Intervention	10.2	4.5	12.6	4.7
Control	9.6	4.6	8.3	5.0
Comparison	6.3	3.0	6.0	2.8
Overall intervention and control	9.8	4.6	10.2	5.3
Overall intervention and comparison	7.7	4.0	8.3	4.8

Table 8.4 Comparison of intervention and control group, effect sizes for overall and listening gain scores

Groups	Gain score, overall	SD	"Effect" size	Gain score, listening	SD	"Effect" size
Intervention	5.2	7.1	+0.77	2.4	4.7	+0.68
Control	−1.0	8.8		−1.2	5.8	
Overall	1.8	8.6		0.4	5.6	

Table 8.5 Comparison of intervention and comparator group, effect sizes for overall and listening gain scores

Groups	Gain score, overall	SD	"Effect" size	Gain score, listening	SD	"Effect" size
Intervention	5.2	7.1	+0.75	2.4	4.7	+0.69
Comparison	0.9	4.8		−0.4	3.5	
Overall	2.5	6.1		0.6	4.2	

between mean scores for each group divided by their overall standard deviation). These make it clear that the intervention group clearly made more progress than both the control and comparator groups (Tables 8.4 and 8.5). This is true both for the overall English score and the listening section. "Effect" sizes of 0.7 or greater are on a different scale to those found at the outset (see above). Also, because the group that was already ahead made the largest gains, the result cannot be due to regression towards the mean.

The headline findings suggest that metacognitive instruction for the Thai EFL learners in the study was effective.

A sensitivity analysis was conducted to estimate the number of counterfactual cases that would be needed to disturb the finding (NNTD). This was estimated as the effect size multiplied by the number of participants in the smaller arm (Gorard, 2021). The smaller arm in each comparison has N of 197. This means that around 152 additional counterfactual cases would be needed to reduce the "effect" size of 0.77, comparing the intervention and control groups on overall English scores, to zero. Since this comparison has only 33 missing cases then, even in the extreme situation that all of them were counterfactual to the overall finding, there would still be a sizeable positive "effect" size. There are the same number of missing cases in the listening scores, with an NNTD of 134. This again means that the substantive finding could not be altered by inconvenient scores for those missing cases. The results are robust, even with respect to missing data.

Process evaluation

Classroom observation suggested that the intervention teachers tried to follow the intervention guidelines and materials given, with some practical adaptations to fit the time and situation.

Students were largely positive about the intervention. They reported that it guided them with useful strategies for learning. The strategies usually mentioned were planning, directed attention, and problem-solving, which helped them to have less panic when dealing with tasks. Some students think that it helped increase their understanding from listening, to analyse the tasks and tackle the tests better.

> In real tests, we can't expect to know everything, so we need to know what to focus first and what to do next.

However, some possible flaws in the intervention were reported. The two most mentioned drawbacks were its time-consuming nature and the use of unfamiliar terms in the intervention guidebook. As the intervention has many details, covering all of them in the presentation phase took a lot of time. In the classroom, some students appeared less confident to complete the metacognitive task at first, perhaps because of the unfamiliar concepts and terms. Pair and small group discussions later on in the session helped them proceed with the task better.

> This approach doesn't help much with the accent we are not familiar. Also, it takes time.

The teachers who delivered the intervention found the intervention a good approach for teaching. One of them had already been interested in applying concepts from cognitive science in teaching and was willing to use the intervention. The other teacher found the intervention completely new, but a systematic and helpful approach. Planning and task analysis are the most obvious beneficial skills which both teachers agreed on. They suggested that the strategies help students feel more ready, and encourage attention during the listening task. Both report that the approach can be applicable to reading skills and could be used in other English courses.

> At least, the planning strategies are obviously applicable in real use. I have recommended the students to apply them in real tests and other courses.

However, they also reported some drawbacks. Both teachers agreed that the intervention had excessive details, similar to the students' view. It takes time to follow the guidelines fully while time is limited (partly due to the reduced teaching time caused by the COVID 19 outbreak). Teacher B thinks the intervention involves several terms which the students find difficult. From the classroom observation, the teacher had to skip some details or shorten time for practice. Teacher A advised that the contents in each session seem to follow the same pattern, causing students who were attentive in the first few sessions to pay even less attention in the later sessions.

> I can notice students feel less engaged in later sessions. It could be because the design of the intervention seems repetitive.

Some implications for policy and practice

The findings suggest that the metacognitive intervention is at least partly responsible for the improved outcomes of intervention students compared to the control and the comparator students. Intervention students then passed the university's English requirement in higher proportion than the control participants and the non-trial students. Therefore, it is reasonable to say that metacognition and self-regulatory promotion shows promise as an appropriate approach for tertiary EFL learners, perhaps especially for the less-proficient learners with pre-intermediate and intermediate levels.

The practice of applying metacognitive and self-regulatory approach to teaching is not yet common practice in a Thai EFL context. One of the main barriers seems to be the complexity associated with the concept of meta-cognition, as expressed above by the trial teachers. But it is not the ultimate aim for teachers to teach complex concepts or terms to the students. What should be emphasised are the strategies and positive dispositions such as reflective and strategic thinking and self-efficacy which play a pivotal role in improving learning (Moseley et al., 2005) and can also be transferred across contexts (Perkins and Salomon, 2012). An important role for teachers, apart from providing sources of knowledge and opportunities for practice, is to support students' self-regulation and agency by developing their self-efficacy, self-reflection, and strategic thinking.

At a policy level, there are multiple valid reasons to advocate this approach in higher education policy. From the evidence of this study and other sources (e.g., Lui and Li, 2015), the metacognitive approach is a high-potential methodology for improving English learning capacity. It is economical to implement (Education Endowment Foundation (EEF), 2018). Teacher training is required to equip teachers with better understanding and applicable techniques for instruction.

Reflections on the doctoral journey

Doing a doctoral degree is a long journey, full of experiences. One core value I have learnt from this journey is the exercise of criticality in doing and using research. This notion was emphasised throughout my studentship by the module convenors, supervisory team, and the institution. It is very important for me as a researcher and for policy makers, educators and academics to carefully examine the evidence before accepting any argument.

The essence of a doctoral degree is the research. Having spent several years on a research project should have equipped one with knowledge and skills to conduct "good" research. What is meant by "good" research may provoke very divergent views, especially among those indulging the quantitative/qualitative schism. In reality though, the paramount consideration is the alignment between research question, research design, and the claims being made (Gorard, 2013). It is not a particular research method which makes good research but how the research is designed to provide evidence for the questions being asked and so warrant any claims being made.

As importantly, the experiences learned along the journey are priceless and probably more valuable than the final product. Several good values have been learnt along the way such as trying to go big and create real impact. My personal value is "believe and give it a try". I tried many new things I have not done before in my research such as doing a systematic review or a meta-analysis, running regression analyses by myself, and reporting effect sizes. I used to view some of these things as difficult. But with self-belief and due support, I tried different ways and eventually managed to learn to do them. These experiences and the newly developed skills are highly applicable and beneficial to my future research and academic career. Giving myself a chance to be a little more ambitious and being open to learn new things made my doctoral journey a valuable experience.

References

Abdelhafez, A. (2006). *The effect of a suggested training program in some metacognitive language learning strategies on developing listening and reading comprehension of university EFL students.* Doctoral dissertation. Exeter, United Kingdom: University of Exeter.

Altay, I., and Altay, A. (2017). The impact of online reading tasks and reading strategies on EFL learners' reading test scores. *Journal of Language and Linguistic Studies,* 13(2), pp. 136–152.

Bozorgian, H., and Alamdari, E. (2017). Multimedia listening comprehension: Metacognitive instruction or metacognitive instruction through dialogic interaction. *ReCALL,* 30(1), pp. 131–152. doi: 10.1017/S0958344016000240

Chamot, A.U., and O'Malley, J.M. (1994). *The CALLA Handbook: Implementing the Cognitive Academic Language Learning Approach.* White Plains, NY: Longman.

Chou, M. (2017). A task-based language teaching approach to developing metacognitive strategies for listening comprehension. *International Journal of Listening,* 31(1), pp. 51–70. doi: 10.1080/10904018.2015.1098542

Coe, R. (2002). It's the effect size, stupid: What effect size is and why it is important. Paper presented at the *Annual Conference of the British Educational Research Association,* Exeter, 2002. Available at: http://www.leeds.ac.uk/educol/documents/00002182.htm. Accessed 21 December 2019.

Cross, J. (2011). Metacognitive instruction for helping less-skilled listeners. *ELT Journal,* 65(4), pp. 408–416. doi: 10.1093/elt/ccq073

Dignath, C., and Büttner, G. (2008). Components of fostering self-regulated learning among students. A meta-analysis on intervention studies at primary and secondary school level. *Metacognition and Learning,* 3(3), pp. 231–264.

Education Endowment Foundation (EEF). (2018). *Teaching and learning toolkit.* Available at: https://educationendowmentfoundation.org.uk/public/files/Toolkit/complete/EEF-Teaching-Learning-Toolkit-October-2018.pdf. Accessed on 15 July 2019.

Efklides, A. (2008). Metacognition: Defining its facets and levels of functioning in relation to self-regulation and co-regulation. *European Psychologist,* 13(4), pp. 277–287.

Flavell, J. (1976). Metacognitive aspects of problem solving. In L.B. Resnick (ed.), *The Nature of Intelligence* (pp. 231–235). Hillsdale, NJ: Lawrence Erlbaum Associates, Inc.

Gorard, S. (2013). *Research Design: Creating Robust Approaches for the Social Sciences.* London: Sage.

Gorard, S. (2014). A proposal for judging the trustworthiness of research findings. *Radical Statistics,* 110, pp. 47–59.

Gorard, S. (2021) *How to Make Sense of Statistics: Everything You Need to Know about Using Numbers in Social Science.* London: SAGE

Hayes, D. (2010). Language learning, teaching and educational reform in rural

Thailand: An English teacher's perspective. *Asia Pacific Journal of Education*, 30(3), pp. 305–319.

Higgins, S., Hall, E., Baumfield, V., and Moseley, D. (2005). *A meta-analysis of the impact of the implementation of thinking skills approaches on pupils, Project Report.* London: EPPI-Centre, Social Science Research Unit, Institute of Education, University of London.

Hutchison, D., and Styles, B. (2010). *A Guide to Running Randomised Controlled Trials for Educational Researchers.* Slough: NFER.

Kaur, A., Young, D., and Kirkpatrick, R. (2016). English education policy in Thailand: Why the poor results? In R. Kirkpatrick (ed.), *English Language Education Policy in Asia* (pp. 345–361). Cham, Switzerland: Springer.

Livingston, J. (2003). Metacognition: An overview. ERIC Database. Retrieved from https://files.eric.ed.gov/fulltext/ED474273.pdf

Lui, P., and Li, L. (2015). An overview of metacognitive awareness and L2 reading strategies. In R. Wegerif, L. Li., and J. Kaufman (eds.), *The Routledge International Handbook of Research on Teaching Thinking* (pp. 266–279). Oxon: Routledge.

Moseley, D., Elliott, J., Gregson, M., and Higgins, S. (2005). Thinking skills frameworks for use in education and training. *British Educational Research Journal*, 31(3), pp. 367–390. doi: 10.1080/01411920500082219

Msaddek, M. (2016). The effect of metacognitive strategy instruction on Moroccan EFL learners' strategy use and reading achievement. *Arab World English Journal*, 7(3), pp. 287–301.

Perkins, D., and Salomon, G. (2012). Knowledge to go: A motivational and dispositional view of transfer. *Educational Psychologist*, 47(3), pp. 248–258.

Pintrich, P. (2002). The role of metacognitive knowledge in learning, teaching, and assessing. *Theory into Practice*, 41(4), pp. 219–225.

Prachathai. (2017). *Education in Thailand's deep south: Not a secular matter.* Retrieved 25 July 2019 from https://prachatai.com/english/node/7087

Quigley, A., Muijs, D., and Stringer, E. (2018). *Metacognition and self-regulated learning.* London: Education Endowment Foundation. Available at: https://educationendowment.foundation.org.uk/public/files/Publications/Metacognition/EEF_Metacognition_and_self-regulated_learning.pdf

Rahimirad, M., and Shams, M. (2014). The effect of activating metacognitive strategies on the listening performance and metacognitive awareness of EFL students. *International Journal of Listening*, 28(3), pp. 162–176. doi: 10.1 080/10904018.2014.902315.

Razı, S., and Çubukçu, F. (2014). Metacognition and reading: Investigating intervention and comprehension of EFL freshmen in Turkey. *Procedia – Social and Behavioral Sciences*, 158, pp. 288–295. doi: 10.1016/j.sbspro.2014.12.090

Roohani, A., and Asiabani, S. (2015). Effects of self-regulated strategy development on EFL learners' reading comprehension and metacognition. *GEMA Online Journal of Language Studies*, 15(3), pp. 31–49.

Seifoori, Z. (2016). Metacognitive awareness and the fluency of task-based oral output across planning conditions: The case of Iranian TEFL students. *Iranian Journal of Language Teaching Research*, 4(1), pp. 11–26.

Tavakoli, H., and Koosha, M. (2016). The effect of explicit metacognitive strategy instruction on reading comprehension and self-efficacy beliefs: The case of Iranian university EFL students. *Porta Linguarum*, 25, pp. 119–133. doi: 10.30827/digibug.53893

Teng, F., and Reynolds, B. (2019). Effects of individual and group metacognitive prompts on EFL reading comprehension and incidental vocabulary learning. *PLoS ONE*, 14(5), pp. 1–24. doi: 10.1371/journal.pone.0215902

Trowler, P. (2003). *Education Policy*, 2nd ed. London: Routledge.

Tsai, Y.R., and Talley, P.C. (2014). The effect of a course management system (CMS)-supported strategy instruction on EFL reading comprehension and strategy use. *Computer Assisted Language Learning*, 27(5), pp. 422–438. doi: 10.1080/09588221.2012.757754

Vandergrift, L. (2004). Learning to listen or listening to learn? *Annual Review of Applied Linguistics*, 24, pp. 3–25.

Vandergrift, L., and Goh, C. (2012). *Teaching and Learning Second Language Listening: Metacognition in Action*. New York, NY: Routledge.

Vandergrift, L., Goh, C., Mareschal, C., and Tafaghodatari, M. (2006). The Metacognitive Awareness Listening Questionnaire (MALQ): Development and validation. *Language Learning*, 56, pp. 431–462.

Wang, M., Haertel, G., and Walberg, H. (1990). What influences learning? A content analysis of review literature. *The Journal of Educational Research*, 84(1), pp. 30–43.

Wudthayagorn, J. (2019, March 9–12). English exit examinations for Thai university students: A closer look at the policy implementation [Paper presentation]. *Conference of the American Association for Applied Linguistics (AAAL)*, Atlanta, GA.

Zenotz, V. (2012). Awareness development for online reading. *Language Awareness*, 21(1–2), pp. 85–100. doi: 10.1080/09658416.2011.639893

Zimmerman, B. (2000). Attaining self-regulation: A social cognitive perspective. In *Handbook of Self-Regulation* (pp. 13–39). San Diego: Academic Press.

Zimmerman, B. (2002). Becoming a self-regulated learner: An overview. *Theory into Practice*, 41(2), pp. 64–70. doi: 10.1207/s15430421tip4102_2

Can Philosophy for Children improve critical thinking and attainment for Chinese secondary students?

Caiwei Wu

Introduction

In recent years, an important goal of China's educational reform has been to amend the disadvantages of the score-only theory, that is, exam-oriented education. This has over-emphasised academic attainment and neglected students' ability to learn with enjoyment and practice independent thinking. In addition, the cramming teaching method makes classrooms lose vitality. It is however difficult to change traditional teaching methods without introducing major reforms in the curriculum, teacher training support, and assessment methods. These problems have persisted in Chinese education for decades.

In 2010, the Chinese government released the The National Guidelines for Medium and Long-Term Educational Reform and Development (2010–2020), which emphasised skills such as independent inquiry, cooperation, communication, and problem solving as well as fostered cognitive skills (Yeung, 2009). To meet the aims of the reform, professional training was needed to help teachers access new pedagogical approaches and skills.

Although the government has provided some teacher training to incorporate wider thinking skills at classroom level, researchers have criticised it as insufficient (Jin et al., 2016; Yan, 2012). It has been very theoretical and consisted largely of hours of listening to government policy and regulations. Teachers complained of having to listen to theory-based lectures in large groups. There was little training in practical application of the new approaches, and specific guidance for practical learning activities was lacking. For example, in the training programme, teachers were simply told the importance of thinking skills and why they are beneficial for the development of children's cognitive skills but were not given any practical examples of how to develop thinking skills for students. Therefore, despite the provision of teacher training, implementing new pedagogies is still challenging for many teachers.

DOI: 10.4324/9781003201366-11

An effective teacher development programme should be one where teachers learn and experience different types of activities and lessons that can be be practiced in the classroom (Harcombe, 2001). The training should have high applicability, a practical orientation, participation, and interactivity (Jovanova-Mitkovska, 2010). Training can be a useful process if it interlaces and complements theory and practice. This was not the case in China. Education reform was introduced without an accompanying effective professional development programme. It is possible that those responsible for the training were ill-equipped to teach the new curriculum, not having been exposed to critical thinking themselves.

Philosophy for Children (P4C) is an approach focused on philosophical enquiry and dialogic teaching. The aim of the intervention is to help children develop their abilities to reason, question, construct arguments, and communicate collaboratively with others (Vansieleghem and Kennedy, 2011). For teachers, training in P4C pedagogy and practice is also an opportunity to improve their dialogic abilities and teaching skills to promote thinking development. This programme for improving critical thinking and communication skills. Prior research has suggested some benefits for children's thinking, classroom engagement, collaboration, and communication skills (Siddiqui et al., 2019), and even slight improvements in academic achievement (Gorard et al., 2015).

Evaluating P4C in a Chinese secondary school context has academic importance and relevance to China's educational reforms intended to improve children's classroom engagement, dialogic skills and critical thinking skills.

In general, P4C has been reported to have benefits for cognitive test scores, reasoning skills, classroom engagement, the level of respect for others' opinions, and the ability to express views clearly (Gorard et al., 2015; Lord et al., 2021; Trickey and Topping, 2004; Yan et al., 2018). The picture for indirect benefits in student maths or languages attainment is not so clear. Some prior studies have been tiny and/or have high attrition. For example, the study by Lipman et al. (2010) included only 20 pupils. The larger the study the smaller the attainment gain appears to be. The most that can be said is that using curriculum time for P4C, to achieve the aforementioned benefits, does not do any harm to attainment.

The number of studies on P4C in Chinese educational contexts has increased in the last 10 years. However, many of these have been conceptual, exploring the possibility of combining Confucian dialogue and communities of inquiry (Gao, 2019), and developing themes and topics suitable for the Chinese classroom (Xiurong, 2017). Again, the empirical studies have tended to be small or poorly designed. A study involving only 28 first-year secondary students in Hong Kong showed that P4C students made bigger gains on the New Jersey Test of Reasoning Skills (Lam, 2012). The treatment group was taught by the researcher and the control group by their normal teacher. A quasi-experimental study conducted in Taiwan randomly assigned two classes of secondary school students to P4C or not (Tian and Liao, 2016). P4C was delivered as part of an after-school activity. The results showed that the control group made bigger gains between pre- and post-test than P4C students. The impact of P4C on Chinese-origin students is therefore inconclusive. A bigger and better designed study is needed.

How the study was conducted

At the start of my PhD no P4C evaluations had yet been conducted in China, even though several schools and had adopted the programme. This approach to teaching is new to Chinese teachers and their students who have traditionally relied on rote learning and dissemination of knowledge. Independent thinking and questioning are rarely encouraged. I attempted to change that in a small way.

Participants

Four public middle schools in China were successfully recruited and agreed to carry out the intervention for a full school year. A total of 14 teachers agreed to take part, and they involved 453 Year 7 students.

Traditionally, multi-school projects in China are initiated by the Government or research institutes. As a PhD researcher, I relied on personal contacts and relatives who were associated with school education. During this phase, I realised that the challenge of school recruitment may be the reason that so many Chinese PhD researchers prefer to conduct small-scale case studies based on tiny sample sizes. However, a small sample size would have challenged my ambition to learn advanced skills for a robust analysis, and later draw some useful conclusions.

Design

The study design was a two-group pre- and post-test randomised control trial. Randomisation was at the class/teacher level. Classes in all schools were randomised and allocated to treatment and control groups. There were 223 students in the treatment and 230 in the control group classes. Random assignment of the classes was used to help create groups with an unbiased distribution of any confounding variables. Also to avoid bias, group allocation was revealed only after the pretest. There is evidence suggesting that knowledge of group assignment could influence the way students perform on the pre-test in trials (Kendall, 2003).

The intervention

The P4C training for the 14 teachers followed the same framework as adopted by the Society for the Advancement of Philosophical Enquiry in Education (SAPERE). This includes demonstration of P4C lessons, sharing of available resources and teaching materials. P4C trained teachers then implemented the programme regularly for a full lesson once a week for four months Figure 9.1.

However, the two-day P4C training alone was not sufficient for teachers who do not have prior experience with P4C. Additional monitoring support was offered. I helped teachers to prepare lesson plans, select topics and stimuli, designing question enquiry and discussion parts, and I observed lesson delivery as far as possible. I provided feedback on the lessons, and encouraged reflection.

There are no P4C textbooks focused on a Chinese content. Most materials were translated directly from the textbooks created based on a Western educational background (Leng and Gao, 2020). This may lead teachers to think that the content of P4C is not related to Chinese curriculum requirements, and is thus not suitable or helpful for Chinese students. In this

Figure 9.1 Preparing for P4C

study, the training provided skills in how to design modules and materials, and provide rich P4C topics.

The Level 1 P4C course lasted two days. Eighteen participants from different provinces attended the course. The training included the following elements:

• Introduction to P4C, key principles and methods;
• Demonstration of P4C lessons and key practice;
• Sharing of available resources and teaching material;
• Advice and support.

In a P4C class, the dialogue generally includes asking questions, giving examples and evidence, discussing and critiquing, summarising, and evaluating. To improve the quality of the dialogue, the Socratic method of questioning was suggested. For example, "Do you mean...?" to clarify students' questions, and "Do you think your question is similar or different from others?" to help analysis. Some cards with Socratic questions were provided in the training, that could be used for both teachers and students during the discussion with questions such as:

• Can someone give an example?
• Do we have any evidence?
• Is that always the case or only sometimes?
• What if...?
• Have we reached any conclusion?

Participants were given the opportunity to practice the steps and questioning techniques. They were also provided with instructional materials, including a P4C handbook, a booklet of lesson plans and extracts, and videos of recorded P4C classes in a Taiwan secondary school.

Data collected

Three main forms of data were collected in the trial.

The primary outcome measured was students' critical thinking skills. The pre-test was administered before randomisation and before the first session was delivered. The purpose of the pretest was to asses baseline equivalence between groups. A post-test was taken after the last P4C lesson. It's purpose was to gauge the average progress made by each group. I used a bespoke critical thinking skills test in which the items assessed skills for interpretation, inference, assumption, non-verbal reasoning, and deduction. An independent test was chosen, as it has no direct relevance with the P4C method. However, it assesses all major dimensions of critical thinking skills that make the core methods of P4C process.

This test had to be validated and appropriate for the language ability of first-year secondary school students for whom English was not their first language. I created a test from components from three commonly used tests for critical thinking: the cognitive attainment test (CAT), Cornell Test Level 1 (Ennis et al., 2005), and Watson-Glaser test (Watson and Glaser, 1980). Each of these tests was too long, too expensive, and/or not age-appropriate. As a compromise, the researcher selected appropriate questions from these existing tests and developed and piloted a test that was suitable for students in the study. It includes items on inferences, assumptions, deduction, interpretation, arguments, and verbal, nonverbal, spatial, quantitative, analogical, and inductive reasoning. There were 12 multiple-choice questions to be completed within 30 minutes. As the test is of critical thinking and not language skills, the researcher prepared the questions in both Chinese and English Figure 9.2.

P4C lessons were observed, and observations were recorded as field notes by the researcher. The focus was on interaction among students with the teacher, and the level of student engagement in terms of asking and

Figure 9.2 Critical concentration

answering questions. It was a way of assessing the quality of the training and subsequent delivery of the programme,

Students and the teachers were also asked about their experiences of P4C lessons. These brief interview included questions about whether they enjoyed the sessions, which parts of P4C they liked or disliked, the quality of dialogue between peers and with the teacher, and what challenges they faced.

In China, it is not a standard practice to ask young children (age 11–12) for consent in this kind of research. The lessons were delivered as part of the school curriculum with consent from the school leaders. No personal sensitive data was collected in this study.

Summary of the key findings

Impact

I conducted the post-test after four months of implementation using all students in the initial sample. The primary outcome measure was critical thinking skills, based on the difference between gain scores from pre-test and post-test for each group, converted to a standard "effect" size (Table 9.1).

The control group was slightly ahead at the outset (which is why gain scores are used). The control group demonstrated no improvement in average test score for critical thinking. The treatment group did make a small improvement after only four months, equivalent to 0.14 standard deviations. This overtaking the score of the control group is an indication that the intervention holds promise for improving students' critical thinking skills.

As a sensitivity test, I computed the number of counterfactual scores that would be needed to disturb this finding (NNTD, see Gorard, 2021). This was 31 cases, indicating a modestly robust finding. Given that there was no missing data, this makes the finding of a difference between groups more trustworthy.

Monitoring the intervention

I observed P4C implementation in a few British schools at the outset, and then took the UK SAPERE training myself. This experience was useful for my own understanding, and helped later in providing support to teachers.

Table 9.1 Comparing critical thinking results of both groups

	N	Mean (pre)	Pre SD	Mean (post)	Post SD	Gain score	SD	Effect Size
Control	230	9.5	2.4	9.5	2.5	0	2.2	
Treatment	223	9.3	2.5	9.6	2.6	0.3	2.1	0.14
Overall	453	9.4	2.5	9.5	2.6	0.1	2.2	

Teachers who attended the subsequent training in China said that they benefited a lot. They reported being confident in the development of the project after two days.

The biggest problem with using training materials wass lack of relevance with Chinese syllabus and curriculum content. Due to traditional teaching habits, the teacher was more likely to choose stimuli relating to factual knowledge than controversial topics. From the feedback of the interview, students agreed that the modules are helpful for their talking and thinking, while the teacher hoped to be closer to the textbook. However, as they became more experienced teachers overcome their initial hesitation of using a topic just for dialogue and communication.

> I think the training is good. It not only introduced the principles of the P4C approach, but a large part of the training included classroom simulations. The trainer worked as a facilitator modelling the delivery of P4C, while I acted as a student. This allowed me to see how the P4C pedagogy works in practice. It also helped me to think about the actual situation and the challenges we may encounter in the classroom.

Chinese students are typically quiet and passive learners. For most of the time in class, they are more likely to receive knowledge from the teacher as an authoritative figure than to contribute to the discussions. Classroom observations of the P4C lessons were used to assess the changes in classroom dialogue. The students initially found it difficult to engage. Over four months, it was observed that students' engagement in the classroom, and willingness to express themselves, increased. The teacher gradually handed over control of the class discussions to the students. Students talked more, and the lessons became more student-oriented and less teacher-focused (see examples in Wu, 2021). Teachers became better at probing, and asking open-ended questions to get the discussion going. Discussions began to include more students, and they were keen to provide a reason for their responses. A teacher said:

> I think the most positive impact was classroom engagement. I can see that the students' participation has greatly increased during this time. There was a clear difference between their active performance in my P4C class and their tendency to remain silent in the past. And I think that is a great beginning for facilitating thinking because if they talk more, they will think more.

Students generally agreed. Three key words that were prominent among the students' feedback were "relaxed", "respectful", and "learn from others". Other comments included:

I like the P4C class because I have a lot of amazing idea to share with my classmates.

I'm very happy because the topics are interesting. It also makes me relaxed because the teacher does not judge me at the moment.

I progressed a lot. I learned how to present my ideas and theories, and how to use evidence to support them.

However, while the students enjoyed the new programme and teaching style and appreciated the opportunity to learn from one another and to exchange opinions, some students doubted whether P4C classes could help them reach their academic goals. They mirrored the concerns of some teachers. As one student expressed:

I don't understand what the relationship between the P4C lessons and exam requirements is.

Implications and reflections

Regarding why I chose this topic – it was not decided overnight. Like many Chinese students who choose to study abroad, I was attracted by the reputation of high-quality higher education in Britain. And my early career goal was to become a teacher. Therefore, I went to study in Britain to see what is good about education in Britain? What are the differences to China? I was impressed by two things. One is that Westerners emphasise critical thinking, and generating ideas without simply following authority. In classes we were all encouraged to express different opinions. Another thing is that the way teachers talk to students in classes in Britain is quite different. In China, students usually answer closed questions and only need to state knowledge. English teachers' questions often have no standard answers, but tended to arouse my thoughts. I searched the literature which revolved around critical thinking, thinking skills, classroom dialog, and metacognition. I was interested in how to use classroom dialogue to promote thinking skills. After discussion with my supervisors, I settled on a consideration of Philosophy for Children.

Through conducting this project, I learnt a lot about the UK model of classroom education where pupils' critical thinking and communications skills are more emphasised in the curriculum and in teacher training frameworks.

The results of this study achieved the research aims and objectives I wanted. It demonstrated that it is feasible to train and deliver P4C lessons in Chinese classrooms. Unlike previous studies that focused more on kindergartens and primary schools, this study indicates that students in secondary school are willing to accept this new teaching pedagogy.

In terms of the measurement tool, the modified English–Chinese version of the Critical Thinking Test was found to be appropriate to the language ability and age of the students. They were able to understand the meaning of the questions and to complete the test within the specified time. The test results showed that the experimental group made some improvements in their critical thinking compared to the control group. After considering what factors may have affected the results, the strongest would seem to be the teachers' enthusiasm for the approach.

However, embedding something like P4C in the curriculum is a challenge. Future studies should also assess the impact on academic achievement. If achievement in language or maths improves even slightly then the approach will be treated with less suspicion. It is more likely that a dialogic approach will be more widely promoted. Exam scores do seem irreplaceable in China's education system. Teachers had felt that implementing planned P4C topics would delay other learning plans for the class. So they preferred to design their own stimuli, more aligned with the curriculum and teaching topics.

The content of previous teacher training for education reform initiated by the government has generally been too theoretical. It seldom gives front-line teachers specific guidance on how to implement the new methods. For example, when schools want to introduce something like P4C teaching methods, traditional Chinese teacher training involves hundreds of teachers sitting in a large classroom to learn what P4C is, its focus, steps, and what teachers should do in class. But few trainers pay attention to the specific details, and the teachers lack follow-up guidance. That is to say, the help teachers get is not enough to implement the programme properly.

This problem cannot be solved by one person or one study. Nevertheless, in my project I tried to make the training more specific and useful. We avoided discussing only abstract theories and concepts. Instead, the SAPERE trainer involved the teachers in several classroom simulations, illustrating the possible problems and opportunities in how the new method should be carried out. I arranged a seminar once a month, where the experimental group teachers communicated with each other. The trainer also joined in to give some feedback, such as what common problems we have, and what can we pay attention to in the next stage. Teachers reported that they learnt a lot. I think this was done well.

Any wider reform will need to be instituted in stages. Helping teachers set short-term goals and providing targeted training in dialogue skills are necessary. The first step may be to ask teachers to move slowly from a teacher-centred to a student-centred approach, and then to introduce Socratic questioning techniques to encourage students to engage in class. Teachers could then be gradually encouraged to develop high-quality discussions, giving students the opportunity to apply more higher-order thinking skills.

References

Ennis, R., Millman, J., and Tomko, T. (2005). *Administration Manual: Cornell Critical Thinking Tests.* Seaside, CA, USA: The Critical Thinking Co.

Gao, Z. (2019). Confucian dialogue and the reconstruction of the community of inquiry in Philosophy for Children. In *Philosophy for Children in Confucian Societies: In Theory and Practice.* London, UK: Routledge.

Gorard, S. (2021). *How to Make Sense of Statistics.* London: SAGE.

Gorard, S., Siddiqui, N., and See, B.H. (2015). *Philosophy for Children: Evaluation Report and Executive Summary.* London, UK: EEF.

Harcombe, E. S. (2001). Science teaching/science learning: Constructivist learning in urban classrooms, Vol. 14. New York: Teachers College Press. Colombia University.

Jin, H., Wei, X., Duan, P., Guo, Y., and Wang, W. (2016). Promoting cognitive and social aspects of inquiry through classroom discourse. *International Journal of Science Education*, 38, pp. 319–343.

Jovanova-Mitkovska, S. (2010). The need of continuous professional teacher development. *Procedia-Social and Behavioral Sciences*, 2(2), pp. 2921–2926.

Kendall, J. (2003). Designing a research project: Randomised controlled trials and their principles. *Emergency Medicine Journal*, 20, p. 164.

Lam, C.M. (2012). Continuing Lipman's and Sharp's pioneering work on philosophy for children: Using Harry to foster critical thinking in Hong Kong students. *Educational Research and Evaluation*, 18, pp. 187–203.

Leng, L., and Gao, Z. (2020). The development and contextualization of philosophy for children in mainland China. *Teaching Philosophy*, 43(3), pp. 254–280.

Lipman, M., Sharp, A., and Oscanyan, F. (2010). *Philosophy in the Classroom.* Philadelphia, PA: Temple University Press.

Lord, P., Dirie, A., Kettlewell, K., and Styles, B. (2021). *Evaluation of Philosophy for Children: An Effectiveness Trial.* London, UK: EEF.

Siddiqui, N., Gorard, S., and See, B.H. (2019). Can programmes like Philosophy for Children help schools to look beyond academic attainment? *Educational Review*, 71(2), pp. 146–165.

Tian, S., and Liao, P.F. (2016). Philosophy for children with learners of English as a foreign language. *Journal of Philosophy in Schools*, 3, pp. 40–58.

Trickey, S., and Topping, K. (2004). "Philosophy for children": A systematic review. *Research Papers in Education.*, 19, pp. 365–380.

Vansieleghem, N., & Kennedy, D. (2011). What is philosophy for children, what is philosophy with children-after Matthew Lipman? *Journal of Philosophy of Education*, 45(2), pp. 171–182.

Watson, G., and Glaser, E. (1980). *Critical Thinking Appraisal: Manual.* New York, NY: Psychological Corporation.

Wu, C. (2021). Training teachers in China to use the philosophy for children approach and its impact on critical thinking skills: A pilot study. *Educational Sciences*, 11, p. 206. doi: 10.3390/educsci11050206

Xiurong, G. (2017). On the thematic features of Philosophy for Children inquiry activities. *Journal of Beijing Institute of Education*, 6, pp. 6–12.

Yan, C. (2012). "We can only change in a small way": A study of secondary English teachers' implementation of curriculum reform in China. *Journal of Educational Change*, 13, pp. 431–447.

Yan, S., Walters L., and Wang, Z. (2018). Meta-analysis of the effectiveness of philosophy for children programs on students' cognitive outcomes. *Analytic Teaching and Philosophical Praxis*, 39, pp. 13–33.

Yeung, S.Y.S. (2009). Is student-centered pedagogy impossible in Hong Kong? The case of inquiry in classrooms. *Asia Pacific Education Review*, 10(3), pp. 377–386.

Evaluating the impact of instruction on the critical thinking skills of English language learners in higher education

Nada El-Soufi

Introduction

Some critics believe that critical thinking (CT) is a cultural practice that cannot be taught in cultures that do not encourage independent thinking. Many theorists also argue that CT cannot be taught as a set of generic skills at all. This study examines whether instruction in CT can develop the CT skills of undergraduate English language learners. A systematic review was conducted to synthesise impact evidence of teaching CT on the CT skills of undergraduate English language learners (ELL). Of the 1,830 records identified, only 36 studies were considered relevant. The review provides indicative evidence that instruction in CT may be beneficial. However, because of major methodological flaws across all studies, the strength of the evidence is weak. To test the effectiveness of this approach more powerfully, a cluster randomised control trial was carried out in a university in Lebanon involving 29 English classes (413 students). The trial was conducted over one term in which 11 lessons in CT were substituted for material from the regular curriculum. The intervention students made bigger gains on the Cornell Critical Thinking Test between pre- and post-test (ES = +0.3). The parallel process evaluation reveals that teachers' positive attitude, training of teachers, and the readily available lesson plans helped make the intervention implementation successful. The barriers observed were some students' attitudes, and lack of general knowledge combined with poor literacy for some.

Background

Some educational systems around the world are still resistant to the concept of independent thought, and young people are not encouraged to challenge ideas or authorities. The education system in the Arab world is a longstanding example of this. The Arab region's social revolutions and political instability since 2011 have wreaked havoc on an already troubled educational

DOI: 10.4324/9781003201366-12

system. The Arab region scores low on the Human Development Index. In 2002, 20% of students were enrolled in higher education, while less than 4% were enrolled in 2008. Education quality is still below acceptable levels as revealed by some standardised international tests, such as the Trends in Mathematics and Science Study (TIMSS) (Arab Human Development Report, 2016).

Lebanon, an Arab country, suffers from political instability that has persisted in the country for years. A report produced by UNESCO (2014) describes Lebanon as "riven by deep sectarian divisions and sharp inequality between its communities, which are further exacerbated by wider tensions across the Middle East" (p. 176). The educational system in Lebanon mirrors all of the conflicts that erupt in the country.

In 1993, the then Minister of Education proposed a reform of education, with the inclusion of CT in school curricula. This reform did not take place exactly as expected for several reasons. The reform was primarily motivated by political considerations (Farah-Sarkis, 1999). Following multiple interviews with members of the education reform committees in Lebanon, including the current director-general, CERD directors, the general inspector, and the dean of the Faculty of Education, it was clear that no education research was involved in making the decision. The reform only involved non-researchers such as schoolteachers and university teaching professors. In Lebanon, education researchers have a low profile, and financing for educational research at the university level is scarce (Farah-Sarkis, 1999). A second reason was that no political agreement existed on what should be taught.

Despite the fact that the reform intended to build a new educational ladder by adopting new curricula and textbooks and providing teacher training, it largely failed due to a lack of agreement on what to teach and how teachers should be selected and trained. Thirdly, both politics and religion have a significant impact on the educational system in Lebanon. Religious sects regulate the knowledge that is disseminated to students in the majority of private schools. History instruction, for example, has remained in the hands of many sects, each of which teaches history from its own perspective in the schools under its control (Frayha, 2009). Another factor that hindered the reform from being successfully implemented was the assessment system which relies on rote memorisation of "facts". Teachers frequently teach to the test, and because critical thinking skills are not tested, teachers do not see the need to teach them (Hilal, 2018).

Finally, because there was no teacher training to implement the new curriculum, the reform goals could not be met. Teachers were informed they needed to include CT in their teaching, but they were not given instructions on how to do so. None of the teachers interviewed by Hilal (2018) stated that they had attended workshops to help them integrate CT into their classrooms. There had been no research done on the best method of CT instruction or how CT may be integrated into the curriculum. Although there was an attempt at introducing an educational reform, the government offered little support on how best to implement it and there was lack of consensus on how to teach CT skills.

Fostering students' CT skills is not an easy task anyway, because the concept itself is problematic. CT has been defined by various theorists. CT may be defined as a set of skills that include the ability to analyse, evaluate arguments, think inductively and deductively, identify biases, make inferences, understand and question underlying assumptions, reach valid conclusions, and synthesise evidence. A major point of contention over instruction in CT is whether it can be seen as a set of generic skills or whether it is domain specific. The general approach considers CT as a set of skills that can be taught independently of any domain (Ennis, 1997). The domain specific approach considers that CT should be embedded in a specific subject such as biology or history (Bailin et al., 1999; McPeck, 1984; Moore, 2011).

Research questions

The research questions are:

- Is there evidence that instruction in CT can help develop CT skills of ELL in higher education?
- What is/are the most promising approach(es) to teaching CT skills to ELL in higher education?
- Can general CT skills be taught to ELL in higher education in Lebanon within the regular curriculum?
- Is it feasible to teach CT skills in an education system which does not generally promote independent thinking and argumentation?

In order to answer the first two research questions, a systematic review was conducted of the literature on the best approach to instruction in CT. The other two research questions, were addressed via a cluster randomised control trial.

Systematic review

The review covered 12 electronic databases in addition to Google Scholar and included some studies already known. I was looking for studies to provide sufficient evidence on the effectiveness or otherwise of any interventions to improve CT for university students. I excluded studies involving only students with special needs, or on the use of technology. Many studies were excluded because they were not empirical, or were related to school-age students, or the outcome did not relate to CT. A protocol was set with a list of inclusion and exclusion criteria and the search syntax. Examples of search words included "critical thinking" or "critical reasoning" and "language learning" or "foreign language" and "experiment" or "randomised controlled trial". The search yielded an initial 1,830 records. Titles and abstracts were screened in order to identify relevant studies. In some cases, the whole article had to be read when the abstract or title did not provide enough information. A total of 36 studies were then deemed relevant to the review. These were classified in terms of the strategies used to teach CT skills to ELL in higher education. The following flowchart is based on the PRISMA flow diagram by Moher et al. (2009). It shows the numbers of records identified at each stage of the search and the number of included and excluded studies (Figure 10.1).

Each of the studies was read for data extraction and evaluation. Evaluation of all studies was conducted based on the sieve approach proposed by Gorard et al. (2017). The ensuing rating of the trustworthiness of

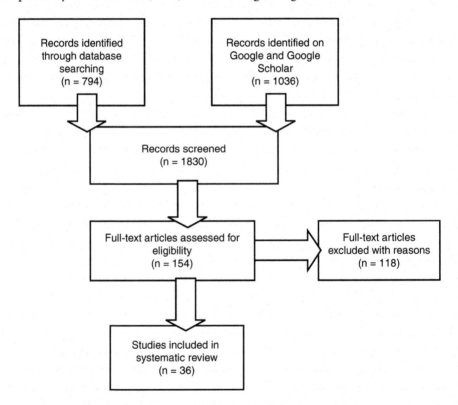

Figure 10.1 PRISMA flowchart

each piece is based on a set of criteria that relate to the study design, sample size, attrition, how outcomes are measured, and other threats to validity.

Most studies that were deemed relevant to the review had serious methodological flaws in the design such as lack of randomisation, different threats to internal validity, small sample size, high attrition rate, or unclear reporting.

The instructional approaches identified in this review concern teaching general CT skills (n = 13 studies), followed by the use of literary and narrative texts (n = 6), and assessment techniques (n = 5) like peer-review, teacher evaluation, and self-evaluation, the use of debates (n = 3), brainstorming techniques (n = 2), journal writing (n = 2), and scaffolding (n = 2). The majority were very weak studies, and most reported a positive outcome.

Instruction in general CT skills involves training students to define arguments, evaluate reliability of sources, identify fallacies and assumptions, use inductive and deductive logic, synthesise information, and make inferences. This approach was evaluated by the largest number of studies, and all, except two, showed a positive outcome. Out of the eleven studies that reported positive effects, four were given a rating of 2* (based on the star rating from 0 to 4). This is still quite weak, but these studies were the highest rated in this review. Despite the lack of clear evidence due to small sample sizes in most studies and attrition in others, it is the most promising method, with the greatest number of 2* studies showing favorable outcomes. The prevalence of low-quality studies in this category, many of which lack suitable comparison groups, random participant assignment, and high attrition, suggests that well-designed randomised control trials with low attrition are urgently needed.

All the other strategies for developing students' CT that were identified are lacking in evidence due to serious methodological flaws in their design like small sample size, lack of randomisation, diffusion of treatment, and very high attrition. I cannot say whether these approaches were effective or not.

Impact evaluation

As there was some evidence, although not strong, which indicates that general CT skills as an instructional approach can improve students' CT skills, it was worth testing the effectiveness of this approach in a randomised control trial. The trial was conducted in a private university in Lebanon. Because students were assigned to classes by university administration and some teachers teach more than one class, this study used a cluster randomise control trial (RCT) in which groups of teachers were randomly assigned to treatment or not. The study involved 29 teaching groups, consisting of 413 students, with 206 students (14 clusters) in the experimental group and 207 students (15 clusters) in the control group. In order to reach this number of students, the trial was repeated over two terms, in Spring 2014–2015 and Fall 2015–2016, involving two distinct cohorts of students. Attrition was low, as only 30 students missed the post-test (9 from treatment, 21 from control).

The intervention lasted one term. Each term had 70 sessions. The control group had lessons based on their regular curriculum for that term. The experimental group had 11 lessons of CT spread over 14 of their 5-minute sessions. These lessons were on CT principles utilising materials generated by the researcher that replaced some of the standard curriculum materials and were integrated into the module.

I designed the material for the intervention, and provided training for the lecturers who taught the experimental classes. I adapted materials from text-books, newspapers, books, and the internet. Some of the materials were modified to suit students' reading abilities and interests. The themes covered were a general introduction to logical fallacies, the difference between causation and correlation, assumptions and stereotypes, the reliability of sources, counter argumentation, and a brief introduction to validity of research and to detecting biases in surveys and statistics.

The primary outcome was CT skills. This was measured using the Cornell Critical Thinking Test (CCTT), Level Z. The same version of the CCTT was used as a pre-test and a post-test as it was deemed to be the most appropriate for the level of the students.

The difference between the pre- ad post-test scores for each group were computed, and presented as average gain scores. The difference between the gain scores for each group was converted to an "effect" size (Table 10.1).

The two groups are reasonably balanced at the outset in terms of pre-test scores. The experimental group showed a slight improvement in the post-test (+0.98) while the control group showed a decline (-1.79). The eventual effect size is +0.27. This means that around 60% of students in the control group are performing worse than students in the experimental group, on average (Coe, 2002). This suggests clear evidence of benefit from the in-tervention for CT as assessed by the CCTT.

The number of counterfactual cases that would be needed to disturb this effect size is 56. Since this is more than total number of missing cases (40), it

Table 10.1 Comparison of progress in critical thinking by treatment groups (combining both cohorts)

	N	Pre-test	SD	Post-test	SD	Gain score	SD	Effect size
Experimental	198	41.98	9.08	42.96	9.70	0.98	10.40	0.27
Control	185	41.74	7.48	39.95	8.89	-1.79	10.08	
Overall	383	41.86	8.28	41.45	9.29	-0.41	10.24	

means that even if all of the missing cases were antagonistic to the finding, there would still be signs of benefit from the intervention (Gorard, 2021).

Process evaluation

Observations of lessons reveal that all of the teachers followed their training and presented the lessons as planned. The lesson materials were put to good use. The teachers who delivered the intervention had little trouble incorporating the CT lessons into their courses. The lessons seemed to captivate the students, and the teachers were able to explain the new concepts effectively to them. Teachers appeared to be quite confident while implementing the CT lessons.

Students were also generally very positive about the lessons. Students' comments show that CT skills were valued:

> It was good, beneficial like I really, things that we learned it was really new to me like reliability and the statistics and things like that I used to believe them right away but now no I have another opinion.

> For me, I enjoyed really like looking at sources. Before I used to believe everything that I read but now when seeing stuff I think twice before just saying that it could be reliable, so I'm better at this now.

> The statistics uhhh we should know about statistics all the conditions related to do this kind of study or research uhhh for example the time, the place, the category of people we're asking, and the type of question we're asking. We did a lesson about the type of question which can be emotional, contain emotions or not. It should be an objective question, not a subjective question.

> Now we can also think about hidden factors like maybe we didn't really think about it when somebody just states a reason of why a specific thing happened so now we can think like maybe it's not the cause there are like other hidden factors.

The process evaluation supports the findings of the trial indicating that teaching CT is possible in an educational system where students and teachers have limited experience and learning opportunities for practicing CT and where CT is not commonly encouraged.

The main barrier to implementing CT instruction, based on observations of classes and focus group interviews with experimental teachers and students, was students' attitude towards CT. A few students showed resistance to learning CT because they did not believe it was relevant to their university major studies. Students' lack of general knowledge about current events, lack of interest in reading, and frustrations caused by limited English ability can all be obstacles to studying CT. A few teachers speculated that the instructional materials were too advanced for some students.

Implications of research, policy, and practice

The systematic review suggested that current empirical research on teaching CT in English language classrooms in higher education is immature, and the evidence of impact is inadequate. Research in this field should be improved, with particular attention paid to design issues in any future studies.

The trial in this study was a relatively small one. As a follow-up, a bigger, independently-funded study could be commissioned to evaluate the generic explicit approach to CT more broadly, by including a greater variety of higher education institutions and faculties. The approach could also be trialled in more Arab countries to see if it works in other jurisdictions with similar laws.

This study shows that teaching CT in Lebanon is possible, and that teaching CT to students who have had no prior exposure to such concepts can help them develop CT skills. Even one term of teaching seems to make a difference. This study has demonstrated that it is possible to integrate CT into the normal curriculum time, in a simple and cost-effective manner. There is no need for expensive instructional materials or new textbooks. The course materials were inexpensive and simple to create. CT can be taught with stimuli from everyday resources like newspaper articles and internet content. The course materials can be updated with more recent materials on a regular basis.

If the government is serious about encouraging CT among its population, deliberate attempts must be made to introduce CT more strategically. The findings of this thesis have implications for both preservice teacher training and professional development of teachers.

References

Arab Human Development Report. (2016). *Youth and the prospects for human development in a changing reality.* http://www.arab-hdr.org/Reports/2016/2 016.aspx

Bailin, S., Case, R., Coombs, J., and Daniels, L. (1999). Common misconceptions of critical thinking. *Journal of Curriculum Studies*, 31(3), pp. 269–283.

Coe, R. (2002). *It's the effect size, stupid: What effect size is and why it is important.* Paper presented at the Annual Conference of the British Educational Research Association, University of Exeter, England, 12–14 September. www.leeds.ac.uk/educol/documents/00002182.htm

Ennis, R. (1997). Incorporating critical thinking in the curriculum: An introduction to some basic issues. *Inquiry: Critical Thinking Across the Disciplines*, 16(3), pp. 1–9.

Farah-Sarkis, F. (1999). Education policy making and research: The case of Lebanon. In R. Wanda (ed.), *Educational Documentation, Research and Decision Making: National Case Studies in Comparative Education*. Geneva: UNESCO International Bureau of Education.

Frayha, N. (2009). *The negative face of the Lebanese education system*. Lebanon Renaissance. http://www.lebanonrenaissance.org/assets/Uploads/0-The-negative-face-of-the-Lebaneseeducation-system-by-Nmer-Frayha-2009.pdf

Gorard, S. (2021). *How to Make Sense of Statistics*. London: SAGE.

Gorard, S., See, B.H., and Siddiqui, N. (2017). *The Trials of Evidence-Based Education: The Promises, Opportunities and Problems of Trials in Education*. London: Routledge.

Hilal, Y. (2018). Do programmes delineating critical thinking as a learning outcome facilitate its teaching? International Baccalaureate Diploma Programme and Lebanese Baccalaureate Programme. *Topoi*, 37, pp. 201–217. doi: 10.1007/s11245-016-9409-9

McPeck, J. (1984). Stalking beasts, but swatting flies: The teaching of critical thinking. *Canadian Journal of Education*, 9(1), pp. 28–44.

Moher, D., Liberati, A., Tetzlaff, J., and Altman, D. (2009). Preferred reporting items for systematic reviews and meta-analyses: The PRISMA statement. *PLoS Med*, 6(7), p. e1000097. doi: 10.1371/journal.pmed1000097

Moore, T. (2011). Critical thinking and disciplinary thinking: A continuing debate. *Higher Education Research and Development*, 30(3), pp. 261–274.

UNESCO. (2014). *Teaching and learning: Achieving quality for all—EFA global monitoring report 2013/4*. Paris: UNESCO.

CHAPTER 11

Can improving the "academic buoyancy" of secondary school students improve their school attendance?

Sophie Anderson

Introduction

This project on the idea of academic buoyancy in schools was carried out in three stages, each utilising different research designs and methods to answer the research questions "as unambiguously as possible" (De Vaus, 2001, p. 9). Academic buoyancy is seen as young people's coping ability to tackle negative experiences in daily school life. In this research I examined academic buoyancy in relation to patterns of pupils' school attendance and exclusions. Stage one of this research was a systematic review of the academic buoyancy construct itself, involving systematic searches, screening, and synthesis of existing research evidence. Stage two was based on a longitudinal cohort design with secondary data analysis of pupil-level and school-level characteristics and school attendance data from the National Pupil Database (NPD). Data from the NPD is collated by the Department for Education (DfE) and includes the School Census, in England. In stage three, a cluster randomised controlled trial (RCT) was designed to test the relationships between improved mindfulness, academic buoyancy, and school attendance. This experimental design tied the findings from the first two stages together to answer the overriding research question, "can improving the academic buoyancy of secondary school students improve their school attendance?" This chapter explores the designs and methods utilised in each stage, offers some exemplar findings which were influential in the design of the RCT in stage three, and considers the implications of this ongoing research for stakeholders including academics, educational practitioners and policy-makers. Additional opportunities to conduct research whilst undertaking my PhD are discussed to outline how a multi-design thesis has been beneficial to my professional development through enhancing desirable research skills.

DOI: 10.4324/9781003201366-13

Background

Inspiration for this PhD thesis originated from my first-hand experiences working as a secondary school teacher, located in an area of high deprivation in the North East of England, where school absence was above the national average. Alongside my teaching role, I also held leadership responsibilities to improve students' school attendance in line with national statistics. Implementing evidence-based interventions to improve school attendance became a fundamental aspect of my role. This experience initiated my interest in character education and constructs such as resilience amongst the wider student population. I wrote a research proposal in 2017, with aims aligned with the Economic Social Research Council's priority for funding research, which focused on improving student wellbeing. I was fortunate to secure a three-and-a-half-year ESRC studentship to fund this research project. My detailed research proposal was planned strategically to fit within this time frame, whilst using the time productively and ambitiously to implement a three staged approach to answer the research question which forms the title of this project.

In line with Gorard's (2013) description of the research cycle, this project begins with two evidence syntheses. Stage one reviews existing research literature and stage two analyses a population-level dataset to produce summaries of what is already known in relation to two key constructs – academic buoyancy and school attendance in English schools. Stage three was designed to pilot trial the most promising intervention to improve academic buoyancy as identified in stage one and ascertain any possible effects on students' school attendance. In the initial planning stage it was not possible to specify what this best intervention would be without a thorough review of the existing evidence, but a smaller-scale pilot trial would ensure that resources would not be wasted on a large-scale definitive study and would minimise the risk if there was no chance of success (Gorard et al., 2017).

A systematic review of studies exploring the educational construct academic buoyancy

A systematic review was considered the most appropriate approach to identify existing literature about the academic buoyancy construct and provide an objective and comprehensive summary of available evidence (Mulrow, 1994; Petticrew and Roberts, 2006; Torgerson, 2003). This review had four research questions:

1 How is academic buoyancy defined?
2 How is academic buoyancy measured?

3 Is academic buoyancy malleable?
4 What is the evidence from existing RCTs of a promising intervention for improving academic buoyancy?

A scoping review rapidly synthesised existing academic buoyancy literature and identified that this review is the first of its kind to be undertaken in this topic area. The objective of this review was to provide researchers, educational practitioners, and policy makers with a non-biased, accessible summary of evidence to ascertain what is currently known about the construct to make evidence-based and informed decisions to identify a promising intervention and directions for future research.

Prior to undertaking the systematic review, a protocol was written explicitly stating the rationale for the study and outlining the pre-planned methodological and analytical approaches to be taken. The protocol was drafted using the Preferred Reporting Items for Systematic Reviews and Meta-analysis Protocols (PRISMA-P, Moher et al., 2015). An electronic literature search of the EBSCOhost, Web of Science, and Scopus databases was conducted. The search strategy was built around two groups of key words: the construct ("academic* buoyan*" OR "educat* buoyan*" OR "daily resilien*" OR "everyday resilien*") AND setting (academic* OR school* OR college OR universit* OR educat* OR schola* OR pedagog* OR pupil OR student OR learn*).

Conducted in two phases, phase one included papers if they provided a definition or measure of academic buoyancy. Phase one included studies focusing on students, with all research designs, across all age phases and in all academic settings. Published and unpublished texts in the public domain were included if they had been written between 1998 and 2020 to minimise the potential for publication bias. For phase two, phase one papers were re-screened to identify studies with RCT designs, to answer research questions three and four. Screening on titles and abstracts and full texts was completed by an independent first reviewer and 20% of texts were double screened by an independent second reviewer. The same quality assurance process was also adhered to for the data extraction.

The methodological quality of the RCTs was assessed using items from the Consolidated Standards Of Reporting Trials (CONSORT) statement. This tool was developed by the reviewers to judge the overall quality of papers in relation to three domains – relevance to the research question, and internal and external validity.

The thesis has a PRISMA flowchart showing the number of papers at each stage of the review (Moher et al., 2009). From the 74 papers eligible to answer research questions one and two it was clear that Martin and Marsh's (2008) original definition of academic buoyancy had strongly influenced how the construct had been defined over a decade of research. It is conceptually defined as, "the students' ability to successfully deal with academic setbacks and challenges that are typical of the ordinary course of school life (e.g., poor grades, competing deadlines, exam pressure, difficult schoolwork)" (Martin and Marsh, 2008, p. 54). Six papers directly quoted Martin et al.'s (2008) original definition and 53 closely resembled this quotation using similar language and phrases. Nine definitions included less of the original language and phrases, but cited papers written by Martin and his colleagues. Five definitions were not linked to cited papers and one study did not explicitly define the construct.

In total, 59 papers utilised the Academic Buoyancy Scale (ABS) created by Martin and Marsh (2008). This 4-item scale is often used in its original format or a closely adapted version of the scale. The items include:

"I'm good at dealing with setbacks at school (e.g. bad mark, negative feedback on my work)";

"I don't let study stress get on top of me";

"I think I'm good at dealing with schoolwork pressures"; and

"I don't let a bad mark affect my confidence"

Seven papers utilised other measures which claimed to measure buoyancy, for example, the Buoyancy Questionnaire, EFL Student Buoyancy Scale, and the Student Buoyancy Instrument. One paper claimed to measure buoyancy, but it measured distinct wellbeing constructs instead. Nine papers did not actually measure academic buoyancy. To date there are no studies which assess the rigour or psychometric properties of any of the self-reported buoyancy scales identified in this review.

Only two RCTs were found. Youth COMPASS (Puolakanaho et al., 2019) and BePART (Putwain et al., 2019) are multi-component RCTs which explore elements such as mindfulness, self-compassion, adaptation skills, cognitive behavioural therapy, positive psychology, physical exercise and goal-setting theory, and their effect on academic buoyancy in secondary and Higher Education students. Results indicate very early evidence that academic buoyancy could be malleable to intervention, but any effects seen in these interventions were time-specific and will require further investigation. Mindfulness was a common feature appearing across both interventions, but it was not tested or measured as an independent component in either. Puolakanaho et al.'s (2019) Youth COMPASS provided a high weight of evidence for relevance to the research question, moderate internal validity and high to moderate external validity. The overall quality judgement given to this RCT was high to moderate. Putwain et al.'s (2019) BePART offered a high weight of evidence for relevance to the research question and moderate internal and external validity judgements, the overall judgment is that this RCT presented moderate to high quality of evidence. The designs of these studies provide a rationale for directly measuring the impact that mindfulness could potentially have on improving students' academic buoyancy.

A secondary data analysis of attendance data from the National Pupil Database

The National Pupil Database (NPD) in England is a population-level administrative dataset, with information about students across all age and stages in state-funded schools. The School Census also includes a large quantity of information about individual pupils attending state-funded schools and is collected on a termly basis, three times per calendar year. Secure researcher training was successfully completed to comply with strict terms and conditions relating to confidentiality, handing data, security arrangements, and use of this sometimes sensitive individual data. The data was only available through an ONS secure area. Longitudinal attendance, exclusion, school, and background information for one complete cohort of students was requested, for every year they had attended compulsory schooling.

This secondary data analysis addressed three research questions:

1 What patterns of missing data exist within the NPD according to pupils' individual-level characteristics?
2 What patterns of school absence and exclusions exist within the selected cohort?
3 Where should an attendance intervention be targeted?

Question one is answered by a descriptive analysis of several pupil-level characteristics including age, ethnicity, free school meals (FSM), gender, language group, and Special Educational Needs (SEN). This analysis highlights the percentage of missing data for each key variable for each National Curriculum Year Group. As students get older, the percentage of missing data decreases. Where it is out of the school's control to specify responses to key variables such as ethnicity and first language, it is plausible to see how refusal and non-response from guardians could leave data missing for some students. Likewise, a previous analysis of children with missing FSM data in the Pupil Level Annual School Census (PLASC) has outlined how children with missing FSM scores are also more likely than their peers to be mobile

(Gorard, 2012). Geographical mobility is another possible cause of dropout or attrition in large social datasets and this increases the potential for entire cases to be missing from the dataset before or after they are mobile (Gorard, 2020). Mobility can prove problematic for students arriving from outside of the UK, from other home countries of the UK, and those who transfer from private sector schools in England (Siddiqui et al., 2019).

There are many methods for analysing missing data discussed in research literature (Little and Rubin, 1989). Nevertheless, for variables with less than 10% of missing data, values were replaced with an appropriate default value, such as the sample mean for continuous variables. Replacing missing vales with an appropriate default allowed all cases to be included in the analysis, without disproportionately influencing the outcome. The limitations of this method were considered such as a reduction of variance within the sample, however, this was overcome by using the standard deviation of complete cases when measuring effect sizes. Variables with more than 10% of data missing, such as attendance data for students in the reception year group, was treated as non-feasible and not appropriate to be used in the analysis. Gorard and Siddiqui (2019) state that these techniques are "not entirely satisfactory" but replacing missing values with national averages leads to less bias than predicting missing values and allows all relevant cases to be retained in the analysis (p. 4).

To answer research questions two and three a similar descriptive analysis method was used, which included the comparison of means for various subgroups and cross-tabulations to compare variables (gender, ethnicity, FSM, language group, and SEN) between groups. Percentages of students with at least one session of authorised, unauthorised, overall absence, and fixed term exclusion were compared to understand the kinds of students who were more likely to be absent from school, and the types of absence they registered. Generally, as students grew older the average number of sessions absent from school increased, with the highest reported sessions of school absence recorded in National Curriculum Year 10. A proactive approach to improve school attendance would therefore consider implementing an intervention before students reach Year 10.

Furthermore, students who were entitled to FSM or reported having SEN were more likely to be absent as they got older. Ensuring that any attendance intervention is inclusive of disadvantaged students may help to improve overall attendance levels. Based on the average number of sessions missed for different types of absence and pooled standard deviation scores, Cohen's D effect sizes were calculated to understand the magnitude of differences between groups of students. Question three focused on school-level characteristics, such as geographical region, local authorities, and school types. The North East of England reported a repeatedly high average number of sessions missed for all types of absence and may be a geographical region which would benefit from an attendance intervention.

It is claimed that regular school attendance can increase the possibility of successful school outcomes, such as improving students' chances of long-term employment and reducing their potential for social exclusion (DfE, 2016; Fogelman, 1978; Morris and Rutt, 2004). The attendance data analysed here supports the idea that absence rates are highest during a student's final years of compulsory schooling. This is a period of schooling where students work towards and sit important national examinations which may be influential in determining their future life outcomes. It is possible that some students do not have the mechanisms and support to cope with the demands and pressures of everyday school life during a phase where expectations for students to succeed are high. As such, the school attendance of these students may be impacted. Providing children with the necessary skills and tools to navigate the stresses and challenges associated with school could have the potential to improve their school attendance. A robust RCT is planned in stage three to explore how implementation of a mindfulness intervention could improve academic buoyancy and so school attendance.

A randomised controlled trial to explore the relationships between mindfulness, academic buoyancy, and school attendance

Data gathered in stages one and two were instrumental in the design of the RCT. Unfortunately, the final 18 months of this PhD were impacted by the disruption caused by COVID-19 pandemic and the national closure of schools in England for the wider student population. Therefore, the RCT was paused following completion of prerequisite training courses, study design, and recruitment stages. Instead, the RCT is written as a protocol and features in the designs and methods chapter of the thesis. This is an area for further research when fieldwork in schools is deemed feasible again.

Based on the findings in stage one, testing the effectiveness of a mindfulness-based intervention was considered promising for improving students' academic buoyancy. A cluster RCT offers a robust research design to evaluate whether a mindfulness curriculum can benefit Year 9 students' levels of academic buoyancy and school attendance (Connolly et al., 2017). Through random allocation of cases to treatment and control groups, selection bias is minimised and differences observed between groups can more easily be attributed to the effects of the intervention as opposed to selection characteristics that are unobserved (Torgerson and Torgerson, 2008). This study was designed as a pilot trial because it evaluates "an incompletely developed intervention" (Lancaster et al., 2004; Torgerson and Torgerson, 2008, p. 119). The Mindfulness in Schools Project ".b" (pronounced "dot be") curriculum was selected for further testing as it continues to catch the attention of educational practitioners, yet the quality of existing research on it varies, and findings are so far inconclusive. Where the outcome of the impact and process evaluations in this trial indicate promise, a justification could be made for a scaled-up version of this small-scale pilot trial in the future.

As an alternative to a simple RCT, this study was designed as a cluster RCT and focused on classes as the unit of study. In discussion with senior leaders at volunteering schools it became apparent that randomising at the individual pupil-level was not practical nor feasible due to a lack of resources available, such as teacher facilitation, size of teaching environments, access to technology, and potential disruption to teaching and learning for the control group. Following the recruitment phase, 44 classes, from 9 schools, across 3 local authorities in the North East of England were eligible to be assigned at random to receive the treatment or continue with their normal curriculum.

This research design can be illustrated using design notation (Gorard, 2013). As time moves from left to right: "R" indicates random allocation of classes to groups, "O" illustrates an episode of measurement and data collection from the same classes, and "X" signifies the point at which the intervention is delivered and received by the treatment group only.

(Time →)				
R	O_1	X	O_2	(Treatment Group)
R	O_1		O_2	(Control Group)

At O_1 schools had agreed to anonymously assign students with unique identifier codes and provide access to their pupil characteristics including gender, ethnicity, first language, FSM, and SEN. Schools would also provide each eligible students' school attendance percentage on the day of data collection. During this episode of data collection students would measure their academic buoyancy using the ABS scale (Martin and Marsh, 2008) and their level of mindfulness. For data collection at O_2 students' mindfulness, academic buoyancy and school attendance would be measured again for both treatment and control groups to ascertain any changes between groups and the size of an effect, if an effect exists. Conducting trials in educational settings can be complex and outcomes and effects could be due to factors that are not the focus of the impact evaluation (Siddiqui et al., 2018). Research questions to be answered in a process evaluation survey for classroom teachers facilitating the project would include perceptions about how successfully the intervention was implemented, facilitators and barriers to implementation, any unintended consequences, amongst many others.

Implications

The implications for researchers, educational practitioners, and policy makers were considered at the end of each stage of the research. This was important to reflect on what the research findings would mean for a variety of stakeholders. With regards to academic buoyancy research, there is an urgent requirement for researchers to turn their attention to the conceptual and operational definitions of the construct before further intervention work can progress meaningfully and findings can report with confidence that the effects seen in students cannot be attributed to errors pertaining to the construct's definition or measurement.

Educational practitioners require easy access to interventions which have the potential to impact a range of student factors such as attainment but also other education-related behaviours such as school attendance and student wellbeing. Whilst an intervention may show evidence of an effect, the size of the effect, quality of the evidence, feasibility, and cost-effectiveness should be considered carefully before further recommendations can be made.

Finally, language used by policy makers in official documents, which have addressed the DfE's strategy for including character education in the curriculum, may have had the potential to cause confusion about which non-cognitive skills to target amongst the wider student population, how best to make changes to these skills, and lead to public funding being misspent by schools on the wrong interventions. Awareness should be brought to the distinctions made between conceptual and operational definitions of several non-cognitive skills such as academic resilience and academic buoyancy. Language used in policy documents should be considered carefully and drawing distinctions between different types of resilience, for example, may be beneficial to provide further clarity for educational practitioners and ensure interventions are fit for purpose.

Opportunities

I have learned a multitude of research skills whilst undertaking my PhD and have had the opportunity to implement these skills in settings outside of academia. I was fortunate to undertake a 3-month policy internship with the Behavioural Insights Unit at the DfE. Whilst undertaking this placement I worked on rapid literature reviews, evidence syntheses for non-specialist audiences, quality assurance of data analysis based on large datasets, helped to design RCTs for various policy teams and training policy makers about the benefits of utilising RCTs to understand the impact of their interventions. I was also asked to deliver training to policy makers to increase knowledge within the department about robust evaluation methods. My confidence and ability to carry out these tasks was due to my experiences as a PhD student and the range of designs and methods I had engaged with to carry out my thesis.

As a post-doctoral research associate, I am continuing to utilise the research skills I have learned as a PhD student and am expanding on them further to learn new skills. In my current role as an employed researcher, I am undertaking a systematic review, doing statistical modelling, and continuing to expand my knowledge of experimental research designs to conduct discrete choice experiments, which are commonly used within health economics. Engaging with robust research designs and methods as a PhD student has given me valuable experience and demonstrated my ability to work on various types of projects.

Conclusion

This three-stage thesis utilises robust research designs and methods, and has taught me many valuable research skills. I am grateful to have been supervised by experienced academics with expertise in the research designs and methods which underpin my project. Their guidance has provided me with valuable insights and helped me to develop as a researcher. Student behaviour and improving student wellbeing continue to influence my research interests but the skills I have gained in systematic reviewing, secondary data analysis and experimental designs can be applied to investigate other topic areas. Engaging with several robust research designs and methods has been instrumental in my development as a researcher and my ability to apply them with confidence has afforded me opportunities in academia beyond PhD life.

References

Connolly, P., Keenan, C., and Urbanska, K. (2017). The trials of evidence-based practice in education: A systematic review of randomised controlled trials in educational research 1980-2016. *Educational Research*, 60(3), pp. 276–291. doi: 10.1080/00131881.2018.1493353

De Vaus, D. (2001). *Research Design in Social Research*. London: SAGE Publications Ltd.

DfE (2016). *The link between absence and attainment at KS2 and KS4: 2013/14 academic year*. Retrieved from https://assets.publishing.service.gov.uk/government/uploads/system/uploads/attachment_data/file/509679/The-link-between-absence-and-attainment-at-KS2-and-KS4-2013-to-2014-academic-year.pdf

Fogelman, K. (1978). School attendance, attainment and behaviour. *British Journal of Educational Psychology*, 48(2), pp. 148–158.

Gorard, S. (2012). Who is eligible for free school meals? Characterising FSM as a measure of disadvantage in England. *British Educational Research Journal*, 38(6), pp. 1003–1017. doi: 10.1080/01411926.2011.608118

Gorard, S. (2013). *Research Design: Creating Robust Approaches for the Social Sciences*. London: SAGE Publications Ltd.

Gorard, S. (2020). Handling missing data in numeric analyses. *International Journal of Social Research Methodology*, 23(6), pp. 651–660. doi: 10.1080/13 645579.2020.1729974

Gorard, S., See, B.H., and Siddiqui, N. (2017). *The Trials of Evidence-Based Education: The Promises, Opportunities and Problems of Trials in Education*. London: Routledge.

Gorard. S., and Siddiqui, N. (2019). How trajectories of disadvantage help explain school attainment. SAGE Open, pp. 1–14. doi: 10.1177/215824401 8825171

Lancaster, G., Dodd, S., and Williamson, P. (2004). Design and analysis of pilot studies: Recommendations for good practice. *Journal of Evaluation in Clinical Practice*, 10, pp. 307–312. doi: 10.1111/j..2002.384.doc.x

Little, R., and Rubin, D. (1989). The analysis of social science data with missing values. *Sociological Methods and Research*, 18(2&3), pp. 292–326. doi: 10.11 77/0049124189018002004

Martin, A.J., and Marsh, H.W. (2008). Academic buoyancy: Towards an understanding of students' everyday academic resilience. *Journal of School Psychology*, 46, pp. 53–83. doi: 10.1016/j.jsp.2007.01.002

Moher, D., Liberati, A., Tetzlaff, J., Altman, D.G., and The PRISMA Group. (2009). Preferred reporting items for systematic reviews and meta-analyses: The PRISMA statement. *British Medical Journal*, 2009(339), p. b2535. doi: 10.1136/bmj.b2535

Moher, D., Shamseer, L., Clarke, M., Ghersi, D., Liberati, A., Petticrew, M., Shekelle, P., Stewart, L.A., & PRISMA-P Group. (2015). Preferred reporting items for systematic review and meta-analysis protocols (PRISMA-P) 2015 statement. *Systematic Reviews*, 4(1), pp. 1–9. doi: 10.1186/2046-4053-4-1

Morris, M., and Rutt, S. (2004). *An analysis of pupil attendance data in excellence in cities (EIC) areas and non-EIC EAZs: Final report*. Retrieved from https:// dera.ioe.ac.uk/5697/1/RR657.pdf

Mulrow, C. (1994). Systematic Reviews: Rationale for systematic reviews. *British Medical Journal* 1994(309), p. 597. doi: 10.1136/bmj.309.6954.597

Petticrew, M., and Roberts, H. (2006). *Systematic Reviews in the Social Sciences: A Practical Guide*. Malden, MA: Blackwell Publishing. doi: 10.1002/97804 70754887

Puolakanaho, A., Lappalainen, R., Lappalainen, P., Muotka, J.S., Hirvonen, R., Eklund, K.M., Ahonen, T.P.S., and Kiuru, N. (2019). Reducing stress and enhancing academic buoyancy among adolescents using a brief web-based program based on acceptance and commitment therapy: A randomized controlled trial. *Journal of Youth and Adolescent*, 48, pp. 287–305. doi: 10.1 007/s10964-018-0973-8

Putwain, D., Gallard, D., and Beaumont, J. (2019). A multi-component well-being programme for upper secondary students: Effects on wellbeing, buoyancy, and adaptability. *School Psychology International*, 40(1), pp. 49–65. doi: 10.1177/0143034318806546

Siddiqui, N., Boliver, V., and Gorard, S. (2019). Assessing the reliability of longitudinal social surveys of access to higher education: The case of the Next Steps survey in England. *Social Inclusions*, 7, p. 1. doi: 10.17645/si.v7i1.1631

Siddiqui, N., Gorard, S., and See, B.H. (2018). The importance of process evaluation for randomised controlled trials in education. *Educational Research*, 60(3), pp. 357–370. doi: 10.1080/00131881.2018.1493349

Torgerson, C. (2003). *Systematic Reviews*. London: Continuum.

Torgerson, C., and Torgerson, D. (2008). *Designing Randomised Trials in Health Education and the Social Sciences*. Basingstoke: Palgrave McMillan. doi: 10.1 057/9780230583993

CHAPTER 12

Understanding the moral values of primary school children: A comparative study

Pian Shi

Introduction

School education worldwide usually involves children understanding and development of good behaviour and high moral values. A general expectation is that children have the opportunity to learn about moral values and uphold them in real-life circumstances, although of course these values might differ in different contexts. Existing research literature suggests that cultural and contextual differences in education systems have differential implications for children's learning about moral values and real-life implementation of moral values. However, there is a lack of robust evidence demonstrating differences in children's perceptions of moral values and actual behaviour after school education in different country contexts and education systems. This PhD project fills that gap in existing literature, presenting comparative findings of 1,950 children in primary schools of England and China. The project involved developing and implementing a survey to indicate children's perceptions of moral values, followed by a game activity observing the difference between perceptions and actual moral behaviour. The study concerns the link between intentions and actions, and the differences between countries.

One of the issues moral education faces is to evaluate students' moral values accurately. Even quite young children seem to portray strong moral values when these are checked through test papers. Cognitively they know "right" and "wrong" and understand how they are expected to behave ethically. However, students' actual behaviour may deviate from the moral values they report when they are away from the supervision of teachers and parents. Moral behaviour is an external demonstration of one's moral values. It can be understood that solid moral values would drive strong behaviour commitment under various contexts. However, the goal of moral value education is not achieved if consistent moral behaviour has not been

DOI: 10.4324/9781003201366-14

developed. Therefore, studying a behavioural commitment to moral values in real-life situations is, or at least should be, critical for assessing moral values.

Background

Researchers in this field have generally used two types of measurements of moral behaviour:

- Self or other reported past behaviour (e.g. Aldridge et al., 2015; Atif et al., 2013; Hardy, 2005; Hart et al., 1998)
- Self-reported behaviour intentions (e.g. Crimston et al., 2016; Gotowiec, 2019; Ring et al., 2018)

There are limitations in both types of measures. First, social desirability (wanting to appear good) could invalidate the results of self-reported measurements. Second, there may be a gap between one's report/intention and actual behaviour. Considering Turiel's (2002) research as an example, young adolescents had different moral views and judgements on actual and scenario moral events. Participants are more likely to violate ethical rules in actual events than in hypothetical scenarios. However, it is argued that sometimes moral behaviours in daily life are not observable to outsiders (Shao et al., 2008).

Some researchers have conducted natural observations of behaviour such as donation and allocation tasks (e.g. Conway and Peetz, 2012; Mulder and Aquino, 2013; Sanders et al., 2018). However, few studies focus on the consistency between moral intention and actual moral behaviour. Therefore, one of my purposes is to develop a measurement of moral values that involves evaluating the consistency between moral behaviour intention and corresponding behaviour.

Another issue is that the research on morality within cultural contexts is weak in terms of robust and large-scale comparisons, especially for young children. Nevertheless, social and cultural differences between Western and East Asian countries might suggest differences in children's moral behaviour expressions (Samuels, 2018).

How the research was conducted

This PhD study presents a general picture of the difference and similarity in moral values and behaviour of young people between China and England, in the contexts of English and Chinese primary schools. There is no space to describe all of it in detail here.

The participants are primary school students between 8 and 12 years old (4th, 5th and 6th grades in China). I recruited 8 public primary schools in China, involving 1,768 children. The eight schools are located in a capital city (Beijing) and three smaller cities (e.g. Lan Zhou, Bei Hai and Tang Shan) in China. One out of the eight schools is located in a rural area in Lan Zhou city. I recuited 2 equivalent schools in England, involving 182 children. This was less than hoped for, due largely to Covid19 lockdown (see below). These schools are located in Durham (a small city) and Newcastle (a big city) in the UK. Some responses in England (75) were via the internet, mainly again from Newcastle and Durham, with a few responses from London (the capital city). The sample from the north east of England comes from a region of relatively high disadvantage (compared to Beijing, for example) and this needs to be recalled when the two are compared. Any differences might be partly due to differences in socio-economic status rather than country or culture. In China, 2 schools refused to let their children take part in the game, and 254 participants were chosen randomly from the rest. In England, 24 children from one school took part in the game (again affected by Covid lockdown).

The survey of moral values concerned students' reports of fairness, helpfulness and honesty, and their behavioural intentions with respect to these moral values. The instrument was developed from the Self-importance Moral Identity (Aquino and Reed, 2002) and 20-item Moral Identity Measures (Black and Reynolds, 2016). Six items were used to check three moral values, with every two items corresponding to each moral value. Taking "fairness" as an example, the two items are: (1) "It is important for me to treat other people fairly"and (2) "It is ok to cheat in a game if the rewards for winning are high". The first item identifies respondents' perceived importance of the moral value, while the other checks the commitment of action. Respondents rate each statement on a 5 degree Likert Scale (from 5-agree strongly to 1-disagree strongly). Some statements were negative to encourage attention, and negative statements were converted into positive ones when the data were analysed Figure 12.1.

Two hypothetical scenarios were presented, and children were asked to make the decision and act accordingly. The scenarios were as follows:

- You are asked to share some small fun gifts between a stranger and yourself. What will you do?
- You get £2 (or 20 RMB) as a reward for joining a game. Some poor children in the world cannot eat healthy food and drink clean water. You are told that your donation of money can help them. You are free to make any decision, what will you do?

Figure 12.1 Setting up the survey in England

The second main part of the study was a game-based activity to observe actual behaviour. Children were allowed to make a decision, and their actions were evaluated for the consistency during the survey and actual behaviour observation in donation and distribution tasks (like those above). Children were selected randomly from the whole class sample present on the school visit for the survey, and individually invited to join the game. In both countries, myself and the chosen child participants were involved in the game. Participant children did not know what the game is before entering the classroom. After finishing the game, they were told not to tell other students who have not yet joined the game Figure 12.2.

Participants were gifted eight colourful bouncing balls, and asked to distribute these between themselves and the researcher (myself). Participants were told they could make any decision. They could keep all the balls to themselves or return all the balls to the researcher. Next, each participant was given £2 (or 20 RMB) as a reward for joining the game. They can then donate none, some, or all of that money. Participants were told that they

Figure 12.2 Preparing for a game observation in China

could take away the balls and money they decide to keep for themselves, after the game.

Summary of key findings

There was little missing data. The mean age of children was 10.2 in both countries. In China 47% were female. In England 54% were female. The biggest differences are in country of origin, and parental education and occupation (Table 12.1). Families in the NE England sample are more mobile, and more likely to be of recent immigrant origin, whereas the families in China are solidly indigenous. The children in the Chinese sample are substantially more likely to have one or more parents with a professional occupation. NE England is an area of relatively high unemployment. All of these factors could influence how children respond, especially in the game where real money and toys are provided.

The overwhelming majority of respondents from both countries report agreeing with all three moral values – helpfulness, honesty and fairness. And with moral behaviour for helpfulness and fairness (Table 12.2). The differences, represented as odds ratios, are relatively small and could be explained

Table 12.1 Percentage of participants in each country with specific characteristics

	Child born in that country	At least one parent born in that country	At least one parent in professional occupation
China	100	100	57
England	89	80	45

Note: for the purposes of clarity in all tables, the small number of missing values is ignored. Full figures appear in the thesis.

Table 12.2 The percentage of the importance of moral values and behaviour

Items	Country	Agree	Disagree	Odds Ratios
Helpful (value)	China	88	8	1.8
	England	82	14	
Helpful (commitment)	China	89	5	1.9
	England	90	3	
Honesty (value)	China	93	4	1.0
	England	85	4	
Honesty (commitment)	China	82	7	5.2
	England	45	21	
Fairness (value)	China	91	6	2.1
	England	84	11	
Fairness (commitment)	China	94	2	2.0
	England	86	4	

by the nature of the sample. The Chinese children report slightly more agreement for all items than the English ones (except for the behavioural commitment to helpfulness).

The Chinese children gave very similar levels of agreement to the values and commitment items, as did the English ones. But for helpfulness and fairness the English children reported slightly more commitment than their values suggested. Chinese children, on the other hand, reported slightly less commitment to honesty than their values suggested.

However, the striking feature of Table 12.2 is low (45%) reporting of commitment to behavioural honesty by the English sample. This is considerably less than the Chinese sample (odds ratio of 5.2). The difference may be due to the nature of the items. The questions about helpful and fair behaviour are "I will not go along with a group decision to hurt others" and "It is not ok to cheat in a game if the rewards for winning are high". The first has the highest agreement of all items for the English sample. It contains the word "hurt" which signals a wrongdoing fairly strongly. The second is probably more trivial, and several children probably have cheated in a game, but the word "cheat" could again be a clear signal of the desirable answer.

The statement for the behaviour commitment to "honesty" moral value goes is "If I know that my best friend did something bad in my classroom, I will tell the teacher when asked about it". Here the word bad is a clue, but in this item it is not the respondent who has been "bad". Bad could mean that the best friend has committed a serious crime (including hurting someone) or it could mean that the friend made a face at the teacher, for example. In the latter case, the moral value of friendship or loyalty to friends (not snitching in English parlance) may supercede the pull towards honesty. It can also be imagined that not saying something is not in itself dishonest (as distinct from denying it if asked by the teacher). It may be that something in the context, or the language of the translated question, is responsible for the marked difference here between the two country samples. This could also explain why both Chinese and English students agree strongly with honesty as a value, but there is a difference between them on whether to tell a teacher. Another explanation could be a genuine difference in culture. Maybe the Chinese students are more motivated to give the socially desirable answer, and/or the English students are prepared to be less honest about issues that are unimportant (to them). It is also the case that the Chinese children responded face-to-face in school, so that although their responses are reported anonymously they might have felt under pressure to respond in a certain way. A large proportion of the English children responded to the survey on-line (but the differences between the on-line and other Engoush responses are small).

Either way, it is encouraging to see that the English sample did not just automatically repeat their reported values in their reported behaviour. What will it look like when we compare reports of intentions and actual behaviour?

In the survey, given a hypothetical £2 or 20 RMB most children offered to donate most of the money for poorer children. The mean intended donation in China was £1.8 and £1.6 in England. The distribution of responses appears in Table 12.3. Children in England were more tempted than those in China to give some part (such as half) away and keep the rest. Most children across both countries intended to donate all of the money.

However, a more marked difference appears in the game itself involving an actual £2 (Table 12.4). Most children in the Chinese sample actually donated the same amount that they reported they would, and a reasonable number donated more. Most children in the English sample, a clear majority, actually donated

Table 12.3 Percentage intending to donate, and how much

	All (£2)	£1.50	Half £1	£0.50	Nothing
China	78	13	6	1	2
England	57	13	18	8	3

Table 12.4 Percentage donating the same or differently in the game to their intention in the survey

	Intention < Action	Intention = Action	Intention > Action
China	13	76	10
England	4	13	79

Table 12.5 Percentage intending to share toys, and in what proportion

	All	More	Equally	Less	No sharing
China	10	10	75	3	2
England	2	2	60	8	26

less than they said they would. On average, Chinese participants actually donated around 0.01 pounds more than they were inclined to donate. However, the participants from the UK actually donated 0.9 pounds less than what they reported to donate in the survey. There are several possible reasons for this. The timing or context of the game in relation to the survey may have encouraged consistency or social desirability in one setting more than the other. The sum involved might have meant more to the English sample living in a more deprived area, and less to the Chinese sample who might not need or receive pocket money. It is worth looking at the other game before discussing more.

In both country samples, most children suggested sharing the bouncy balls equally (Table 12.5). The Chinese sample was more likely to retain fewer balls for themselves, while the English sample was more likely to share none of the balls. Across both games, the English children are reporting an intention to be less generous than the Chinese children.

Unlike in the donation "game", more English children actually shared more balls than they had suggested they would, although an even higher proportion shared fewer balls. The Chinese sample was more consistent across the two games, mostly acting as they had said they would. They were either more generous or less motivated by the cash and fun toys. In the thesis, I explore the observation and interview data that may help understand this Table 12.6.

Table 12.6 Percentage gifting the same or differently in the game to their intention in the survey

	Intention < Action	Intention = Action	Intention > Action
China	20.5	66.5	11.8
England	45.8	37.5	16.7

Discussion

Here it is noted that participants from the two countries showed somewhat different attitudes towards money during the game observation. When Chinese participants were asked why they would like to donate the money, at least half of them replied something like:

I do not need money. If I want something, my parents will buy me.

Money is useless for me.

None of the English participants responded like that to the same question. Most participants from both countries donate the money because they said that the needy children need the money more than they do, and they want to help. And the reason they may keep some money for themselves is because they want to buy something for themselves or their siblings.

In the distribution task, the most popular explanation among participants from both countries is that "distributing equally or fairly is the best solution". The eight bouncing balls are in four colours, and even in number. Many participants even paid attention to distributing the colours evenly. Respondents' similar reaction to the distribution of the balls from the two countries is consistent with their shared "equity" tendency that the statistics show. Most of the participants from both countries said they liked the bouncing balls. A few participants said they were not interested in them, and gave all the balls to the researcher. Perhaps they felt the toys were too childish. There is a considerable difference between children of age 8 and age 11.

Some participants' behaviour did indicate social desirability in the game observation. For example, some children were very hesitant about whether or how much to donate. The expressions on their face suggested that they wanted to keep the money rather than donating it. One participant decided to take all the reward money away and went back to the classroom. However, she came back a few minutes later and wanted to donate all the money without any reasons. Another participant also decided to keep all the money and told the researcher that they had already donated to another charity recently. Some participants saw the researcher as a kind of teacher, and they seemed to care about what the researcher thought of their behaviour. For example, a few Chinese participants distributed more bouncing balls to the researcher and even kept the balls in the colour that they did not like. They said something like:

Teacher [referring to the researcher] deserves more balls and I want to give the balls in their favourite colour to the teacher

Teacher works hard and deserves more balls

Participants' different attitudes towards money and the potential social desirability may have influenced their actual behaviour during the observation. The survey and observation only provide a general picture of any differences and similarities in moral values between the two samples. Of course, apart from the observed details, the family background, parenting, school climate, gender and cultural values and norms could also contribute to the similarity and differences. This needs to be explored further.

A key finding from the research is that the assessment of moral values focusing on the behaviour commitment to the values can and does work with children. The questionnaire about cognitive moral values is understandable for children at least eight years old. The returned questionnaires are valid. The game observation is operational in the school environment. Each participant takes 5 to 10 minutes to complete the tasks, which is acceptable for most school gatekeepers. None of the selected participants wanted to quit the game observation because of discomfort. Participants behaved in different ways during the observation even though possible social desirability exists.

The differences and similarities in the moral values between the two countries provide a starting point for researchers interested in comparative research on morality to study further.

Another key finding is that self-reports of moral values do not necessarily match self-reports of intended moral behaviour, and are even less consistent with actual behaviour (even when known to be under observation). Future research should rely less on self-report/introspection, and focus more on moral behaviour itself. Perhaps the same is true for those interested in moral education.

It is even clearer than it was at the outset of the PhD that morality is a tricky concept to pin down and research – although this is not an argument for not doing so. The possibility of a clash between generosity to unknown others or to a friend or sibling, or between strict honesty and loyalty to a good friend, is fascinating. It shows again that trying to understand the principles of justice deployed by young people is endlessly fascinating (Gorard and Smith, 2018).

Conclusion

In this final section, I want to share my reflections on developing large-scale PhD research as an international student in the UK. Some challenges were predicted when I was thinking about the topic of my research. For example, access to the target groups, especially schools in the UK, game observation which was time-consuming and required support from staff at school, and surveying young adolescents was more complicated than with adults. Besides the predictable difficulties, I also met some unexpected challenges, such as the lockdown due to Covid 19 pandemic and more complex ethical implications for researching with participants under the age of 18. However, I was not demotivated by these challenges. On the contrary, I was driven by the idea that this research project would seem different once I overcame these challenges. So, I will tell my story and reflect on what can be improved in my further study.

An extensive sample increases the probability of robust research. Considering my existing resources for the study, I set a reasonable goal for myself, but with a bit of ambition. I had worked with several primary schools in China as part of an education research program, making it easier for me to access Chinese primary school students. However, it was difficult for me to access British primary schools since I did not know anyone who worked in primary schools in the UK. Even though my supervisors said they could help me access the target group when we discussed my research topic, I still wanted to try all my ways before I turned to them. I thought about several possible ways to achieve my goal initially and started to try all of them when I was doing the literature review in my first year.

First, I volunteered to help in a local primary school through Durham University. This would have provided me with a chance of working with teachers and gatekeepers in local schools., and an opportunity to practice communicating with primary school students in English. However, the Disclosure and Barring Service, UK requirement for school visitors, took me a long time to negotiate, and I missed the chance to volunteer. It is worth noticing that the DBS check was beneficial to me. It gave me permission to do the game observation with students individually later. I also tried other ways to access local primary schools. I made friends on social media who are working with local schools. I also got some tips from peers. I learnt how to make calls and email schools to take part in a survey. To make the gate-keepers interested in my survey, I thought about how my survey would benefit their students and if there is anything I can help with their teaching and learning. Before the lockdown in my second year, I got two local schools.

Another challenge is to persuade the gatekeepers of schools to get their students to join the game observation. The biggest concern of the gate-keepers is that game observation is time-consuming and would interrupt their teaching. Some gatekeepers were happy with the game observation and were happy to give me one or two hours to complete the observation with their students. For others, I used students' break time to finish the observation or reduces the number of students involved. In a word, I tried all the ways before I gave it up. Finally, I got five schools in China and two schools in the UK to do the game observation.

Making the survey and game observation understandable for primary school students is another difficulty. The questionnaire was piloted and adjusted ten times to ensure that the expression was clear and readable enough for the target respondents. The questionnaire was also checked by pilots and readability software online (FLESCH INDEX). Finally, it was demonstrated that children older than eight years old can finish the questionnaire independently. The gifts (bouncing balls) involved in the game observation were also pre-investigated among primary school students to check whether the students are interested in the balls. The whole process of the game observation was rehearsed and timed in advance.

Again, I met some unexpected challenges. It is more complicated to get approval of the ethical application from the university when you are researching under-aged participants compared with adults. The research plan has to ensure the privacy and well-being of the participants. Then, the unexpected lockdown for 19-Covid stopped me from collecting more data face-to-face in the UK. I had only finished the survey with two schools and the game observation in one school. I had to turn to the internet to do the survey. I persuaded not only the teachers but also parents to get their children to help with my survey. I asked a local British friend to help me make my survey link and message seem friendly and eye-catching online. And then, I joined to as many the community clubs or school groups as possible. I posted my survey link anywhere it was allowed by the social media rules. At first, I was worried that no one would respond to my survey. However, the result was much better than I expected. I got a lot of supports from strangers online. Some of them are teachers who are working at local schools. They helped with posting my survey link in their parents' group online or on the website of their schools. Some of them are parents. They got their children to finish my survey and sent my link to their friends' group as well. Finally, I got a further 75 valid responses online by the end of my second year.

My original research design almost has been realised. However, there are still limits, and they need to be improved for my further study. The sample from the UK could be larger to match the sample from China better. No students from rural areas were involved in the game observation. Therefore, the sample should be more diversified in my further study on this topic. Second, there should be a long time interval (two weeks to one month) between the survey and the game observation to minimise the potential of social desirability in the game observation. According to the brief interview with some participants from one Chinese school, a few students recalled what they responded to the related questions in the survey when they did the tasks in the observation. Students who behaved like this probably take the initiative to keep their words and deeds in line. However, the probability of social desirability can never be ruled out. Finally, the questionnaire for primary school students should be as short as possible. Even though the percentage of missing data for most items is below 5%, the non-response rate of the items in the second half of the questionnaire is higher than that of the first half.

I have learnt a lot from the whole process of conducting research. It goes far beyond pure research technics. It is more about the confidence and persistence of a research designer. And how to establish communication with your target groups and gain trust from them. A researcher should not only master the skills of academic research but also explore and coordinate all resources to make a research design realised. The only tip I can recommend to students who are about to do academic research is to act as soon as possible. Supports will be around you as long as you move on your way. Finally, I would like to express my appreciation for the super support from my supervisors Stephen Gorard and Nadia Siddiqui. Thank you for the invitation to tell my research story here. My family, friends and all the people who helped with my research (especially the lovely participants) deserve loads of thanks from the bottom of my heart.

References

Aldridge, J., Ala'i, K., and Fraser, B. (2015). Relationships between school climate and adolescent students' self-reports of ethnic and moral identity. *Learning Environments Research*, 19, pp. 1–15.

Aquino, K., and Reed, A., II (2002). The self-importance of moral identity. *Journal of Personality and Social Psychology*, 83, pp. 1423–1440.

Atif, M., Charfi, A., and Lombardot, E. (2013). Why do some consumers consume ethically? A contingency framework for understanding ethical decision making. *Journal of Marketing Research and Case Studies*, 2013, pp. 1–20.

Black, J., and Reynolds, W. (2016). Development, reliability, and validity of the Moral Identity Questionnaire. *Personality and Individual Differences*, 97, pp. 120–129.

Conway, P., and Peetz, J. (2012). When does feeling moral actually make you a better person? Conceptual abstraction moderates whether past moral deeds motivate consistency or compensatory behaviour. *Personality and Social Psychology Bulletin*, 38 (7), pp. 907–919.

Crimston, C., Bain, P., Hornsey, M., and Bastian, B. (2016). Moral expansiveness: Examining variability in the extension of the moral world. *Journal of Personality and Social Psychology*, 111(4), pp. 636–653.

Gorard, S., and Smith, E. (2018). *Equity in Education: An International Comparison of Pupil Perspectives*. Chinese translation, East China Normal University, ISBN 9787567572621, 195 pages.

Gotowiec, S. (2019). When moral identity harms: The impact of perceived differences in core values on helping and hurting. *Personality and Individual Differences*, 151, pp. 1–9.

Hardy, S. (2005). Identity as a source of pro-social motivation in young adulthood. *Dissertation Abstracts International: Section B: The Sciences and Engineering*. University of Nebraska.

Hart, D., Atkins, R., and Ford, D. (1998). Urban America as a context for the development of moral identity in adolescence. *Journal of Social Issues*, 54(3), pp. 513–530.

Mulder, L., and Aquino, K. (2013). The role of moral identity in the aftermath of dishonesty. *Organisational Behavior and Human Decision Process*, 121, pp. 219–230.

Ring, C., Kavussanu, M., Simms, M., and Mazanov, J. (2018). Effects of situational costs and benefits on projected doping likelihood. *Psychology of Sport and Exercise*, 34, pp. 88–94.

Samuels, W. (2018). Nurturing kindness naturally: A humane education program's effect on the pro-social behaviour of first and second graders across China. *International Journal of Educational Research*, 91, pp. 49–64.

Sanders, S., Wisse, B., Van Yperen, N., and Rus, D. (2018). On ethically solvent leaders: The roles of pride and moral identity in predicting leader ethical behaviour. *Journal Business Ethics*, 150, pp. 631–645.

Shao, R., Aquino, K., and Freeman, D. (2008). Beyond moral reasoning. *Business Ethics Quarterly*, 18, 513–540.

Turiel, E. (2002). *The Culture of Morality: Social Development, Context, and Conflict*. Cambridge: United Kingdom: Cambridge University Press.

PART **III**

Evaluating Education Policy

In Part III we have included chapters examining education policy, using administrative datasets, experiments, systematic reviews, documentary analysis and interviews.

Evaluating education policy

There are chapters covering:

- Does absence from school influence attainment, and what is the best way to handle it?
- Do expensive Science, Technology, Engineering, and Mathematics (STEM) enrichment activities make any difference to science and maths outcomes at school?
- What did the policy of Free Schools achieve in England?
- The role of contextualised admissions to higher education in China
- Internationally, are official surveys of school-leavers and graduates actually used?
- How can we best encourage teachers to appreciate and use research evidence?

The findings in this section, evaluating government policies in many countries, are again valuable for being largely negative. They suggest ways in which governments could save money and effort, and deploy these elsewhere to help improve education. In this section, we learn that the policy for dealing with school absences and exclusions in England is not really based on evidence (Chapter 15). It is extremely hard to find any impact on attainment and participation in STEM subjects from schools' widespread use of enrichment activities by universities and organisations (Chapter 16). The policy of encouraging parents to open local Free Schools did not work as planned (Chapter 17). The timing and lack of official data probably make it

DOI: 10.4324/9781003201366-15

too soon to tell whether admissions to higher education are getting fairer in China (Chapter 18). The resources spent on official surveys of school-leavers are not always used well in practice (Chapter 19). It is very hard to get teachers and other supposed users of publicly-funded research to use evidence well, or at all (Chapter 20). These studies have been widely disseminated, and often picked up by the media.

CHAPTER 13

Free schools in England: Researching a (controversial) new policy reform using a mixed methods approach

Rebecca Morris

Introduction

Thinking back to the very start of the PhD, I recall a range of emotions. It was September and the school term had started. Yet I was not required to be in the classroom. Instead, I was back at the university where I had completed my undergraduate and master's degrees, trying to figure out what the next three or four years might look like. The empty stretch of time ahead felt both daunting and satisfying. I knew I had to complete a big piece of work and that this would be a major challenge – academically, but also perhaps socially and career-wise too. I had loved my previous role as a full-time English teacher in a Birmingham secondary school, and had left some fantastic friends, colleagues and students to start the PhD. But the freedom ahead was also exciting too.

Having completed my MA a few years before, I knew that I was ready for more research. My small-scale study then had explored mixed ability teaching and learning in the secondary English classroom. I learnt so much, had my previously held views challenged and altered, and begun to realise the potential value of research for improving education practice and policy. Through the PhD I was hoping for more of this. But this time, my study would be bigger, more ambitious and focusing on a topic which I felt that the education community needed to know more about. Free schools were still a relatively new phenomenon in England when I started my doctoral studies. The first schools had opened in 2011, following the election of the Conservative-led coalition in 2010. By 2012, and the start of my PhD, there was a lot of media coverage of free schools but very little in the way of robust research and evidence.

So why free schools? Prior to my doctorate, I had been working in a community secondary school which was consulting on conversion to academy status. Academisation was a policy area I had followed with interest during the general election campaign and through my membership of the

National Union of Teachers (now part of the NEU). Free Schools were an extension of this policy. As a flagship education initiative for the Tory party, they were viewed by advocates as a radical and promising way of affecting change in the English system, raising standards, promoting innovation, and encouraging parental choice. Others were more sceptical, however, challenging the government on the rationale for introducing such an approach, questioning the effectiveness rationale, and arguing that more diversity of schools in the system could lead to greater social selection and inequalities. Understandably, research on free schools within the English context was scant. And so, while preparing my proposal for the PhD, it seemed like this topic area combined two key elements. It was both a topic that I personally really wanted to know more about, and an area with a developing evidence "gap".

Securing a scholarship from the School of Education at the University of Birmingham also helped to confirm that my chosen area was of interest and value to others. Without this scholarship, it would not have been possible for me to undertake the PhD, and receiving it further cemented the idea that my project needed to do something more than just keep me entertained for three years. I felt lucky to have been awarded the funding and knew that I should try to make the most of it. I wanted to be contributing to knowledge and asking interesting and difficult questions. I wanted to produce research that others would want to read and know about. Like many new social researchers, I hoped that my work might be "useful" (whatever that means) and would contribute to positive changes in society. I could see the power in research, but I was also unaware at this stage of how complex the whole social research process is and how much I had to learn in the years ahead. Despite recognising this now, I still hold on to the view that the PhD is the time to be bold and ambitious. It is the chance to craft a study – led by *you* – that is different and challenging. And while it might not change the world on its own (however brilliant it is), the PhD is a great opportunity to follow your interests, learn about your chosen area, to hone your abilities as a researcher and perhaps to have some impact on the field.

The following sections of this chapter will provide an outline of my PhD study and reflections about each stage of its design and development. I discuss some of the benefits and challenges of carrying out a relatively large-scale research study on a contentious new policy area. I also emphasise that, while meeting the requirements for a doctoral-level study (according to my two excellent viva examiners, at least) my PhD was definitely not perfect. Like most research it included aspects which did not go to plan, or which could have been improved. I found the PhD to be three years of complex decision-making – about research questions, design, methods, accessing participants, ethics, analysis, data presentation, my career, amongst many,

many other things. I often worried about getting it wrong – and sometimes did. But with the support of good supervisors, you learn that this is all part of the process and that by taking (some) risks and being a little bit braver, you can complete a significant and interesting piece of work which can open up myriad future opportunities.

Design and methods – what did I do and why?

For most Education PhD students, a training course in research design and methods will form a core part of the early stages of their studies. Looking back, I realise that I was lucky to be enrolled on a number of different modules across my first year. They were interesting, challenging and helpful in encouraging me to think deeply about my planned project and what I wanted to do. At the same time I was feverishly trying to read anything on free schools that I could lay my hands on. The policy was developing at a rapid rate at this stage with new schools opening, some schools being closed, and various scandals being reported in the media too. I was trying to balance this contemporary awareness with wider, international academic literature linked to the topic. And I had gone back to teaching for a couple of days a week too.

There was so much to take in and so much to do in terms of narrowing down a focus for my study in that first year of the PhD. Working out how to do this given the vastness of the area was challenging, but challenging in a good way. In some ways I felt lucky that with a relatively new policy area, there were lots of questions to ask and lots of unknowns for me to explore. Looking to the literature on related education policies and contexts, both in the UK and internationally was important here. This existing work was highly influential in helping me to design my own study. I could see the kinds of research that other authors had conducted on academy schools, charter schools, admissions policies, local authorities, segregation and clustering and parental choice – and I looked at how this could be adapted and developed for the new policy initiative that I wanted to examine. It sounds obvious, but reading widely in these early stages was crucial for me. It allowed me to develop confidence in the area I was researching, slowly building understanding and expertise in my rather niche little field of study. Of course, I sometimes ended up down "rabbit holes", reading pieces which perhaps weren't completely relevant but were just interesting or new. But again, this was part of the fun – you cannot tell what is relevant until you read it, and if you have the luxury of time for reading widely, then why not do as much as you can? During the later data collection, analysis and write-up stages (and definitely in the academic job stages!), the time for engaging as thoroughly with the literature evaporates, and so getting stuck-in early was really beneficial for providing these solid foundations of knowledge.

A lot of this reading was happening at the same time as the doctoral methods training programme, and I can see now how important it was that the two were linked. This was a view that was enthusiastically reiterated by my supervisors, meaning that there was rarely a time when we would talk about the content of a piece of research without also scrutinising how it had been conducted and what that meant for the conclusions being presented. When drafting and developing my research questions, I was asking myself both *what* it was I wanted to find out but also questioning *how* that was going to happen.

Determining my research questions was not completely straightforward though. Armed with Patrick White's excellent "Developing Research Questions" (read it), I was brimming with ideas and had pages of potential options for studies. Narrowing these down was a crucial next step. While I was being encouraged to be ambitious, my supervisors were clear that I also could not do it all. And so, with some further reading and thinking, I worked to reduce my questions and refine them, ensuring that I had a coherent project with questions that could be answered through the data I wanted to collect. I chose to have an overarching research question which would form the basis for my study as a whole and would provide an "umbrella" for my sub-questions and mixed methods approach. This question was "Who attends English free schools and why?", and was centred around issues of equity and social justice. In the early years the free schools policy was criticised for being potentially socially selective and favouring access, opportunities and outcomes for more affluent, advantaged children and families. There were also concerns that the initiative could lead to the increased clustering of richer and poorer pupils between schools too. Without empirical data and analysis on these topics we could not know whether the policy was contributing to these existing inequities, and so this seemed like a good place to locate my study.

It was important to me that I should try to present a holistic perspective on this element of the free schools policy, and this involved engaging with information from different sources and at different time points. Scale was also important. There had been no study in England at that point which had sought to look at the policy on a national level, involving schools and parents from right across the country. I was also hopeful that by taking this approach I would be able to capture and understand some of the diversity of free schools, a central feature of and rationale for their introduction.

This chapter can only outline the work and its findings. For further details, readers can also refer to the published articles on each section or my full thesis. I have separated the following into the three sections for clarity. The actual execution of these elements did not always happen in neat, compartmentalised sections nor in a linear fashion.

How were free schools prioritising access? Using school admissions policies for documentary analysis

A key part of my PhD study was to examine the actions and intentions of free schools in relation to their student intakes. I wanted to know how they were prioritising access, and what impression this presented in terms of the values, aims and ethos of each school. Admissions policies are one way of looking at this issue. They are an "official" document in the sense that admissions authorities (such as individual schools and local authorities) are legally required to publish their admissions arrangements on their school websites. This means that the documents are freely and publicly available. It also means that this is their agreed stated intentions in terms of how they plan to admit children to the school. Of course, the enactment of these policies could be somewhat different in reality but the documents themselves provide a relatively stable and straightforward dataset for understanding the declared aims of the admissions authorities. In this case, I was particularly interested in the oversubscription criteria i.e. the ranking and methods used to determine which children can attend each school should there be more applicants than places.

I started having an informal look at free school admissions policies over the Christmas break of the first year of my PhD. After reading much of Anne West's work (e.g. West et al., 2011; West, 2014) on the topic of school admissions and inequalities, I was intrigued to see what these policies might look like for free schools. Pioneering studies by Fitz et al. (2002) and White et al. (2001) also highlighted the methodological possibilities, and provided helpful frameworks for planning a systematic study in this area.

Sometimes people assume that documentary analysis is a bit dull, not quite as exciting as "getting out there" and talking to people. I would wholeheartedly disagree. Documents are rich sources of information, and products of their specific contexts. Moreover, they have all been created by someone's hand. They are not neutral in the way that some seem to assume. In the case of free schools, these documents provided a valuable window into the mindsets and priorities of the founders of these new schools, and the political background against which the schools were being opened. They also provided a really important basis for understanding the two other foci of my study: parental choice of free schools and the characteristics of children attending them. And so, after some scoping of the availability of these policies and their content, I developed a strategy for coding both the type and ranking of oversubscription criteria used by free schools and analysed the policies accordingly. I viewed this as a piloting approach, knowing that later I also wanted to include a comparative element (including local authorities where the free schools were situated), and examining new waves of free schools as they opened.

This initial approach worked well, and after conducting the analysis on the first groups of free schools, I realised that I had an interesting and original dataset. I had found that the majority of new schools were adhering to the legislation in the Admissions Code. There were, however, a minority who were not. I also found that some free schools were using some of their "freedoms" to include methods such as lotteries, random assignment, or prioritisation of founders'/teachers' children in their oversubscription criteria. These approaches were not permitted to be used by local authorities at the time, and so signalled an important divergence. With these findings, and the wider discourses that were emerging in the academic literature and media about admissions and unequal school access, I was encouraged to publish this analysis.

At the time, I really had no idea what this meant. I had obviously read lots of journal articles but had not thought about what it might mean to write one. My supervisor was encouraging and told me to look at some examples of articles I liked and use those for inspiration. Writing this up seemed to make sense as a way of organising my thoughts about school admissions and documenting the small study that I had undertaken. And so, after a few weeks of drafting, I submitted my first journal article to the *Oxford Review of Education*. Unsurprisingly it came back from the peer reviewers with some pretty substantial suggestions for improvement, but these were genuinely helpful, and I sought to address them all before resubmitting, eventually getting the article published in the second year of my PhD (Morris, 2014). This felt like an achievement, and it was a contribution on a topic which, at the time, had very little in the way of evidence. Later that year, I won a university postgraduate researcher award for this publication too. The book voucher prize was very welcome but even more importantly, this award gave me confidence. Perhaps I could conduct research that others were interested in reading, and perhaps there was a place for me to carry on researching within this strange academic world.

Why would parents choose a brand-new school for their child? Questionnaires and interviews for exploring school choice

Since the early 1990s there has been a growing body of education research which has looked at issues relating to parental choice of schools in England. This work covers a wide range of topics including the reasons why parents' (and children) choose schools, the information used to make choices and the role of admissions arrangements, the influence of local "markets" and the outcomes of choice policies on school intakes. It is a large and often complex body of research, and one which sometimes appears to present contradictory findings. Again, navigating this work and considering how it might be relevant for my own area of study was crucial. There had been a decline in the school choice literature in the late 2000s/early 2010s but I felt that the introduction of free schools and the wider context of diversity in the English system presented an original and important landscape for study. I was also inspired by earlier studies (such as Ball and Vincent, 1998; Gorard, 1997; Woods et al., 2005) which had engaged directly with parents in order to understand their experiences of and attitudes towards school choice. This seemed particularly pertinent for my study because, through the free schools policy, the government were promoting "parent power", and encouraging parents to set-up and run new schools themselves.

I decided to conduct a questionnaire with parents who had chosen a secondary free school in the early years of the policy. I included a comparison group of parents whose children attended a non-free school in the same local authority as the participating free schools. My questionnaire was adapted from successful studies which had looked at similar issues. I used a number of the same question items but also included questions relating to a key element of the free school choice: the "newness" of the school. With no local reputation and no history of exam success or inspection grades, I wanted to know why parents would select these schools and what information they used to make these decisions. The survey was complemented by a series of 20 interviews with parents of Year 7 (age 11–12) children in free schools across the country.

Probably one of the most challenging parts of the PhD came next – accessing participants to complete the questionnaire. I wanted my questionnaire to be seen (and completed) by as many parents as possible but reaching this group was not straightforward. I decided that asking schools to distribute the questionnaires was probably my best option as they were in a position to ensure that all Year 7 children (my target group) were given a questionnaire to take home to their parents. And so, I set about contacting every secondary free school in the country in 2013. At this point, there were only 92 schools. However, I was quickly introduced to the concept of "gatekeeping" and the challenges that come with it. The schools had almost complete power over whether I could access my selected participants (parents) or not. Reaching the right people to speak to about the questionnaire and to request its distribution was not always easy. If direct contacts on school websites were available, this was helpful, but calling and emailing school offices and asking for relevant staff was more challenging. The default response from receptionists or school leaders was often "no". Some head teachers told me that even though the project sounded interesting, they were wary of participating in research such as this when their school was so new, especially if parents might be able to report negative views. Despite these challenges, a total of 14 free schools did kindly agree to participate, meaning that I could proceed with this phase of data collection.

I learnt a lot during this stage about getting the practicalities right in order to improve the response rate. I had read about this in methods textbooks but had not recognised the importance of this until I was immersed in data collection planning and piloting. Minimising the input and effort for the schools was key. In order to help with this I reassured them that all they needed to do was hand out the questionnaires. I attached stamped addressed envelopes so that parents could return the questionnaires directly to me at university. This also helped with assuring confidentiality and anonymity. After piloting, I recognised the need to shorten my questionnaire and to keep the questions as simple and focused as possible. At the end of the questionnaire, parents were also invited to signal their willingness to participate in an interview, providing a self-selected group who were able to share more detailed accounts of their free school choice experiences.

The 20 telephone interviews involved parents from 9 different free schools across 6 different regions in England and lasted for approximately an hour each. Though only a small sample of free school parents, these interviews generated valuable, in-depth data which contributed substantially to my understanding and interpretation of the questionnaire findings and the other phases of research within my doctoral study. Interestingly, the interviews also pointed towards additional and alternative themes which had been less clear from the questionnaire. Comparisons of free schools with other school types and the issue of school intake as a determining choice factor, for example, came through quite strongly, as exemplified by these parents:

[The Free] School is modelled on grammar and private school educational system which is better than the average state school...Good sports facilities are an important factor and at [Free School] are almost on a par with the local preps.

...you're coming home from work, you see children walking around in their school uniform and it just looks bad. I've always been asking myself, do parents know where these children are, some of them are getting up to no good, so for me the idea that it will be a longer day at school appeals to me...another thing is I wanted [child] to go to grammar school actually, but she'd need her 11 plus...I really wanted her to have a high level of education.

The interviews also pointed to the value that many free school parents were placing on wider educational outcomes and a more holistic view of schooling:

Every Friday they do a drop-down day, so they take them out of the school environment and they take them to museums or they do some sort of like business enterprise with them. It's very much sort of like the whole round person as it were, rather than just focussing solely on academia the whole time.

These parents highlighted the diversity of perspectives and experiences around issues of school choice; their personal stories brought richness to the project and the issues that I was investigating, while also pointing to contemporary views and concerns which are likely to have been more generally relevant to parents involved in the free school choice process. Further details of this element of the study can be found in an article published in the *Cambridge Journal of Education* (Morris and Perry, 2019) or in the relevant chapters of my thesis (Morris, 2016).

Who was attending free schools in England? Using large-scale datasets to examine intakes and social segregation

Alongside the two components described above, I was analysing the intakes of free schools. I was particularly interested in whether the schools were taking a proportional share (based upon local figures) of children with Free School Meals (FSM) and Special Educational Needs (SEN) compared with other schools in their area. Like the two phases above, my rationale for this element and the approaches taken were closely linked to the existing literature and the critiques of the free schools policy that were emerging at the time. To what extent were new free schools contributing to the clustering of pupils with the same characteristics, within the system?

The best way to explore this question was through the use of large-scale datasets. Previous high-quality research in the field had taken this approach and the findings from these studies had contributed to ongoing and lively debates on the influence of educational quasi-markets on school intakes (see Burgess et al., 2005; Gorard et al., 2003). These projects introduced me to new sources of data: the Annual School Census, the National Pupil Database and the Millennium Cohort Study, amongst others. These existing, freely available datasets opened up a whole new world of possibilities for research. This was all very exciting. Except, I had very little clue about what I was going to do with this data if I got it. I did not have a background in using secondary data or statistical analysis. I was an English teacher with a decent maths GCSE and a bit of experience of data analysis while working in school. But I had little confidence when it came to dealing with national datasets.

I need not have worried too much though. A combination of helpful and available supervisors, useful textbooks and Youtube videos for stats novices, short courses at university, and some helpful PhD friends made everything a lot less scary. Yes, there was a lot to learn, and sometimes it was difficult or annoying. But really that was one of the reasons for coming to do a PhD. I should stress at this point that I am still by no means a stats-whizz. My PhD work in this area was relatively simple but I do now have enough competence to understand some of the key approaches to using numerical data and can carry out some of these myself. I can see the value that these data and methods can bring to educational research, and having even this elementary level of knowledge has opened up lots of opportunities for research and teaching since.

My study for this element of the PhD focused on using Annual Schools Census/National Pupil Database data to determine the proportions of children with certain characteristics attending free schools and to compare these with their six nearest schools, and the local authority figures too. I then calculated segregation ratios (adapting similar approaches to those used earlier by Gorard et al., 2003). The available data meant that I could examine this on a national level and longitudinally too, including schools which opened each year between 2011 and 2015 and tracking changes in the intakes over this period too. Interested readers can learn more about the methods and findings from the first stage of this study in an article published in the *British Educational Research Journal* (Morris, 2015). The extended findings of this study and the other sections above can be found in my thesis.

Drawing it all together – what story could I tell?

Once completed, the findings from these three distinct yet linked components of my PhD had to be drawn together and organised so that I could respond to my research question(s), and share the conclusions in an accessible, coherent and (ideally) interesting way. With a large, multi-methods study, this can be difficult. There are multiple datasets, sometimes complementary or contradictory findings, and lots of different perspectives on the best ways to "triangulate" the information that you have. Prior to collecting and analysing my data, I did not know what the overall story of my PhD would look like. So what did I find helpful at this point?

Returning to my research questions was key here, constantly reminding myself of what it was that I had originally wanted to find out. I was also very conscious of relevant new research that was emerging all of the time, and tried to keep up with reading this so that I could draw upon it where appropriate in my write-up. I also enjoyed looking at successfully completed social sciences theses. While usually on completely different topics, and often using very different methodological approaches to those that I had adopted, seeing examples of the "finished thing" was motivating and informative.

Sharing and discussing my work with others was also influential at this stage. My supervisors and their challenging questions pushed me to ensure that the claims I was making and the story I was telling were rooted firmly in the data. Conference attendance and other dissemination activities were also useful. The university postgraduate conferences were an excellent stepping-stone for building confidence and developing my research communication skills. In the second and third years of my PhD I presented at the annual BERA conference too, a forum that I have continued to contribute to since. I also braved going to the Nordic Educational Research Association conference in Gothenburg, Sweden, my first international conference. My free schools topic was relevant to the Swedish context (free schools have existed there since the early 1990s) and I was keen to hear more about other international work in the field. I met some fantastic researchers during this trip, colleagues who I have kept in touch with and met up with at subsequent conferences, and who I hope to work with in the future.

I was also invited to write a number of non-academic pieces, including posts for *The Conversation*, blogs for the university, and for the BERA site. Communicating research with new audiences and responding to questions from academics and the wider public helped to shape and organise the messages that I wanted to convey. It also led to further networks and connections which have proved fruitful and supportive for subsequent research too.

In writing up the final sections of my thesis, I wanted to highlight the empirical, theoretical and methodological contributions of the study. It found that in the early days of the free schools policy, some of the concerns around social selection and unfair admissions practices were justified, and that this new type of school appeared to be contributing to ongoing inequalities within the system. However, I also found that in many respects, free schools were operating in similar ways to other schools in their area (in terms of admissions and intakes), indicating that it was wider policies of autonomy and diversity which were potentially problematic rather than the free schools themselves.

Through my engagement with parents, my study foregrounded the new role of parents as *providers* of education rather than just consumers. Those who had decided to contribute to the setting up and running of free schools were an important and unique group within the parental choice landscape, and one which I was able to shed some light on through my findings. Since this research has been conducted, however, the free schools policy and our evidence base has developed considerably. Despite ongoing political support, free schools remain relatively low in number, and very few now have parental involvement involved in the set-up phases. Recent evidence also builds on findings from my study, confirming that these schools are largely operating in similar ways to other schools, demonstrating little of the innovation or "freedom" that was touted as a major rationale for the policy (Wiborg et al., 2018). Further research examining the role and outcomes of free schools within the wider system, rather than as a distinct group of schools, seems like an important angle for future studies.

Final thoughts and reflections

When I started my PhD, I had not planned on becoming an academic at the end of it. I had not planned anything because spending three or more years on a single research study seemed like enough of a plan in itself! I was lucky to be able to continue teaching during the PhD, both at school and then later as part of the initial teacher education and undergraduate/masters programmes at the University of Birmingham. I was keen that a future role would still include teaching and, doing my doctorate, I realised that pursuing research would be important and enriching too. Working in a university seemed like an ideal way to combine these two interests. I could see that the jobs market was tough though, and even with a PhD and a teaching qualification, there was definitely no guarantee of a clear path to an academic role.

Since submitting my thesis in early 2016, I have worked across three different universities, first in a range of temporary research fellow and lecturing posts, and then securing a permanent Assistant Professorship in January 2019. For each of the roles I have worked in and for all of the research projects that I have contributed to, my PhD training and research has been influential. Completing a large-scale mixed methods study has given me a valuable breadth of knowledge plus experience and enthusiasm for designing and carrying out interesting, ambitious research studies. This has also come in very useful for contributing to teaching about research methods on undergraduate and postgraduate programmes too. Pleasingly, I cannot be pigeonholed as either a "quantitative" or "qualitative" researcher, but instead try to offer flexibility and versatility which I have found helpful when working across studies and collaborating with others. As I note above, I am not particularly expert in anything; I do not have the depth of knowledge that some methodological specialists have. But I have found that in the social sciences, there is a place for the "jack of all (or some) trades", for researchers who are willing to try out new approaches, traverse disciplinary boundaries, and contribute to projects which are outside of their methodological comfort zones.

The same could probably be said of my chosen PhD topic. While I loved researching free schools at the time, I was always conscious that there were lots of other interesting educational issues to research too. Broadly speaking, much of my current work now falls under the more general theme of education policy. The foundational knowledge and skills from my PhD have enabled me to develop and contribute to a wide range of projects, researching topics including grammar schools, teacher shortage and initial teacher education, vocational education, widening participation and the Pupil Premium. I am also interested in more practice-based and pedagogical issues linked to assessment and feedback, literacy and practitioners' use of research and evidence. For some, this may appear to be a case of breadth over depth – and they may well have a point. But with a field as vast, dynamic and interesting as education, it would seem a shame (to me at least) to narrow my focus too much.

And this brings us back, full circle, to the start of this chapter. I started my doctorate because I was interested in the possibilities and power of research. Completing the qualification was of course important, but it was the thinking and doing of the research that was even more motivating for me. I did not see the PhD as just the end-goal, but instead viewed it as more of a starting point for my next steps within the world of education. I feel fortunate that it supported my transition in to a challenging and exciting career which allows me to be curious all of the time, and I hope that others find similar enjoyment through their doctoral studies and subsequent research too.

References

Ball, S.J., and Vincent, C. (1998). "I heard it on the grapevine": "Hot" knowledge and school choice. *British Journal of Sociology of Education*, 19(3), pp. 377–400.

Burgess, S., Wilson, D., and Lupton, R. (2005). Parallel lives? Ethnic segregation in schools and neighbourhoods. *Urban Studies*, 42(7), pp. 1027–1056.

Fitz, J., Taylor, C., & Gorard, S. (2002). Local education authorities and the regulation of educational markets: four case studies. *Research Papers in Education*, 17(2), 125–146.

Gorard, S. (1997). *School Choice in an Established Market*. Abingdon: Routledge.

Gorard, S., Fitz, J., and Taylor, C. (2003). *Schools, Markets and Choice Policies*. Routledge.

Morris, R. (2014). The admissions criteria of secondary free schools. *Oxford Review of Education*, 40(3), pp. 389–409.

Morris, R. (2015). Free schools and disadvantaged intakes. *British Educational Research Journal*, 41(4), pp. 535–552.

Morris, R. (2016). *Free schools in England: choice, admissions and social segregation*. Doctoral dissertation. Edgbaston: Birmingham, UK: University of Birmingham.

Morris, R., and Perry, T. (2019). Private schools for free? Parents' reasons for choosing a new free school for their child. *Cambridge Journal of Education*, 49(5), pp. 535–552.

West, A. (2014). Academies in England and independent schools (fristående skolor) in Sweden: Policy, privatisation, access and segregation. *Research Papers in Education*, 29(3), pp. 330–350.

West, A., Barham, E., and Hind, A. (2011). Secondary school admissions in England 2001 to 2008: Changing legislation, policy and practice. *Oxford Review of Education*, 37(1), pp. 1–20.

White, P. (2017). *Developing Research Questions*. United Kingdom: Macmillan International Higher Education.

White, P., Gorard, S., Fitz, J., and Taylor, C. (2001). Regional and local differences in admission arrangements for schools. *Oxford Review of Education*, 27(3), pp. 317–337.

Wiborg, S., Green, F., Taylor-Gooby, P., and Wilde, R. (2018). Free schools in England: "Not unlike other schools"? *Journal of Social Policy*, 47(1), pp. 119–137.

Woods, P., Bagley, C., and Glatter, R. (2005). *School Choice and Competition: Markets in the Public Interest?* Abingdon: Routledge.

CHAPTER 14

Does absence from school influence attainment, and what is the best way to handle it?

Haifaa Alabbad

Introduction

The study was inspired by my interest in the challenges of school attendance and exclusions – a subject that is both topical and controversial. United Kingdom as a welfare state promises all children free access to state education. However, there are disparities in the benefits of free education when some children do not attend school regularly. There are also school policies which exclude children from attending. This PhD examined the patterns of inequalities among children who miss attendance at school and/or who are excluded. It was a large-scale study based mainly on the National Pupil Database (NPD) for England, presenting links between pupils' background, their school attendance and exclusion, and official attainment measures. The findings draw attention to poverty as a barrier for children in attending school on a regular basis. There are also some indications of unfair implementation of exclusion policies for children with special education needs and disabilities. These findings have implications for education policies for disadvantaged children who cannot fully benefit from school education due to these barriers in attending schools. However, the evidence also suggests that the lack of attendance itself is not the real problem (at least not in the way portrayed by the government), and that addressing it will not be sufficient. The study also involves a systematic review of evidence on the most promising interventions to improve attendance. This suggests that financial incentives for school and parents can be successful approaches in addressing barriers to school attendance.

The chapter describes how a student from Saudi Arabia with no knowledge of education in England, and no experience of NPD, took on one of the biggest issues in UK education. They developed a research design and innovative analysis that led to robust findings which have policy and practice implications, and have attracted both media and policy attention. The study was completed within three years.

DOI: 10.4324/9781003201366-17

Background

In England, levels of school attendance and exclusions became a focus of government interest in recent decades. In 2004, David Miliband, the then schools minister, wrote a letter to the directors of local authorities, noting that it is "because of the strong link between attendance and attainment – and also because of the well-known links between truancy and street crime and anti-social behaviour – that government sees reducing absence from school as a priority" DfES (2004). The same concern was reiterated in a House of Commons Committee of Public Accounts (2006) report, which stated that, "Regular absence from school is damaging, making a young person much more likely to leave school with few or no qualifications and potentially vulnerable to involvement in crime and anti-social behaviour" (p. 3).

This belief, in a causal link between school absences and academic progress on one hand, and between absences from school and antisocial behaviour and crime, on the other hand, has led to increasing school attendance targets to keep children in schools in a bid to address both problems (Sheppard, 2011). The pressure on schools to raise their attendance rates has led to tougher attendance policies.

The Department for Education (DfE) suggested that every day in school matters in term of academic attainment (DfE, 2016a). The national and local press have published news stories about prosecutions and fines for parents who have failed to ensure their children regularly attend school. This high-profile publicity drive sent out a tough and clear message to the parents and the community in general that "truancy will not be tolerated" (Zhang, 2004, p. 27). Despite this, the Guardian newspaper claimed that DfE figures showed a "sharp increase [of] nearly 60,000 pupils" taking term-time holidays compared to the previous year, and "nearly 330,000 children" had been recorded as missing school because of unauthorised family holidays in the 2016 autumn term (Adams, 2017).

In England, schools and parents find themselves under pressure due to the high attendance targets that the government requires. Parents have taken to the courts to appeal against fines imposed by the DfE because of lapses in their children's school attendance. Absence from school or classroom have two major categories – authorised (granted by school authorities for valid reasons such as verified health grounds) and unauthorised (no valid reason or information is apparent to the school).

Perhaps even more attention has been given to school exclusions in which pupils are removed from school and/or classroom by the school authorities on valid reasons of safety concerns,. An analysis by the Programme for International Student Assessment (PISA) showed England as a country suffering from high exclusion rates (OECD, 2017).

The TES claimed recently that "permanent exclusions have skyrocketed by as much as 300% in a year" (Bloom, 2017). And some schools have very high rates of exclusion – "Outcry as academy excludes 41% of pupils" (Perraudin and McIntyre, 2018). The "wild west system of school exclusions is failing pupils, say MPs" (Weale, 2018). An Education Select Committee report claims that many pupils are excluded from schools as a punishment for minor incidents (House of Commons Education Committee, 2018). The government was asked to address the problem of off-rolling within schools, a process whereby some pupils are removed from the school register before sitting their GCSE exams so the school can game league tables scores (House of Commons Education Committee, 2018).

A report by Ofsted and the Care Quality Commission (CQC) on their inspection of the effectiveness of support for children with Special Educational Needs and Disabilities (SEND) indicated that such children experienced a lower quality education and there were instances when "some school leaders had used unofficial exclusions too readily to cope with children and young people who have SEND" (Ofsted Care Quality Commission, 2017, p. 5). "1 in 5 teachers are aware of illegal SEND exclusions" within the schools where they work (Hazell and Ward, 2017). The official figures for school exclusions showed that a high proportion of school excluded pupils came from disadvantaged groups of children (DfE, 2016b).

Disadvantaged children are also seen as most likely to be persistent absentees in official data (DfE, 2015). The common characteristics of persistent absentees are that they live in a family with one parent and are likely to come from a household where the head is not in any form of employment. These absentees are more likely to be bullied, excluded from school and/or be involved in risky behaviours such as drug and alcohol abuse, compared to other pupils. Many of these children are school mobile (for example, from Irish traveller or Roma families), eligible for free school meals (FSM), or have Special Educational Needs (SEN) pupils (DfE, 2011).

All of these issues, and their links to attainment, are the subject of this new investigation.

Outline of the study

The research had three elements – an analysis of the NPD, interviews with school teachers exploring their perceptions of the NPD findings, and a systematic review of interventions to improve school attendance. This study is the first nationwide UK study to adopt a three-stage approach to research the determinants of and relationships between school attendance, exclusions, and academic attainment for pupils by the age of 16.

Figure 14.1 Where are they all?

The NPD is a rich education dataset, covering a wide range of information about pupils at state-funded schools in England. Schools and local authorities are required to provide the information to the DfE three times a year. This includes characteristics of each pupil and of the school attended, attainment, attendance, and exclusion figures for around 600,000 pupils in each age cohort. This study is based on 525,242 Key Stage 2 (KS2) pupils, 544,031 KS3 pupils), and 546,250 KS4 pupils.

The percentage of missing data in each indicator was examined, and any patterns found. It was clear that pupils with missing values, for FSM-eligibility and SEN for example, were among the most disadvantaged in other terms, and least likely to reach any level of attainment at school.

After the data cleaning process, the analyses graduated from simple descriptive analyses and "effect" sizes to more complex regression models for the different outcomes (school attendance, exclusions, and academic attainment).

Cohen's d effect size calculation (standardised mean difference) were used to examine the strength of the differences between groups of children based on overall school absences (number of missing school sessions during the school year) and school exclusions at KS4. The groups were based FSM eligibility, SEN, EAL, ethnicity, and pupil sex. These background characteristics are standard measures, used in other studies as indicators of disadvantage (Gorard, 2018). Comparisons were also made between school types for primary and secondary schools in terms of averages of absence sessions (authorised and unauthorised), and averages of school exclusions.

In the effect size calculations, there was no controlling for other different variables. Therefore, there was a need for a more sophisticated analysis in which the association between the outcome and other independent variables is measured, controlled for other variables included in the analysis. Regression analysis was conducted to predict school attendance, exclusions, and academic attainment at KS4 (Gorard, 2013).

Four binary logistic regression models were run: two to predict/explain school attendance in terms of authorised and unauthorised absences at KS4, one to predict school fixed exclusions at KS4, and one to predict the academic attainment at KS4. The independent variables were entered into the models in three separate "blocks", according to the chronological order which each group of variables impacted on the life of the individual. The first block included characteristics present from birth (age in months, gender, SEN, ethnicities, and EAL). The second block included primary school indicators, namely KS2 maths point scores, English point scores, authorised and unauthorised absences. The last block included secondary school indicators, namely KS3 maths point scores, English point scores, authorised and unauthorised absences, KS4 school mobility, and type of school attended.

I conducted a systematic review on the evidence on effective approaches for the improvement of school attendance. The Campbell Collaboration Review protocol format was followed (Maynard et al., 2012). The quality of all evidence was rated, using the sieve developed by Gorard (2014). Reporting described included studies in terms of design, year, type, source of publication, and where these studies were conducted, targeted groups, and other outcome measures included (other than school attendance and academic attainment). The achieved evidence was then synthesised by comparing the quality of research, the direction of outcomes, and the number of studies to come up with final conclusions.

Further analyses were conducted, and the results are reported in the thesis (Alabbad, 2020) Figure 14.1.

Summary of the key findings

Which pupils in England are recorded as absent, persistently absent, and/or excluded from school?

The number of authorised absences remains about the same across school years (Table 14.1). The marked change over time is in the proportion of

Table 14.1 Percentages of absences by Key Stage

Key Stage	At least one authorised absence session	At least one unauthorised absence session
KS2 (year 6)	92	23
KS3 (year 9)	91	32
KS4 (year 11)	90	40

unauthorised absence. Transition to secondary school, puberty, and the onset of periods for girls, could all be factors here. There may be an element of increased school avoidance, or perhaps parents are less concerned about the whereabouts of older children. Exclusions from school are also more frequent at secondary schools, but peak in KS3. Girls are more likely to be persistent absentees, while boys, especially of Black ethnic origin, are more likely to be excluded. Pupils labelled SEN or who are FSM-eligible are more likely to be persistently absent and/or excluded from school. Some face challenges at home and school that their peers do not.

To what extent do background characteristics, prior attainment, and school-type predict authorised absences, unauthorised absences, and/or exclusions from school?

Prior authorised absences is a useful predictor of future absences (and unauthorised absences can also predict future unauthorised absences). There are differences between schools and types of schools in term of patterns of absence. But these are largely due to differences in school intakes. Pupils' characteristics from birth (age in year, gender, SEN, ethnicity and FSM status) were more likely determinants of authorised absence. This confirms what is already known from the literature.

Around 40.9% of all pupils had at least one unauthorised absence. The logistic regression model used to explain who was an unauthorised absentee and who was not therefore had a base of 59.1% of cases predicted correctly. This rose to 63.4% when pupil characteristics from birth were added. The percentage of cases predicted correctly rose to 65.3% using variables known by the end of primary school, and to 69.5% using variables from KS3. The remaining (30.5%) variation was not explicable in terms of the variables available in the NPD. The strongest single predictors were FSM-eligibility, and moving between schools.

Similarly, for both fixed and permanent exclusions by KS4, the strongest predictors were pupil characteristics set very early in like. These include being a boy (odds ratio of exclusion compared to girls of 2.2), have

SEN or disability (odds ratio of 1.8), and being FSM-eligible (odds ratio of 1.59). School characteristics and attainment are not good predictors of exclusion, once these individual characteristics have been accounted for. SEN pupils, for example, have a range of learning difficulties that could affect their academic performance and behaviour. However, the dataset of this study has not been designed to explore the reasons for school exclusions or even the type and level of SEN that pupils experience. Therefore, although the obtained results of the regression model show a pattern of excluded pupils, explanations underpinning these findings need to be sought otherwise.

To what extent is absence and/or exclusion from school linked to pupils' academic attainment at KS4 once background characteristics and prior attainment are accounted for?

A logistic regression model to predict which pupils would achieve 5+ GCSEs at grade C or above had a base of 57%. A further 12 percentage points were added using variables set at birth (Table 14.2), with 9 added using what was known at primary schools, and a further 3 only for what was known at secondary schools. This all suggests that early intervention could be more effective to promote the academic attainment of pupils from disadvantaged backgrounds.

Table 14.3 shows the coefficients for the variables included in the model above. Again the key factors are pupils' sex, FSM-eligibility, and SEN status. Prior attainment is, as expected, a predictor of later attainment. Absence from primary school, once birth characteristics are accounted for, is not a determinant of attainment at school. This finding is contrary to official accounts, that may be attributing to absences the impact that is realty caused by poverty and learning challenges. The importance of secondary school absences is not much greater (still odd ratios of near 1). It seems that absence from school is more a proxy than a factor in school attainment.

Table 14.2 Percentage of cases predicted to achieve 5 good GCSEs or equivalent, including English and Maths, by stage

No.	Block	Percentage correct
0	Base	57
1	Pupils' characteristics from birth	69
2	Primary school factors, including absence	78
3	Secondary school factors, including absence	81

Table 14.3 Odds ratios from the binary logistic regression model in Table 14.2

Block	Variables in block	Odds
Pupils' characteristics from birth	Age in months	0.99
	Male (vs female)	0.60
	SEN (vs non-SEN)	0.49
	Non-white (vs white)	1.32
	FSM (vs non-FSM)	0.65
	Non-English (vs English)	1.32
Primary school factors	KS2 Maths point scores	1.19
	KS2 English point scores	1.16
	KS2 authorised absence session	1.00
	KS2 unauthorised absence sessions	0.99
Secondary school factors	KS3 Maths point scores	1.06
	KS3 English point scores	1.01
	KS3 authorised absence sessions	0.98
	KS3 unauthorised absence sessions	0.97
	School mobile (vs not mobile)	0.94
	Selective school (vs non-selective)	1.43

Is there any evidence of effective interventions that have improved the school attendance behaviours of disadvantaged pupils and has a positive impact on their academic attainment?

According to the systematic review, there are interventions that have been evaluated and have shown that attendance can be improved. Of the five strongest evaluations (graded 3 or 4), four show positive results. This is promising. Promoting the school attendance of pupils from disadvantaged backgrounds without intervening to improve the background characteristics that underpin disadvantage are unlikely to be successful in promoting school outcomes. But conditional cash transfer payments parents or carers did promote school attendance Table 14.4.

The picture for whether promoting attendance improves attainment is much more mixed (as would be expected from the results of the secondary analysis above). Of the five strongest studies, three showed no impact or worse. See, for

Table 14.4 Number of studies in improving school attendance, by quality of research, and outcome

Quality of research	Positive impact	No or negative impact
1*	4	4
2*	5	2
3*	3	1
4*	1	–

example, Akresh et al. (2013). Conditional cash transfers are not nearly so effective here. They might work to improve attainment more directly, but not through improving attendance as such (Evans et al., 2014). Most of the studies that reported a positive impact on academic attainment after implementing an attendance programme relied on poorer quality evidence.

Of course, attendance is important for many reasons other than attainment. However, attainment matters in education as an indicator and as a determinant of lifelong outcomes. But, the review agreed with the secondary data analyses, that absence from school is not the key driving factor in attainment. It is more a reflection of the struggles that disadvantaged pupils might face in their life.

What are the perceptions of teachers in England about school attendance of the disadvantaged pupils?

The reports from teachers confirmed that FSM status is strongly associated with school attendance.

> The attendance of FSM children is challenging.

> The most problematic children in terms of school attendance are FSM children. They are the most absentees within the school.

The views on whether there is a gender gap in attendance were mixed. The gap is not perhaps systematic, but can have different cause for boys and girls at different ages.

> We do not notice a difference between boys and girls in school attendance. A pupil who used to attend school regularly continues to do so.

> A big effect on girls' attendance is social problems. A girl has had a conflict with a group of friends [and] decides to stay off school for two or three weeks. Girls find it difficult to come back.

> We can say that most of the school absences of girls are because they were hidden young carers.

> We know these girls miss school to take care of someone in the family.

Other than this issue of unpaid caring, participants felt that a lack of parental involvement in their children's education was a cause.

> Low attendance students often have parents that do not engage or push their children to go to school.

Four kinds of interventions were highlighted, such as phone contact with parents, home visits, developing harmonious relationships with students, and attendance rewards. But no school attendance intervention works for all children.

> We contact the parents of the absentee children by phone and accept their excuses more often. In some cases, we do home visits.

> Teachers get open and friendly with students and [try to] be someone that they can rely on and talk to if needed.

> We reward our full attendance students by writing their names on the school display board, taking them on trips, and offering them a free meal such as sandwiches in the morning.

Implications

For future research

The findings of the systematic review raised implications for researchers. In terms of clarity and completeness of reporting researchers should carefully consider their research reports. The reports should be transparent and convey the entire process of the study, including the side-effects of the intervention (e.g. attrition rate, possibility of risks such as spillover effects or other diffusions during the programme's implementation). These limitations matter in evaluating the claimed evidence. Researchers should strive at all times for impartiality and objectivity in their research designs, and transparency and completeness could help others to replicate the work and thereby achieve the most reliable results. Moreover, these reporting issues could prevent the wasting of unnecessary funds by sponsors as well as save the time and efforts of both teachers and pupils.

Future evaluations of interventions should look at long-term impacts of policies. Most of the studies evaluated only short-term impacts of interventions. Future evaluations should also conduct cost-benefit analyses. Many evaluations do not report the costs of implementation. This cost is an essential element for evaluating any intervention because it allows costs to be set against achieved outcomes (i.e. cost effectiveness). Such a systematic analysis would save money by identifying which interventions provide the most desirable effects related to their costs.

More reliable and comprehensive data on the socio-economic circumstances of children from disadvantaged backgrounds would be a step towards improving our understanding of school attendance issues. Existing measures of the background poverty of children through the prism of FSM have their limitations (Gorard and Siddiqui, 2019). They might ignore children who are still suffering from the prior effects of living in disadvantaged circumstances. Therefore, finding new or additional indicators of poverty that show the length of time which a child has been living in poverty and children who are always eligible for FSM is crucial for measuring the impacts of this indicator over time.

In addition, it is necessary to consider schools' intakes (especially those including a high percentage of disadvantaged children) when assessing attendance, exclusions, and academic attainment rates. This consideration could reduce pressures on schools and offer a more balanced judgment of their progress, which may enable them to address the concerns of their pupils' needs rather than being concerned about the data that they need to present to Ofsted.

For dealing with absence

The findings highlighted a range of indicators with associations to school attendance, exclusions, and academic attainment. The strong association between SEN and exclusions needs to be investigated in more depth, including generating specific data related to types of SEN, the schools that pupils with SEN attend, and their home circumstances. Interviews with SEN pupils and their families may be beneficial to see how schools meet the needs of this group of pupils, and how these children and their families perceive the services that they receive. This can determine the factors underpinning absences and exclusions.

Similar things can be said about FSM-eligibility. Addressing the needs of disadvantaged groups of pupils is a priority if schools are to improve both school attendance and academic outcomes. Cash transfers might be helpful in improving attendance for pupils from disadvantaged backgrounds (although this raises the possibility of a false incentive for absence for others). Supporting low-income families with regular stipends may induce them to concentrate more on their children's education and encourage them to attend school more regularly. Providing free meal alone does not help disadvantaged children to attend school more regularly. Pupils from poor background need additional support services that can help in attending schools regularly.

Girls are more likely to miss school days than boys, especially as they get older, with the evidence pointing to a link between gender, poverty, and school attendance (Benshaul-Tolonen et al., 2019; Marsh, 2017). One reason for this may well be "period poverty", and hence providing sanitary pads for girls from disadvantaged backgrounds could help to promote their attendance. However, a range of reasons could explain the school absences of girls, such as caring roles for a younger sibling or disabled parent and different domestic chores. There is also a need to understand long-term impact of period poverty on girls' education experiences and life-long outcomes.

The findings showed that the data for school exclusions were unhelpful in actually predicting school exclusions. The unavailability of essential information related to school exclusions seemed to mask the real situation. The exclusion data was limited to certain school exclusions and types and the reasons underpinning such exclusions (not included in this study). The existing literature relates school exclusions to mental health symptoms and suggests that a high proportion of excluded pupils experience mental health difficulties (Gill et al., 2017). Studies have also attributed school exclusions to racist beliefs (Okonofua and Eberhardt, 2015), parents' mental health problems, poverty, and bad parenting (Cooper and Stewart, 2013). Developing school exclusion data by providing more information on pupils' mental health, ethnicity, experience, and knowledge of the behavioural challenges facing school teachers and headteachers, as well as the mental health and the history of the parents and integrating such information into studies would help in determining the influential factors that lead to school exclusions.

For attainment

This study found a weak link between school attendance and academic attainment. It suggests that the association between school attendance and academic attainment at KS4 is not as strong as the DfE has proposed (DfE, 2016a). Pupils' background characteristics (age in months, gender, SEN, ethnicity, FSM, EAL) and prior academic attainment (KS2 and KS3 Maths and English attainment) are more strongly associated with academic progression at KS4. FSM status is the better predictor of school attendance according to the findings of this study. Therefore, policy and practice need to be cautious when devoting public funds to interventions merely to promote school attendance ignoring the specific needs of pupils from disadvantaged backgrounds.

No evidence was found to suggest that penalising parents increases school attendance (Kendall et al., 2004). However, the DfE insists that every school day matters (DfE, 2016a). Parental penalties are also still being. A parent has been found guilty by the Supreme Court for taking his 7 year-old daughter for a week of holiday (BBC News, 2017). The same report noted that the court ordered the father to pay a fine of £2,000. But missing a small number of school days does not necessarily disturb the learning progress of children. There is thus a need to revise the policy of penalising parents for their children's school attendance. This needs more robust evidence to determine that penalties can improve school attendance. It would also be beneficial to distinguish between parents who provide children with opportunities to learn new things outside the school setting, such as trips and visits to educational sites like museums, and parents who do not.

Schools that have a high proportion of absenteeism might still want to engage parents through regular meetings and discussions that demonstrate to parents the role of school attendance in their children's progress and post-education life chances. Schools could also use the opportunity for engaging parents in identifying the factors behind low school attendance.

Through training courses, based on sound evidence, schools need to provide their teachers with adequate knowledge about the factors that may cause school absences and exclusions, different behavioural problems, and strategies to deal with such issues. The main goal of these courses would be to identify mechanisms that enable teachers to ascertain the needs of at-risk children to mentor their progress and inform local authorities of what is needed.

References

Adams, R. (2017). Unauthorised term-time holidays soar in England after legal challenge. *The Guardian.* https://www.theguardian.com/education/2017/may/18/unauthorised-term-time-holidays-soar-in-england-after-legal-challenge

Akresh, R., De Walque, D., and Kazianga, H. (2013). *Cash transfers and child schooling: Evidence from a randomized evaluation of the role of conditionality.* https://openknowledge.worldbank.org/bitstream/handle/10986/13127/wps6340.pdf?sequence=1

Alabbad, H. (2020). *A study of school attendance and exclusions in secondary schools in England.* PhD thesis. Durham University, UK.

BBC News. (2017). Isle of Wight term-time holiday dad Jon Platt guilty. *BBC.* https://www.bbc.co.uk/news/uk-england-hampshire-40381825

Benshaul-Tolonen, A., Zulaika, G., Nyothach, E., Oduor, C., Mason, L., Obor, D., ... and Phillips-Howard, P. (2019). Pupil absenteeism, measurement, and menstruation: Evidence from Western Kenya. CDEP-CGEG WP, 74. Available at: cdep_absenteeism.pdf (wordpress.com).

Bloom, A. (2017). Exclusive: Permanent exclusions "skyrocket" by as much as 300% in a year. https://www.tes.com/news/exclusive-permanent-exclusions-skyrocket-much-300-year

Cooper, K., and Stewart, K. (2013). *Does Money Affect Children's Outcomes?: A Systematic Review.* York: Joseph Rowntree Foundation.

DfE (2011). *A profile of pupil absence in England.* https://assets.publishing.service.gov.uk/government/uploads/system/uploads/attachment_data/file/183445/DFE-RR171.pdf

DfE (2015). *National tables: SFR10_Main_tables (2).* https://www.gov.uk/government/statistics/pupil-absence-in-schools-in-england-2013-to-2014

DfE (2016a). *The link between absence and attainment at KS2 and KS4 2013/14 academic year.* Department for Education. https://www.gov.uk/government/uploads/system/uploads/attachment_data/file/412638/The_link_between_absence_and_attainment_at_KS2_and_KS4.pdf.

DfE (2016b). *Permanent and fixed period exclusions in England: 2014 to 2015.*

https://assets.publishing.service.gov.uk/government/uploads/system/uploads/attachment_data/file/539704/SFR_26_2016_text.pdf

DfES (2004). Improving school attendance and tackling truancy. *Letter to Chief Education Officers and Directors of Children's Services in England, 25 August, LEA/0237/2004.*

Evans, D., Hausladen, S., Kosec, K., and Reese, N. (2014). *Community-based conditional cash transfers in Tanzania: results from a randomized trial.* The World Bank.

Gill, K., Quilter-Pinner, H., and Swift, D. (2017). *Making the difference breaking the link between school exclusions and social exclusion.* https://www.ippr.org/files/2017-10/making-the-difference-report-october-2017.pdf

Gorard, S. (2013). *Research Design: Creating Robust Approaches for the Social Sciences.* London: Sage.

Gorard, S. (2014). A proposal for judging the trustworthiness of research findings. *Radical Statistics,* 110, pp. 47–59.

Gorard, S. (2018). *Education Policy: Evidence of Equity and Effectiveness.* Bristol: Policy Press.

Gorard, S., and Siddiqui, N. (2019). How trajectories of disadvantage help explain school attainment. *SAGE Open.* Stephen Gorard, Nadia Siddiqui, 2019 (sagepub.com).

Hazell, W., and Ward, H. (2017). 1 in 5 teachers aware of illegal SEND exclusions. https://www.tes.com/news/1-5-teachers-aware-illegal-send-exclusions

House of Commons Committee of Public Accounts. (2006). *Department for education and skills: Improving school attendance in England.* https://publications.parliament.uk/pa/cm200506/cmselect/cmpubacc/789/789.pdf

House of Commons Education Committee. (2018). *Forgotten children: Alternative provision and the scandal of ever increasing exclusions.* https://publications.parliament.uk/pa/cm201719/cmselect/cmeduc/342/342.pdf

Kendall, S., White, R., Kinder, K., Halsey, K., and Bedford, N. (2004). *School attendance and the prosecution of parents: Effects and effectiveness* (1903880653). https://www.nfer.ac.uk/publications/PPT01/PPT01.pdf

Marsh, S. (2017, March 17). Girls from poorer families in England struggle to afford sanitary protection. *The Guardian.* https://www.theguardian.com/society/2017/mar/17/girls-from-poorer-families-in-england-struggle-to-afford-sanitary-protection

Maynard, B., McCrea, K., Pigott, T., and Kelly, M. (2012). Indicated truancy interventions: Effects on school attendance among chronic truant students. *Campbell Systematic Reviews,* 2012, p. 10. Campbell Collaboration.

OECD. (2017). *PISA 2015 Results (Volume III): Students' Well-Being,* Paris: OECD Publishing. doi: 10.1787/9789264273856-en.

Ofsted Care Quality Commission. (2017). *Local area SEND inspections: One year on.* https://assets.publishing.service.gov.uk/government/uploads/system/uploads/attachment_data/file/652694/local_area_SEND_inspections_one_year_on.pdf

Okonofua, J., and Eberhardt, J. (2015). Two strikes: Race and the disciplining of young students. *Psychological Science,* 26(5), pp. 617–624.

Perraudin, F., and McIntyre, N. (2018). "She deserves an education": Outcry as academy excludes 41% of pupils. *The Guardian.* https://www.theguardian.com/education/2018/aug/31/english-school-outwood-academy-fixed-term-exclusions-pupils

Sheppard, A. (2011). The non-sense of raising school attendance. *Emotional and Behavioural Difficulties, 16*(3), pp. 239–247.

Weale, S. (2018, July 25). "Wild west" system of school exclusions is failing pupils, say MPs. *The Guardian.* https://www.theguardian.com/education/2018/jul/25/children-abandoned-after-school-exclusions-say-mps

Zhang, M. (2004). Time to change the truancy laws? Compulsory education: Its origin and modern dilemma. *Pastoral Care in Education, 22*(2), pp. 27–33.

CHAPTER **15**

Do expensive STEM enrichment activities make any difference to science and maths outcomes at school?

Pallavi Banerjee

Introduction

Science and mathematics are two key subject areas in school (DfE, 2014). In recent decades, official UK reports have claimed that a highly skilled science, technology, engineering and maths (STEM) workforce is required for continued economic development (OECD, 2007). In 2010, it was suggested that in the next ten years over 58% of all new jobs would require STEM skills (Behr, 2011; Garnham, 2011). This demand for STEM skills was apparently over and above the national demand at that time (DfE, 2010, but see UKCES, 2015, and Smith and Gorard, 2011). The decline in STEM study after A-levels at age 18 was more pronounced for STEM subjects than for arts and humanities (The Royal Society, 2006, 2008; Vidal, 2007). A comparative account of science and maths subject choices in the UK showed the proportion of students completing full A-levels in science and maths in England, Wales and Northern Ireland was far lower than the equivalent proportion taking Highers in Scotland (Table 15.1).

Factors affecting subject choices at school and beyond are embedded in the social and educational framework, which cannot be easily shifted (Homer et al., 2014). There are no ready policy measures that can change the picture (CBI, 2012). Hence a difficulty was foreseen in meeting the predicted STEM skills demand, in England.

It has been reported that non-STEM subjects such as modern foreign languages, history and geography were more popular subject choices amongst disadvantaged pupils (DBIS, 2010). Therefore, increasing and widening participation in science and maths post compulsory education have been of interest to the UK Government since 2000 (Conway, 2009). Chronic poverty, social exclusion and deprivations linked to ethnicity, conflict, neighbourhoods and disability can interact to place underprivileged groups at extreme educational disadvantage (Gorard et al., 2007). This is evidenced by the fact that the attainment gap between poor pupils and their elite peers in England,

DOI: 10.4324/9781003201366-18

Table 15.1 Percentage of young people taking advanced science qualifications, by UK home country, 2009

A-levels			Highers
England	Wales	N Ireland	Scotland
28	27	37	50

Source: The Royal Society (2011).

termed the "poverty gradient" (Gorard and See, 2013), is wider than gender gap or the gap between ethnic groups.

In England, there were two main areas to focus on – improving attainment in school science and maths (Gorard and See, 2009), and increasing and widening participation in science and maths beyond compulsory education (Gorard and See, 2008). This led to the design and delivery of several outreach programmes which operated at local and national level and were funded by educational charities, government and private organisations (Wynarczyk, 2008). These activities introduced students to fascinating aspects of STEM careers and also tried to break the myth held by young people that science and maths are only meant for the "brainy" (Archer, 2013). Beginning in 2000, the number of STEM enrichment activities, and the funding allocated to them, continued to grow. However, a centrally coordinated database of these STEM activities implemented at local or national levels was not available until 2009.

At the same time, major studies or surveys of participating schools and students, looking at the medium- or long-term impact of these schemes in improving exam results or sustaining interests in science and maths subjects were relatively scarce (Wynarczyk and Hale, 2009). Some activity providers captured experiences of students and teachers immediately after taking part in an activity, in "happy sheets", but these had little to do with solid evidence about whether attainment and participation rates had changed. My PhD project was one of the first robust evaluations of the impact of STEM enrichment activities on longer-term outcomes, such as raising attainment, narrowing the achievement gap, and continued participation in STEM subjects.

Conducting the research

This study consisted of a systematic review of the evidence factors influencing the attainment of disadvantaged students (not described here, but see Banerjee, 2016a), and a quasi-experimental evaluation of the impact of recent STEM initiatives to improve STEM attainment and participation (the focus of this chapter). The study also involved documentary and website analysis, observations in the field and ad hoc interviews. I used a quasi-experimental design as it can provide information about naturally occurring events, behaviour, attitudes or other characteristics of a particular group and can be used to demonstrate associations (DBIS, 2010), without disturbing the formal education system or introducing a bias. Data for the project was collected from existing records of management and information systems of STEM activity providers, national pupil database (NPD) and desk research. Further details appear in the papers published from my PhD work including Banerjee (2017a, 2017b).

Major Government, non-government, charitable organisations and higher education institutions have delivered on-campus STEM outreach activities, and peripatetic workshops, and created web-based resources. Given the scale of these undertakings, one of the earliest tasks for my research was to classify these activities and decide which ones to evaluate. I started by looking at the various STEM enrichment activities being delivered nationally, and chose to evaluate student focused activities. To ensure comparability across evaluations, I followed the public sector guidance for evaluation issued by the National STEM Centre. The definitions the various concepts I used in the thesis were largely from official reports released by DfE and the Parliamentary Office of Science and Technology.

The STEM activity providers included in the study delivered educational programmes by visiting schools and/or by allowing schools to visit STEM centres. Each provider had a set of schools registered with them, which meant a range of activities were delivered throughout the academic year to different schools. Some schools were registered with up to four activity providers at the same time. Registration with many activity providers meant that almost all year-groups of some schools were being enrolled for some kind of STEM enhancement activity. All schools in England that were registered with at least one STEM activity provider for each academic year between 2007 and 2012 were shortlisted for my study.

Identifying intervention schools: original plan, challenges and mitigation

In order to identify school taking part in interventions, I selected state-maintained secondary schools following the national curriculum for England, with a high percentage of FSM-eligible pupils. Then, I looked up the DfE performance tables to identify which of these schools had high-level outcomes (i.e. they were getting good results with relatively disadvantaged intakes). Letters were sent out to the headteachers of all these schools, to request their co-operation in the research project by responding to a few simple questions. The requested information was whether the school had been taking part in any external STEM enrichment activities in the last five years. If so, they were further requested to identify the scheme (by providing the name or web link), the years of participation, and the student year groups involved.

As these schools had been doing exceptionally well, despite being located in an area of disadvantage and having a very high share of FSM eligible pupils, they were clearly examples of good practice. This knowledge exchange would have benefitted students, schools, researchers and policymakers. This was highlighted in the email requests. Naturally, I promised to keep the school and individual identities anonymous.

However, only 3 out of 179 head teachers replied. Two of them said the information could not be disclosed while one said their achievements were solely due to effective in-school teaching. None provided answers to the simple questions asked. All other emails went unanswered despite reminder emails, requests and phone calls. This non-response meant an alternative plan had to be devised for data collection.

The STEM Directories launched by the DfE in 2009 provided details of relevant activities and activity providers (but not schools). In 2013 there were 238 initiatives listed as being delivered for various age groups, delivered by 162 STEM activity providers. These included free schemes as well as those for which schools or parents were required to pay. Some contact details were incorrect or had not been updated on STEM directories. Desk research helped me to collate contact details of all of these STEM activity providers. The lists of schemes did not identify which schools the providers worked with. Therefore, email requests were sent to all of these 162 providers requesting the names of participating schools. The programme leaders were asked for a list of all STEM activities being run, or launched by them, in the past five years along with names of schools and the year groups who participated in them. In the emails I had highlighted how valuable their support would be to future students, schools, researchers and policy makers as the data will contribute to evidence-informed decisions, and as before, anonymity was promised for all stakeholders. No scheme would be identified by name.

However, despite e-mail reminders and phone calls, STEM activity providers generally did not respond. Of the 161 correspondences (one spam entry) only one STEM provider initially shared some school names. A few organisations were worried that revealing school names to third parties would be against the data protection act (this is clearly not so because no individual details or sensitive data were requested). Others claimed that they did not collect any data on schools they worked with (even though the request was for any information even if incomplete). Some promised to get back but they did not. The majority simply did not reply. When reminders were sent, the providers began contacting each other to plan how *not* to respond. Some sent strongly worded emails to me and threatened to complain to the university, and some did complain to my PhD supervisor (who dealt with this by explaining that the request was legal, reasonable and in the public interest). It is interesting that programme leaders responsible for STEM education of current and future generations were apparently so upset by an e-mail request for institution-level information for non- commercial purposes. It raised the possibility that some of them did not want any independent evaluation of their sometimes lucrative activities, other than the post-event happy sheets that they were using.

I volunteered to work for organisations in return for the simple data (however poor). Eventually, ten organisations kindly agreed to share the names of participating schools. I was also allowed to witness sessions run for school children for a couple of months. The way the activities were delivered was that sometimes a team of trained and well-equipped staff from the organisations visited schools and demonstrated science experiments. The demonstrators carried with them all of the required equipment and chemicals. These demonstrations were sometimes part of larger "inspire science learning weeks or days" and at other times for STEM clubs. The organisations also allowed schools to visit on scheduled dates for a day full of STEM activities, ranging from rocket propulsion to DNA finger printing. The teacher supervising the children was requested to complete a feedback form at the end of these sessions.

In order to ensure as large a sample of participating schools as possible, I had looked up the websites of all 162 activity providers in England. Data from the public domain revealed reviews and testimonials from schools which had engaged in these activities and also identified participating year groups. Desk research along with the previous data collection procedure yielded names of about 1,000 participating schools all over England from 2007 to 2012 and these were the schools I started working with.

The evaluation

Out of all state-maintained secondary schools in England listed in the DfE annual school census (ASC), I had eventually identified 800 schools registered with activity providers, and these form the "intervention" schools. Out of these 800 schools, 317 schools had taken part in an activity every year from 2007 to 2014, and these were used for longitudinal tracking (Table 15.2). Another 483 schools had participated in activities on and off, but for at least one complete academic year, and were discontinuous intervention schools. All 2,287 remaining mainstream schools were used as comparator schools.

Of course, many of the 2,287 "comparator" schools will also have undertaken STEM activities. It is just that they were known (to me) to have

Table 15.2 Number of schools known to be participating in STEM activities 2007–2012

Participation status in intervention	Frequency	Percentage
Comparator	2,287	74
Discontinuous	483	16
Longitudinal	317	10
Total	3,087	100

done so. This is less than ideal, but is the best I could achieve under plan c. If the known intervention schools have improved their STEM outcomes as a result of STEM activities, then this should still be reflected in their scores relative to all other schools. Assuming that the schools not known to be undertaking STEM activities (but doing so) would also improve their STEM outcomes to the same extent, this would merely reduce the scale of any difference between schools known and not known to be involved.

Nearly 80,000 students from these intervention schools were known to have participated in STEM interventions. I used unique pupil identification numbers (UPN) and school codes (URNs) to find them in the NPD, and link them from the beginning of Key Stage 3 (KS3) to the end of KS5. I then eliminated the UPNs, and worked with a de-identified anonymised extract of the NPD. I used several student background indicators such as FSM eligibility, speaking English as an additional language (EAL), special educational needs (SEN), sex and ethnicity, to form students sub-groups. The outcome measures for the evaluation were maths and science attainment in GCSE (for schools and pupil sub-groups), and post-16 participation in STEM subject areas.

Students who dropped out of education or left the country could not be followed up as their records were no longer available from NPD. The number of pupils in each group for comparison are shown in Table 15.3.

The outcomes for each group, and each sub-group, were then compared in terms of maths and science KS4 results and KS5 participation in STEM subjects.

Table 15.3 Number of students in sub-groups, STEM activity participation

Sub-groups	End of KS4		End of KS5	
	Numbers	Percentages	Numbers	Percentages
Comparator	555,295	88	554,861	88
Intervention group	76,462	12	76,406	12
Total	631,757	100	631,267	100

Summary of findings and their implications

The secondary data analysis showed that science and maths results had improved nationally for schools, students and disadvantaged pupils since 2007. However, this success could not be attributed to STEM enrichment activities because the improvements were not peculiar to schools known to have been involved in STEM interventions. The findings were similar for the various subgroups marked by poverty, SEN and for ethnic minorities. Schools known to be involved in STEM activities did not, on average, have better outcomes at KS4 or KS5 than the comparator schools.

For example, Table 15.4 shows the percentage of school in each group whose pupils achieved 5 or more GCSEs or equivalent at grade A*–C including in maths and English – the KS4 Level 2 indictor then used by DfE to report school performance outcomes. The number of schools varies over time, and between groups as more school tended to take up STEM enrichment activities. National attainment figures tended to increase annually over the period. The intervention schools start out, in 2007, with higher scores (54%) than the comparator schools (48%). This suggests that schools willing and able to volunteer for STEM interventions are not some kind of random sub-set of all schools. They are the ones with time, stability and extra funds needed. The difference between the groups was probably higher than this in reality since there would have been at least some schools in 2007/8 listed in the comparator group but who were participating in a STEM intervention (i.e. that I did not identify as intervention schools, see above).

The intervention group of schools continued to have higher scores for every year than the comparator schools. However, they did not pull away any further, suggesting that there is no evidence that known STEM intervention schools increased their attainment any faster than other schools. The same is true for individual subject breakdowns. This was not a question of merely dampening the effect size because only some intervention schools were known

Table 15.4 Percentage of pupils in each group of schools meeting the KS4 level 2 performance indicator

Year	Intervention schools, N	Percentage KS4 level 2	Comparator schools, N	Percentage KS4 level 2	Achievement gap
2007/8	390	54	2,720	48	0.06
2008/9	536	55	2,566	50	0.05
2009/10	521	60	2,559	55	0.04
2010/11	601	62	2,422	58	0.03
2011/12	550	62	2.423	58	0.03

Note: The achievement gap here is difference between two percentages divided by their sum (Gorard, 2021).

to be. Known intervention schools did not improve faster than another large group of schools of all those not known to be intervention schools. The achievement gap in favour of intervention schools was 0.06 in 2007/8, and it dropped annually to 0.03 in 2010/11. Far from providing evidence of benefit, if anything this data suggests that schools not known to be undertaking STEM enrichment activities actually made more improvement.

KS4-only interventions appeared to be the least effective. In certain situations, the comparator group schools and students performed better than the intervention sub-group. This calls for further research to investigate if these interventions produce any potentially harmful effects. KS3-only and longitudinal interventions were found to be slightly more effective. This backs up other research which shows that educational interventions earlier on in the life of students are often more effective (Ayoub et al., 2009). Students' aspiration by the age of 14 gives a good indication as to whether they will continue with STEM when they get older (Archer, 2013).

STEM skills are valuable and students should be able to study subjects they are interested in, irrespective of their background. STEM enrichment activities require staff engagement, time and money. If these schemes are not working, perhaps the money should be saved and used elsewhere to get the better effect. It is important for funders and activity providers to conduct robust evaluations in order to understand what works and works better, rather than be "protective" of their reputation or similar.

The systematic review identified some of the potential approaches which have been effective in improving cognitive development, supporting attainment in school science and maths and progression of disadvantaged pupils (Ayoub et al., 2009). Directing resources to effective programmes will encourage better results with a similar or reduced investment.

Fuller details of the methods and results are in my publications from the PhD (Banerjee, 2015).

Dissemination and impact

STEM activity providers claim that their work helps students attain better in school science and maths, and increase their likelihood of taking up STEM subjects for level 3 qualifications. According to the available data, this does not appear to happen. Some STEM activity providers have endorsements on their websites which echo positive views and success stories. There are two main concerns here. There is a limited number of such case studies compared to the huge number of schemes being run. And cherry-picking endorsements, with no comparator group, is not evidence. The National STEM Centre encourages more effective evaluation of STEM initiatives, summarising it as "Better evaluation: better STEM".

The data for this project was collected for England, but the local approach of this study did not however limit the generalisability of research findings as similar activities were being run in many western countries. The recommendations made from my PhD study were of interest to a wide audience. To help increase the impact of the study, I applied for and received an ESRC impact acceleration award. I designed a research briefing in order to translate the main research findings for a lay person to help them understand the findings. This was in an accessible format and had a wide reach (schools and activity providers). I submitted evidence to the UK Parliament, and shared a report with the DfE. The study was cited by the Royal Academy of Engineering. One of the suggestions made by my external examiner was that activity providers are more likely to read a book than a journal article so if I really wanted them to start thinking about robust evaluations, I should write a book and I did (Banerjee, 2017).

Reflections on my journey

Moving from science to education, and beginning to plan a PhD, I started reading more widely. Some of the pieces I first read, understood and liked had been written by Professor Stephen Gorard. When you have been in a job and earning money, it is not easy to give up that financial independence. Writing to a prospective supervisor in a new area took courage. It is even harder being a mature student in a foreign country, speaking English as an additional language, trying to do a PhD with two very young children now unsettled from their former life.

One of the biggest mental blocks I had was that I was not a social scientist. I did not follow a lot of terms used commonly by people at the university and was constantly worried that my area of expertise lay elsewhere. However, even in social science, designing research, evaluating robustly, using numbers effectively and answering the "so what" questions are still scientific and logical. Over the years, I attended several training courses, and grew my confidence. I remember my first BERA conference presentation in 2014. I was really worried, but my PhD supervisor said, "Don't worry, I will be in the audience if someone tries to act funny". It is very reassuring to have a senior mentor stand up for you – which he often did.

At Durham University, I went on to receive the Norman Richardson Award (and the Ustinov travel award) to support the additional unanticipated journeys I had to make for data collection and a small pot of money from BERA for attending conferences. Remember to apply for things. If you do not ask you will definitely not get them.

Given my STEM background, I was familiar with the power of numbers. This project taught me how powerful secondary datasets can be. One of the best pieces of advice I was given by my supervisor was that "…it does not take any more time to analyse 100,000 cases than it does to analyse 100 cases. So, if a census dataset makes your design robust you should go for it".

As I discuss elsewhere, it is important to amend and update your research plans, if required, to ensure that the project is completed on time. Often, things do not go fully as planned but back up plans can help you to answer research questions completely and sometimes in a more robust way than you had first envisaged.

I think an effective supervisor makes a lot of difference to your PhD journey, and associated learning and experiences. I had my first academic job as a post-doctoral research associate at Durham University before submitting the thesis and it lasted for a year. After obtaining my PhD degree I got a lectureship at the University of Exeter. I had my first ESRC grant in 2016 as a co-applicant with Stephen Gorard and Vikki Boliver, and then two more grants funded by the Office for Students the next year. Within a year of joining Exeter, I was promoted to Senior Lecturer where I now lead the MSc programme, teach research methods and supervise Masters' and PhD students. I am still learning but I now feel more comfortable calling myself a social scientist.

References

Archer, L. (2013). *What influences participation in science and mathematics?* TISME briefing paper. www.kcl.ac.uk

Ayoub, C., O'Connor, E., Rappolt-Schlictmann, G., Vallotton, C., Raikes, H., and Chazan-Cohen, R. (2009). Cognitive skill performance among young children living in poverty: Risk, change, and the promotive effects of Early Head Start. *Early Childhood Research Quarterly*, 24(3), pp. 289–305.

Banerjee, P. (2015). *Impact assessment of STEM initiatives in improving educational outcome.* PhD thesis. www.dur.ac.uk

Banerjee P. (2016a). A systematic review of factors linked to poor academic performance of disadvantaged students in science and maths in schools. *Cogent Education*, 3(1), pp. 1–18.

Banerjee P. (2016b). A longitudinal evaluation of the impact of STEM enrichment and enhancement activities in improving educational outcomes: Research protocol. *International Journal of Educational Research*, 76, pp. 1–11.

Banerjee P. (2016c). Does continued participation in STEM enrichment and enhancement activities affect school maths attainment? *Oxford Review of Education*, 43(1), pp. 1–18.

Banerjee, P. (2017a). *Impact Assessment of STEM Initiatives in Improving Educational Outcomes.* United Kingdom: Author House.

Banerjee, P. (2017b). Is informal education the answer to increasing and widening participation in STEM education? Review of Education, 5(2). 202–224.

Behr, N. (2011). *A-level students in England unprepared for entry to STEM degrees*. The Royal Society. www.royalsociety.org

CBI. (2012). Learning to grow: What employers need from education and skills. Education and skills survey. www.cbi.org.uk

Conway, A. (2009). *Widening participation in higher education and the resultant diversity of learners: A review of government policies, the academy and market demands that may influence this trajectory.* Paper submitted for term review as part of the EDD at the University of Sheffield.

DBIS (2010). *Attitudes to science: Survey of 14-16-year-olds*. Report. www.gov.uk

DfE (2014). *What is the most effective way of increasing young people's take-up and attainment of strategically important subjects, especially science and maths?* www.gov.uk

DfE (2010). *Educating the next generation of scientists*, HC492. National STEM Center. Summary of public sector guidance for evaluation with respect to STEM initiatives NAO. www.nationalstemcentre.org.uk

Garnham, D. (2011). *National curriculum: Now and for the future.* SCORE Conference Report. www.score-education.org

Gorard, S. (2021). *How to Make Sense of Statistics*. London: SAGE.

Gorard, S., Adnett, N., May, H., Slack, K., Smith, E., and Thomas, L. (2007). *Overcoming Barriers to Higher Education*. Stoke-on-Trent: Trentham Books.

Gorard, S., and See, B.H. (2008). Is science a middle-class phenomenon? The SES determinants of 16–19 participation. *Research in Post Compulsory Education*, 13(2), pp. 217–226.

Gorard, S., and See, B.H. (2009). The impact of socio-economic status on participation and attainment in science. *Studies in Science Education*, 45(1). 93–129.

Gorard, S., and See, B.H. (2013). *Overcoming Disadvantage in Education*. London: Routledge.

Homer, M., Ryder, J., and Banner, I. (2014). Measuring determinants of post-compulsory participation in science: A comparative study using national data. *British Educational Research Journal*, 40, pp. 610–636.

OECD. (2007). *Providing a highly skilled workforce for continued economic development*. www.oecd.org

Smith, E., and Gorard, S. (2011). Is there a shortage of scientists? A re-analysis of supply for the UK. *British Journal of Educational Studies*, 59(2), pp. 159–177.

The Royal Society. (2006). *A degree of concern? UK first degrees in STEM*. London. www.royalsociety.org

The Royal Society. (2008). *Science and mathematics education, 14-19*, A "state of the nation" report. Available at: https://royalsociety.org/topics-policy/projects/state-of-nation/5-14/.

The Royal Society. (2011). *Preparing for the transfer from school and college science and mathematics education UK STEM higher education* – "state of the nation" report. www.royalsociety.org

UKCES. (2015) *High level STEM skills requirement in the UK labour market.* www.gov.uk. August 2021.

Vidal, R. (2007). *A level subject choice in England: Patterns of uptake and factors affecting subject preferences.* Cambridge Assesment. www.cambridgeassessment. org.uk

Wynarczyk, P. (2008). *An overview of initiatives in science, technology, and engineering across England, Scotland and Wales.* Report commissioned by the UK Resource Centre for Women in Science, Engineering and Technology (UKRC) project Women in SET. www.gov.uk. August 2021.

Wynarczyk, P., and Hale, S. (2009). *Improving take up of science and technology subjects in schools and colleges:A synthesis review.* Report prepared for ESRC and DCSF. London: United Kingdom.

CHAPTER 16

How fair are the indicators used in contextualised admission policies in China?

Yiyi Tan

Introduction

Equality of access to higher education (HE) is a significant issue worldwide, because HE can play an important role in the development of individuals and society (Gorard, 2018; Zhao and Wang, 2020). In order to improve HE access, many countries have implemented policies to widen participation in HE for disadvantaged groups. One such policy is contextualised admissions (CA) which promotes the idea of widening access for disadvantaged groups in HE, by taking account of student background information. This PhD project is a comprehensive exploration of HE participation, especially in terms of indicators for disadvantage prescribed in contextualised admissions policies in China. The study provides an appraisal of the available indicators, and an evaluation of additional feasible and reliable indicators, which could address the aims of widening access for disadvantaged or under-represented groups.

CA policies regard students' background as contextual data and take this additional information into account during admission decision-making (Gorard et al., 2017). One of the underlying principles of these policies is Rawls' theory of justice, which argues any acceptable unequal distributions of social values can only be justified by being for society's benefit, while less-advantaged people such as those "with less native assets and born into less favourable social positions" deserve more attention from society (Rawls, 1999, p. 86). If students are identified as disadvantaged in a way that might affect their prior attainment, then they could be positively-discriminated and enrolled by universities and higher education institutions (HEIs) with lower entry requirements based on their potential to succeed if supported (Boliver et al., 2015).

CA policies are becoming common. All Scottish universities, Russell Group Universities in the UK, the most selective 4-year HEIs in the US, and HEIs in India have implemented CA policies (Boliver et al., 2017; Chauhan, 2008; Kevin and Claire, 2020; Mountford-Zimdars et al., 2016). These

DOI: 10.4324/9781003201366-19

universities use a variety of contextual indicators to identify disadvantaged groups. For example, POLAR and ACORN are UK-based geographical indicators of HE participation rates, and race/ethnicity, gender and caste are group-level indicators used in affirmative action in the US and India. Some indicators can be officially verified, others are accepted as self-reported.

In China, most high school graduates must take the National College Entrance Examination (NCEE) as the first step to be HE applicants. There are some CA policies intended to improve the participation of the disadvantaged students. NCEE scores are classified based on student's Hukou (or household) provinces, and their admission to HEIs is then filtered through the Province-based Quota Admission Policy. This area-based quota system aims at improving HE enrolment for students from socioeconomically poor and remote provinces. Moreover, if students are from minority ethnicities or "martyr" families (similar to families of Armed forces in the UK), they are eligible for an increase in NCEE score of 5 or 10 points, according to Extra Credits Policy. According to the Three Special Plans, students who were born, live and study in poor prefectures or had rural Hukou, could apply for a priority in admission or a looser enrolment requirement from certain HEIs if they pass additional examinations.

However, many of the indicators used worldwide for identifying disadvantage are problematic. In the UK, Gorard et al. (2017) pointed out parents' education level and occupational status might be far from suitable to be an indicator because they are primarily self-reported rather than administratively verified. First generation to attend HE involves about two thirds of students in the UK, which is a very large group (Jerrim, 2021). There is also evidence that shows geographical indicators of HE participation rates (such as POLAR) do not closely correlate with other regional identification markers which measure household socioeconomic poverty. Some of these area-based indicators (e.g. TUNDRA and ACORN) are behind the paywall of companies who produce these measures for the business purposes. This has implications on wider use by HEIs. Furthermore, almost all postcode-based indicators (POLAR, ACORN, IDACI, IMD/SIMD and MOSAIC) and school-level indicators such as school types are vulnerable to an ecological fallacy (Gorard et al., 2017). Most disadvantaged students do not live in the areas of most disadvantage.

Indicators used in Chinese CA policies face similar problems. The geographical-level indicators such as hometown provinces, poor prefecture, or rural Hukou, and group-level indicators such as minority ethnic group can be weak, and insensitive to identification of individual cases of false negatives and false positives (Boliver et al., 2019). Few scholars have paid attention to this issue, especially in China, which has implications for fair access and the admission of disadvantaged students.

According to the preliminary results of my scoping review, there is a considerable body of research about equity and HE access in China. Only a few examples from my fuller review can be cited here. There have been studies of differences in access between provinces (Hamnett et al., 2019; Qin and Buchanan, 2019; Yang and Wang, 2019), ethnic groups (e.g. Cai and Cen, 2018; Xie and Liu, 2019), Hukou identity (e.g. Li, 2019; Wu, 2019; Zhu et al., 2018), prefectures (Cao et al., 2018; Chen and Gao, 2019) and family socioeconomic status (SES) (e.g. Song et al., 2019; Xu and Fang, 2020; Yang, 2020). In summary, research has suggested that there are considerable inequalities in HE admission in China.

However, many of the studies I found are of limited quality – small-scale, with convenience samples in one HEI, inappropriately designed, using incorrect forms of analysis, or mistaking correlation and regression analyses as providing causal evidence. See Gorard (2013, 2021) for more on this. Several studies describe the backgrounds or contents of these policies without evaluating them (e.g. Zhang, 2019). Some research focused on the implementation of these policies rather than their impact (e.g. Shao and Wu, 2018).

Perhaps most dangerously, previous studies discussing HE equity in China primarily focussed on existing HE students, or the candidates in the NCEE who have successfully finished compulsory education, passed the Senior High Schools Entrance Examination, continued to study at high schools and eventually took the NCEE. This ignores the larger population, who could have been eligible to take the NCEE but had dropped out beforehand. This large group might be more disadvantaged in education, but they are largely ignored in the widening access literature (Gorard, 2007).

Accordingly, my PhD includes students who leave education at this earlier period and not just those leaving after NCEE. It evaluates three officially-acknowledged indicators – provinces, Hukou identity, and ethnicity – and compares them other possibly more accurate indicators for disadvantage. The research questions are:

- What are the disparities in HE participation by province, Rural-Urban Hukou identity, ethnicity or other indicators?
- To what extent do these indicators accurately indicate a disadvantaged group of students?
- Are there indicators leading to fairer identification of disadvantaged students?

Outline of the study

This study consists of a scoping review, followed by secondary data analysis to investigate inequality of HE participation and the most useful measures of disadvantage. I used three categories of datasets:

- governmental administrative data, including the nationwide-level data of Population Census, Mini Census, Micro Census, provincial-level data of HE participants and NCEE candidates
- institutional level data including admission quota plans published on the official website of the 42 World Double-First (WDF) HEIs
- individual-level data including three nationally-representative social surveys with sample sizes over 10,000 – the Chinese General Social Survey (CGSS), the longitudinal China Family Panel Study (CFPS) and China Education Panel Survey (CEPS)

These datasets are not ideal. Some are only for aggregate level, used in the descriptive analysis to demonstrate the patterns of HE participation. The admission quotas published by WDF HEIs are only plans, and could differ from the real student intakes. Universities might make an offer to more students than in the plan, or some students might not accept an offer from a university and choose to repeat the last year of high school. Most WDF HEIs publish their provincial admission quotas by subjects, so I calculated the total manually. Despite the large nationally-representative samples of the surveys, there are missing responses and values, and inevitable dropout in the two longitudinal datasets. All missing data provides potential for bias (Gorard, 2021). More systematically, CGSS only cover students aged 18 and over, lacking information on compulsory education and high school and educational aspirations of individuals, all thought to be highly correlated with HE participation. Despite excellent coverage, CEPS only covers middle-school and later, omitting cases who did not even attend middle school. Only two waves of the survey have been completely finished, and inter-viewees are not yet at the age of attending HE.

Finally, some variables are more vulnerable to bias than others. In CGSS, for example, due to the difficulty of asking about family income, respondents were asked "comparing with your contemporaries, which social class do you think your family was located in when you were 14 years old (ranking from 1 to 10)". But the answers to this question might be more biased than asking "how much was your family income". To answer the former question, the respondents are supposed to know not only their own socioeconomic conditions but those of their counterparts' and then, making a comparison, identify their own rankings. This could be more complicated and dangerous than providing an estimated figure about family income.

These limitations, and others, are noted here to provide a caution. However, there is no national dataset of all student trajectories providing the real background and enrolment data for all. These alternatives are reasonably authoritative and able to demonstrate a nationally- or provincially-macro-level picture, or are reasonably sampled, designed and conducted to reveal representative and comparable individual information. Cleaning and linking these disparate datasets before analysis, in itself, makes this a very ambitious project.

There is only space in this chapter to summarise some of the results, and consider what they mean. The focus is on who enter HE, with some comparative frequencies, and a logistic regression model (described in the next section).

Missing values in categorical variables (other than attending HE or not), for whatever reason (not applicable, refused, unknown and so on) have been recoded as missing. Missing values in real-number variables, including family income, educational expenditure and standardised cognitive ability scores, have been assigned the average of all existing data. Some variables were reorganised. For example, cognitive ability scores have been standardised by age. The dozens of parental occupation types have been reduced to four categories – "skilled agricultural & fishery workers", "elementary occupations", "higher skilled/professional labour" and "missing" for a clearer regression model.

Summary of results and implications so far

Just over 24% of all young people, and 31% of high school attendees, entered HE (Table 16.1). As suggested above, not going on to high school is a crucial barrier to attending HE. In the dataset, no young person attended HE when they had not previously attended high school. This does not seem unreasonable. But if we are genuinely concerned with equality of access to later educational opportunities, then this situation of only 70% of young people

Table 16.1 The number of students entering HE by attendance of high school education (or equivalent)

	Did not enter HE	Entered HE	Total
Not attended high schools or equivalent	550	0	550
Attended high schools or equivalent	1,330	610	1,940
Total	1,880	610	2,490

Source: CFPS.

attending high school in China must be addressed urgently. This kind of simple political arithmetic exposes inequalities and under-development that governments and international comparisons rarely notice/mention.

Within the group attending high school there are further differences in HE enrolment between different types of high schools that students went to (Table 16.2). Only students who studied in ordinary high schools ("Pugao" in Chinese), which refer to the high schools that primarily provide students with academic knowledge and exercises, have a substantial proportion of students attending HE (44%). Attending any other kind of high school – adult high schools, ordinary specialised high schools, specialised adult high schools, vocational high schools and technical high schools – means very, very little chance of accessing HE. It seems that one of the keys to HE entry is not just high school education but also winning a place in an ordinary high school.

In order to clarify the link between prior education, student background, and Hukou status on the one hand and HE participation on the other, likely predictors were entered into a logistic regression model. The binary outcome was whether a student entered HE or not.

Most (75.5%) students do not attend HE. Therefore the base model for logistic regression is far from 50:50 at the outset. This study employed a method introduced by Gorard (2021, p. 243). This involves treating the smaller group (HE participants) as one group and then randomly selecting a subgroup of the same size from the larger group (non-HE participants). After merging these two groups into one, a dataset with a reasonable base model (50:50) is created. This process has then been repeated 10 times and the results are the average of those 10 goes.

There were five blocks of variables added to the regression model in steps. Block 1 looks at participation in ordinary high schools and HE access. Block 2 focuses on some individual-level indicators including sex, ethnicity, Hukou type (rural/urban/army/other), birth month, daily-used languages with classmates/family, annual expenditures on education and cognitive test scores. In Block 3, family-level indicators such as parents' education levels,

Table 16.2 The percentage of students entering HE by attendance at different categories of high school education

	Entered HE
Ordinary high schools	44
Adult high schools	0
Ordinary specialised high schools	3
Specialised adult high schools	0
Vocational high schools	4
Technical high schools	2

Source: CFPS.

parents' political status, parents' occupations, annual family income and educational aspirations were added. Block 4 was the Hukou province. Block 5 involves school-level indicators. These include school types "key schools" (state-run selective schools), "ordinary schools" (state-run non-selective schools), "private schools" (civilian-run schools where students fail to be received by state-run schools for any reasons) and "schools for internal migrant workers' children". Class type is classified as "currently in a key (selective) class", "currently not in a key class" and "the school attended does not distinguish between ordinary and key classes". All predictors in each block used a Forward (conditional) method, to eliminate unnecessary ones.

Table 16.3 shows the quality of the model (predictions) after each block. Most of the gain in prediction comes from knowledge of the kind of high school attended (as suggested previously by Table 16.2). Most of variation in continuing to HE can be explained by prior continuation to ordinary high schools, as with continuation to Key Stage 5 in England (Gorard, 2018). The individual-level indicators improve the model a little further, but once they are accounted for, there is little difference relating students' family, neigh-bourhood or school backgrounds. After that there is very little improvement. In fact, knowledge of a student's Hukou province (rather than its nature as in Block 2) makes no difference at all to predicting whether a student attends HE. Of course, this does not necessarily mean that student background and family characteristics are not important to earlier selection, for example, to entering ordinary high schools.

Table 16.4 summarises the coefficients of predictors included in the model by Block 5. Young people's total amount of education expenditure in the last year made no difference, nor did their Hukou province, father's occupation (if mother's occupation was known), or birth month within the year. Perhaps because of scarcity, having an ethnic minority origin was not related to outcomes. This is odd because ethnicity is commonly used CA indicator. For clarity, Table 16.4 also omits odds for missing values. The full

Table 16.3 Percentage of cases predicted correctly, for HE entry or not, by blocked predictors

Predictor variables/block	Percentage correct	Percentage explained
0: Base	50.0	–
1: Type of high school	73.2	46.4
2: Individual characteristics	75.4	4.4
3: Family background	75.8	0.8
4: Hukou province	75.8	0
5: School level	76.5	1.4

Table 16.4 The average coefficients of variables in final step of the model

Variables	Odds (ExpB)
Attend ordinary high schools (vs not)	3.97
Male (vs female)	0.73
Urban Hukou (vs Rural Hukou)	1.21
Daily communication with classmate in Chinese dialect (vs Mandarin)	1.33
Daily communication in minority ethnic language (vs Mandarin)	0.21
Daily communication with classmate in other languages (vs Mandarin)	0.51
Daily communication with family in Chinese dialect (vs Mandarin)	0.70
Daily communication with family in minority ethnic language (vs Mandarin)	0.98
Daily communication with family in other languages (vs Mandarin)	0.38
Math cognitive test scores, standardised by age	1.09
Verbal cognitive test scores, standardised by age	1.06
Elementary occupations (vs Skilled agricultural & fishery workers)	0.45
Higher skilled/professional occupations (vs Skilled)	1.17
At least one parent completed post-compulsory education (vs neither did)	1.52
At least one parent completed HE (vs neither beyond compulsory education)	2.08
Parents' educational aspiration for child-junior high schools (vs primary)	0.68
Parents' educational aspiration for child-senior high schools (vs primary)	1.08
Parents' educational aspiration for child-vocational colleges (vs primary)	1.14
Parents' educational aspiration for child-HE (vs primary school)	2.45
Parents' educational aspiration for child-Master's degree (vs primary school)	2.83
Parents' educational aspiration for child-Doctoral degree (vs primary school)	1.98
Key/selective school (vs non-selective school)	2.69
Private schools (vs non-selective school)	0.53
Currently in a key class (vs not)	1.60
School does not distinguish between ordinary and key classes (vs not)	0.86

figures appear in the thesis. In general, cases with missing data for any key variable are less likely than average to attend HE.

As expected the odds of attending HE is one attended an ordinary high school are much higher than for any of other kind of school (nearly four times as much, all other things being equal). It also helps to be female, living in an urban area, and communicate with classmates in a Chinese dialect or with family in Mandarin. Naturally higher cognitive test scores are linked to entry to HE (the odds increasing by 9% for every age standardised score in maths, for example). Students whose mother worked in a higher-skilled or professional occupation, and/or whose parents received higher levels of education themselves, and/or have high educational aspirations for their child, are more likely to go to HE. As a meritocratic tracking system, key schools and classes have already completed their selection of more advantaged students, and these are also more likely to enter HE.

Of course, other than high school none of these predictors makes much difference to the accuracy of the predictions (as in Table 16.3).

If students do not take high school they have no chance of HE entry, whatever their other context and characteristics. If students do not enter an ordinary high school, they have very little changes of HE entry, again whatever their other context and characteristics. As the pipeline of selection or exclusion, including key schools and classes, continues the chances of taking, and having success in, NCEE become clearer and more stratified by socio-economic and other characteristics. It is a shame that current CA policies and scholars in the area mainly focus on the later stages of NCEE examination and admissions to HEIs. A large group of disadvantaged students have been excluded from concerns about why they are excluded and what to do about it.

Contextualised admission policies can never be truly effective if they only concern HE applicants, or consider inappropriate (but perhaps convenient) measures of disadvantage (Gorard et al., 2017). These policies would work best with non-applicants, and identify the disadvantaged long before the application or selective examination. And, although there is no evidence in this study, to help HE participants who are enrolled through CA policies in academic achievement, life or career preparation. Therefore, the indicators employed in CA policies will be problematic if they can only identify disadvantage in the final selection to HE.

The evidence presented here suggests that the indicators used in current Chinese CA policies are inaccurate and may be ineffective. Things like parental education and occupation, minority ethnicity, province and Hukou identity have not been shown to be key indicators. The work has to start at entry to high school or before. And this is about much more than raising aspirations or expectations (Gorard et al., 2011). The key issues are likely to be structural.

There is another thing that might deserve to be questioned – the effectiveness of standardised tests. Selections via standardised tests such as the examination for transition to high schools and NCEE, like an inferior "veil of ignorance", might portray a superficial procedural justice in China (and elsewhere). Educators claim a preference for talented students and give them offers to enter ordinary high schools, key schools/classes and even HE based on their standardised test scores. Nevertheless, these talents are to a large extent stratified by individuals' background. In other words, educators select their target students indirectly based on their characteristics. However, if it is unfair or illegal for educators to directly select their potential students on the basis of their backgrounds, how could it be fair that this selection is based on the substitute variables of these background characteristics (Gorard, 2018)? CA policies in China had intended to rectify the problem of superficial equality and dreamt of realising substantive justice in HE participation, but missing out the most potentially-disadvantaged groups and the inaccuracy of indicators to a large extent make their goals very difficult to achieve. At least according to the results so far.

Academic development

During my ongoing PhD journey, besides the completion of the project, it has been important to improve my academic skills. For me, the first and one of the most valuable lessons was the importance of research design. This is about far more than techniques or procedures but is really a pursuit of safe evidence-based conclusions (Gorard, 2013). Without robust design, research is seldom of high-quality. Secondly, I have learned about statistics. I was worried that I am not good at mathematics so that it would be difficult for me to handle numbers. But, as Gorard (2021) pointed out, I find statistics to be more like the real-life daily arithmetic used by everyone, than abstract and complicated mathematics. Furthermore, the operations in the statistics tools are like playing games!

I realise the importance of making things easier rather than more complex. For example, for many real problems which need to be analysed by statistic techniques, simple models such as linear regression and logistic regression are adequate to disclose how indicators and outcome variables are correlated or to what extent indicators could accurately predict the outcome variables. There is little need to employ more elaborated and sophisticated models, as these cannot rectify the shortcomings of raw data and might even confuse readers.

Another improvement is my ability in critical thinking. When I read any arguments or conclusions in papers or books, I now evaluate and critique these ideas more objectively and critically, based on the research design, the quality of conduct in these studies, regardless how well-known the authors or sources are.

I have obtained a far deeper understanding of HE, education equity and social mobility in a Chinese context. For example, HE admission decisions based on students' scores in the NCEE seem to shield the admission process from subjective and biased selection, and to be just and fair, but this is a superficial procedural kind of justice instead of substantive justice. It ignores a larger group of potentially-disadvantaged students who could not even take the NCEE or attend high school. Disadvantage, in fact, does not start to become barriers to HE after the NCEE but hinders students since the early years. Disadvantage also contributes to the stratification of students' educational attainment, their aspirations for education and perhaps even the willingness to work academically. Thus, it would be far from sufficient if HE admission policies which aim for HE equity only focus on contextualised admissions *after* the NCEE.

References

Boliver, V., Crawford, C., Powell, M., and Craige, W. (2017). *Admissions in context: The use of contextual information by leading universities*. Project Report. London: Sutton Trust.

Boliver, V., Gorard, S., and Siddiqui, N. (2015). Will the use of contextual indicators make UK higher education admissions fairer? *Education Sciences*, 5(4), pp. 306–322. MDPIAG. Retrieved from 10.3390/educsci5040306

Boliver, V., Gorard, S., and Siddiqui, N. (2019). Using contextual data to widen access to higher education. *Perspectives: Policy and Practice in Higher Education*, 25(1), pp. 7–13. doi: 10.1080/13603108.2019.1678076

Cai, W.B., and Cen, L.Y. (2018). The discourse institutionalism analysis of points adding policy of college entrance examination for ethnic students [少数民族高考加分政策的话语制度主义分析]. *Journal of Shihezi University (Philosophy and Social Sciences)*, 32(2), pp. 43–50.

Cao, Y., Zhang, R.J., and Hou, Y.N. (2018). Compensation or selection? Accuracy analysis of the provincial allocation for the compensatory opportunity from the "National Special Plan" in China [补偿还是选拔？"国家专项计划"补偿机会在地区间分配的精准性分析]. *China Higher Education Research*, 8, pp. 23–29.

Chauhan, C.P.S. (2008). Education and caste in India. *Asia Pacific Journal of Education*, 28(3), pp. 217–234.

Chen, J.H., and Gao, H. (2019). The research on the differences in HE participation between countries and the indicators – based on the empirical analysis of HE enrolment data in Gansu from 2007 to 2016 [我国高等教育入学的县域差异及其影响因素研究——基于甘肃 2007–2016年高考录取数据的实证分析]. *Higher Education Exploration*, 1, pp. 1–16.

Gorard, S. (2007). *Overcoming the Barriers to Higher Education*. Stoke-on-Trent: Trentham Books.

Gorard, S. (2013). *Research Design: Creating Robust Approaches for the Social Sciences*. London: Thousand Oaks, CA: SAGE.

Gorard, S. (2018). *Education Policy: Evidence of Equity and Effectiveness*. Bristol: Policy Press.

Gorard, S. (2021). *How to Make Sense of Statistics*, 1st ed. London: SAGE.

Gorard, S., Boliver, V., Siddiqui, N., and Banerjee, P. (2017). Which are the most suitable contextual indicators for use in widening participation to HE?

Research Papers in Education, 34(1), pp. 99–129. doi: 10.1080/02671522.201 7.1402083

Gorard, S., See, B.H., and Davies, P. (2011). *Do attitudes and aspirations matter in education? A review of the research evidence.* Saarbrücken, Germany: Lambert Academic Publishing.

Hamnett, C., Shen, H., and Liang, B.J. (2019). The reproduction of regional inequality through university access: The Gaokao in China. *Area Development and Policy*, 4(3), pp. 252–270.

Jerrim, J. (2021). Measuring disadvantage. *Research Brief*. The Sutton Trust.

Kevin, J.D., and Claire, C. (2020). Comparing and learning from English and American higher education access and completion policies. *Policy Reviews in Higher Education*, 4(2), pp. 203–227. doi: 10. 1080/23322969.2020.173959

Li, A. (2019). Unfulfilled promise of educational meritocracy? Academic ability and China's urban-rural gap in access to higher education. *Chinese Sociological Review*, 51(2), pp. 115–146.

Mountford-Zimdars, A., Moore, J., and Graham, J. (2016). Is contextualised admission the answer to the access challenge? *Perspectives: Policy and Practice in Higher Education*, 20(4), pp. 143–150, doi: 10.1080/13603108.2016.12 03369

Qin, X.L., and Buchanan, R. (2019). Policy and public preferences regarding the university enrollment quotas system across Chinese provinces. *High Education Policy*. doi: 10.1057/s41307-019-00170-0

Rawls, J. (1999). *A Theory of Justice* (rev. ed.). Oxford: Oxford University Press.

Shao, G.H., and Wu, W.W. (2018). Investigation and research on the college entrance examination comprehensive reform situation – based on the 2017 college freshmen attending CEE in Zhejiang province [我国高考招生制度综合改革的成效与问题研究——基于浙江省2017年高考录取学生的调查]. *China Higher Education Research*, 6, pp. 50–55.

Song, B., Liu, H., and Wang, L. (2019). Higher education expansion, social stratification and the decisions on HE attendance made by peasants – based on analysis of CGSS [高校扩招、阶层分化与农户高等教育投资决策——基于CGSS数据的分析]. *Education Research Monthly*, 12, pp. 101–108.

Wu, W. (2019). The latest evolution of urban-rural inequality in higher education in China – based on the analysis of CGSS 2015 data [新中国成立以来我国高等教育城乡不均衡的最新演变——基于cgss2015数据的分析]. *Journal of China Agricultural University (Social Sciences)*, 36(5), pp. 129–136.

Xie, Z.J., and Liu, H.J. (2019). Evaluation on the effect of the preferential policy that awards bonus points in National College Entrance Examination for Ethnic Students – based on a comparative investigation of Han and ethnic students at four ethnic colleges in western China [少数民族高考加分政策实施效果评价——基于西部四所民族院校汉族学生与少数民族学生的对比调查]. *Journal of Research on Education for Ethnic Minorities*, 30 (2), pp. 31–41.

Xu, W.Q., and Fang, F. (2020). Study on the access to the higher education: Dual perspective based on household registration status and family background

[谁获得了高等教育——基于户籍身份和家庭背景的双重视角].
Chongqing Higher Education Research, 8(1), pp. 14–26.

Yang, P., and Wang, R. (2019). Central-local relations and higher education stratification in China. *Higher Education*, 79(1), pp. 111–139.

Yang, T. (2020). The relationships between family capitals, education attainments and social stratifications – based on CGSS2015 dataset [家庭资本、教育获得与社会分层关系研究——基于CGSS15年的数据]. *Ability and Wisdom*, pp. 175–176.

Zhang, H.J. (2019). The gap between scientificity and acceptability of Gaokao and the breakthrough of the governance dilemma – taking the implementation of the standard score system as an example [高考科学性与受众接受度的断裂及治理困境的突破——以标准分制度的沿革为例].
Journal of National Academy of Education Administration, 6, pp. 43–50.

Zhang, X.L. (2015). The research on the determinants of the opportunity of HE participation [高等教育机会获得的影响因素研究]. *Journal of Zhengzhou Institute of Aeronautical Industry Management*, 33(2), pp. 127–132.

Zhao, L.X., and Wang, L.M. (2020). Promotion or suppression: The influence of HE on social class mobility [促进还是抑制：高等教育对社会阶层流动的影响——基于CGSS混合截面数据的实证分析]. *Higher Education Exploration*, 9, pp. 5–11.

Zhu, J., Xu, L., and Wang, H. (2018). Research on urban-rural differences in education transition between generation – evidence from CGSS data [教育代际传递的城乡差异研究——基于中国综合社会调查数据的验证]. *Education & Economy*, 34(6), pp. 45–55.

CHAPTER 17

International comparisons at the crossroads of policy, practice and research: The case of school leavers' and graduates' information systems

Rita Hordósy

Introduction to researching research

My doctoral research compared how school leavers' and graduates' data are produced in different national contexts, and to what extent the data are then applied in educational policy planning, institutional decision-making and informing students.

This chapter looks at the "inception" of the research idea, the research design and methods used, and the main findings and takeaway points. I close the chapter by reflecting further on the PhD experience and my research career since finishing.

Where did my research ideas come from?

During my MA in Sociology at the Eötvös Lóránd University in Hungary I worked as a student researcher in a wide array of social science research projects. These included the first major national study on school aggression, exploring teachers' perception of school poverty, and researching the audience and cultural consumption at a summer art and music festival. My main goal was to become a researcher in the field of education. To continue on this path, I wanted to gain a doctoral degree.

On finishing my MA, I worked as a research assistant in a larger team at the Hungarian Institute for Educational Research and Development (HIERD). One of my research foci was to compare examples of school leavers' tracking surveys from different national contexts (Figure 17.1). This was intended to inform policy thinking for potential information systems that cover secondary schools and vocational education, to complement the Graduate Career Tracking Program that was being set up at the time. This prompted the idea of looking at these information systems more broadly. How is data on important policy issues, such as students' destinations, actually used, if at all? Does it

DOI: 10.4324/9781003201366-20

Figure 17.1 A tale of visiting three cities – Helsinki, Amsterdam and London

filter into national or institutional decision-making? Is it ignored or even abused? To address these questions, I applied for a full-time PhD at the University of Birmingham in the UK.

Conducting a comparative study

I have long been fascinated with the similarities and differences between educational systems across national settings. I believe that understanding the logic of different regimes can help expose what we usually take for granted about the school system we grew up in. This deep-seated interest prompted the idea of using an internationally comparative design for my PhD. That, and the hope to travel a bit too! I decided to use the European Union and affiliated countries as a geographical frame to explore the process of Europeanisation of education as well (Ladrech, 2010; Lawn and Grek, 2012; Vink, 2003).

Comparing across national, societal and cultural boundaries is rewarding, although it has its own challenges relating to our understanding of the context, as well as the language used (Hantrais, 2009; Phillips and Schweisfurth, 2006). A systematic and profound examination of the broader societal setting is necessary so that a deeper understanding can be reached. Researching our native contexts allows some assumptions to be made, that are often missing when comparing countries that we are unfamiliar with. Beyond rapid reviews of how schooling works in the selected case-study countries, for this study I drew on interviews with educational researchers to point me to pertinent debates and issues within each system. Regarding language, I had to acknowledge that English as a common medium of communication throughout this project can only be an imperfect substitute for direct communication, with some data loss occurring. Although this was my first major project where I interviewed in English, I could draw on my substantive experience from doing so in Hungarian.

The research strategy consisted of two key phases – an exploratory first phase using a cross-sectional design, followed by a second in-depth comparative case study design. This international comparative research project employed a mixed-methods approach for collecting and analysing data – triangulating between different types of evidence and sources.

Given the paucity of evidence, I used the initial cross-sectional design to explore what type of *school leavers' and graduates' information systems* exist – abbreviated as the rather clunky SLGIS. Throughout this phase I used documentary data, drawing on content analysis. I had to employ both my diverse language skills – Hungarian, English, and a little bit of Spanish and German. But where not feasible, I utilised online translation tools. The key research questions in this phase revolved around the aims and methodology of the SLGIS across Europe. Based on the key characteristics of research designs and sampling frames of SLGIS, I created a typology to serve as the basis for selecting the case study countries for the second phase.

To explore how these information systems are set up, and how the resultant outcomes are drawn on by different stakeholders, I decided to focus on three countries, namely England, Finland and the Netherlands. Throughout the roughly two-week field visits to the Netherlands as well as Finland, and over the course of several weeks traveling around in England I collected data from a total of 60 experts in 44 personal or group interviews. As Table 17.1 shows, I interviewed ministerial civil servants; school or university teachers, academics and professionals with a portfolio in careers and employability; and research institute representatives. As suggested earlier, I also talked to several educational research experts, both about the schooling and university system in the given country, and their experiences of using the SLGIS as a source of secondary evidence. Throughout the

Table 17.1 Number of interviews and interviewees in each case-study country

	Netherlands	*England*	*Finland*
Research Institute	5	3	3
Ministry	3	2	3
School/University	5	5	5
Research expert	2	3	5
TOTAL number of interviews	15	13	16
TOTAL number of interviewees	18	19	23

fieldwork I also collected a wide array of further documentary data, especially grey literature partly suggested by the interviewees.

The semi-structured interviews were broadly similar in scope within the groups of interviewees, and had comparable elements between them. Tailoring the interviews to the interviewees meant a high number of variables to work with whilst preparing for fieldwork, but it helped in gaining detailed and comprehensive information.

The number of interviews conducted was deemed appropriate, given I had to be able to assess both how SLGIS are set up and utilised in each country. The 44 interviews took several months to transcribe, and resulted in a 200,000-word corpus for analysis. I decided to transcribe the interview audio files myself partly due to lacking the funds to pay for professional transcription, and partly to ease the process of analysis. As a result, I came to know my data very well, aiding me substantially throughout coding, analysis and writing up. I used thematic analysis, focusing on the key areas of interest in the research. Although I had very good NVivo training, I decided to run my coding in a simple Word file, because the coding tree I used was fairly straightforward.

To ease the comparison at a later stage, I initially wrote national case studies, structuring the three texts in the same manner. These documents were then offered for checking to the interviewees, who on some occasions asked for some omissions to be made in the final text. This process of course was part of my ethics application to both my home institution, and some of the local institutions where I interviewed.

The three case studies were prefaced in the thesis with a brief discussion of how the national school and university systems and the local SLGIS are structured. These country profiles helped locate the key issues of the three education systems, such that the subsequent analysis could then focus on comparing different features of the SLGIS.

Through the initial, exploratory phase of the research, I very quickly had results to discuss, and as such, I got over the initial fear of writing early. In fact, I turned the chapter in which I published these results into a journal article before finishing my PhD (Hordósy, 2014). This meant that I arrived to my viva with the acceptance letter of my first publication from this research. The subsequent two papers were a "harder sell", given they seemed to fall between journal interests. However, I published the key findings on the discrepancies of data production and utilisation (Hordósy, 2017), as well as on Europeanisation of data systems (Hordósy, 2016).

Key findings: SLGIS in Europe

The key findings of this research are summarised around the aims, research design and methods, the history, institutional set up and financing, utilisation by groups of stakeholders and the European view. The school leavers' and graduates' information systems (SLGIS) in this research were defined by three key criteria, such as:

a. Collecting and analysing data at the national level;
b. Provide evidence on outcomes from secondary as well as tertiary levels of education; and
c. Gather data from more than one cohort, or contact the same cohort several times.

Using these criteria, my research distinguished four key types of SLGIS in regard to what they *aim to capture*, (1) transition process from school-to-school or school-to-work; (2) lifespan of young people more generally; (3) destinations of the leavers or graduates; and (4) young people's first impressions of being in the labour market. Mostly these information systems did not provide in-depth information on socio-economic background of students, or much contextual information about their school or university. This meant that "schools and universities that have more non-traditional or low socioeconomic-status students, or are situated in economically deprived areas, may appear not to be performing as well as they actually are". The emphasis of SLGIS was on the short-term labour market outcomes, without much contextualisation based on student characteristics, concentrating on the monetary gains of education rather than a broader view of outcomes. As an interviewee at an English university remarked:

> It's a trade-off, really: six months is long enough for people to have gone and got a job and still the contact details held by the institution are good enough to get into contact with these people, but six months isn't long enough for them to have necessarily got the job that recognises the job that they were capable of getting following the qualification that they've got…

Regarding the *different research strategies*, SLGIS were categorised using the dichotomies of longitudinal OR cross-sectional designs, and sample-surveys OR censuses. The optimal design depended on the aims, and how the data gathered will be utilised. An information system that is used in the audit and evaluation process of educational institutions should collect data on virtually every former student or graduate. A data collection that feeds back to the institution the perception of how useful the former education was, should use a questionnaire to reach a part of the cohort. An information system serving national policy planning should make causal claims possible through a longitudinal design; a data collection that is used in career guidance should provide longer-term up-to-date information on transitions from school to work. In terms of permitting the analysis of returns of education and training, comparability between the different levels and sectors of the educational system over a longer period of time is desirable.

However, changes in how the SLGIS were set up, run, and the issues they focus on were constrained by the benefits of prior points in the time-series that the new data can be compared against, as suggested by a Dutch interviewee:

> There was much debate about the questionnaire that [they] have to change it completely. And then [a research organisation] said: please don't! Because (…) we cannot make our monitor on student drop-outs.

The interest of the different stakeholders did not always align; there were some discrepancies of data production and utilisation. Because these information systems tended to be centrally funded, the interests of government, and national policy makers impacted strongly on the design and focus. Their interest tended to centre on short-term labour market outcomes, with the option to compare institutions, whilst gaining national level trend-data. One issue then was that a short-term view on wages and type of employment did not provide sufficient information to practitioners working in careers information, advice and guidance, or researchers interested in exploring the broader context and socio-economic determinants of school leaving and graduate outcomes. Similarly, institutional stakeholders were more interested in longer-term outcomes, providing information on satisfaction with school or university, as well as skills and competences gained and used.

Beyond the discrepancies of data production and whose interests the SLGIS with different designs satisfy, my research identified further issues relating to their utilisation. Such discrepancies were especially clear when the SLGIS were employed in a manner they were not designed for (Hordósy, 2017). For instance, some of the SLGIS used to *inform students* at the institutional level, suggesting career pathways others from the student's school or university took recently. Given the increased policy interest on school and university outcomes, the national policy level followed suit, for instance using the English university level survey to "inform student choice". They provided data on recent graduates' outcomes to current secondary school students. Note the difference in timeframes here: the gap between data-collection and "informing" in the latter case is much longer, and the realities of both the university experience and the labour market outcomes could be very different several years on. A second example of discrepancies of data utilisation relates to using the SLGIS in *evaluating education*, whereby institutions had to react to the shifts in national policy approaches. Using the same English example on the Destinations of Leavers from Higher Education (DLHE), one interviewee from an English research institute suggested:

(...) when [the DLHE] started it was very much designed by the careers people as a tool for (...) evaluating their own work, and also to provide them with information for the next cohort through. Whereas these days, and I think the big switch was round about 2000 to be honest, there is much more of an emphasis on... or there was that stage what became the new emphasis was performance measurement. It suddenly became about measuring the performance of the universities.

A third example on the discrepancies relates to *monitoring the educational system*, whereby the distance between data custodians, such as statistics agencies, and researchers in academic institutions often made data sharing problematic. As one of the researchers at a Finnish university remarked:

> I had these big dreams of getting this huge pile of data and the [statistics agency] do have it, they have the data, it would be quite easy to give it to us. But because of these strict privacy policies, I decided that it wasn't worth the money and the effort.

Given the SLGIS closely mirrored the structure of the corresponding educational systems, I could not observe substantive convergence between the SLGIS across Europe. As such, it was not just school-to-work transitions that were path-dependent (Raffe, 2008), but also the SLGIS that capture information about them (Hordósy, 2016). The international comparative view over school leaving and graduation could be seen in other sources, such as the Labour Force Survey. Further, some convergence could be observed on more specific policy issues such as young people not in education, employment or training, or graduate outcomes in Bologna-process across the European Higher Education Area.

Taken together, this research showed that there was a clear rationale to include a broader set of information-needs when setting up the SLGIS, beyond that of central governments. Otherwise educational institutions could not be expected to respond to the presented outcomes meaningfully, and the resultant data would not be used widely as secondary evidence by researchers. Without a commitment to making sure that the SLGIS work for a broader set of stakeholders, their value for money could be called into question.

Reflections on the PhD

I thoroughly enjoyed setting up this project, organising the various interviews, and talking to a diverse group of people in 9 to 10 cities in three different countries. It is an incredible feeling to start understanding an array of different education systems, and I found writing the case studies very easy. The harder aspect was editing the text to fit the word limits of a thesis, and working out how the comparisons across the cases can be presented best. Substantive parts of what I intended to have in the main text had to be relegated to the appendices, making these "extras" add another 200 pages to the already lengthy text.

I received the School of Education scholarship from the University of Birmingham to carry out this project. This meant that I could focus on this research full-time, without the concerns of other work commitments. I managed to save some of my maintenance funds and money from smaller research projects, thus creating a very tight, but sufficient budget for the fieldwork in Finland and the Netherlands, and the train fares within England. Travelling across Europe was relatively cheap and easy. To a degree I could draw on friends, or friends of friends for accommodation, although I am unsure how safe this would be deemed by a stricter ethics board.

There were many people I could draw on for support. I had experienced supervisors, who provided suggestions and encouragement where useful. They helped me both with the research, as well as broader career development whilst being a PhD student – such as supporting me in my first teaching engagement and conference talks, providing feedback on my papers, and tips for job applications. The projects I worked with them on taught me new skills and gave me further research experience, as well as English language publications.

Throughout the PhD I was part of a very good postgraduate community, with regular socials, and colleagues who became great friends to this day. Being able to share the isolating experience of a PhD was very important to me – in this sense, it did not matter whether we were in the same discipline or not. I also believe that an early exposure to international conferences helped build my confidence in presenting my research findings, whilst gaining insights into different perspectives on my own work, and broadening my networks.

What did I gain through this research experience?

This large-scale, international comparative study proved my capacity in gathering, organising and analysing substantive amount of data, as well as working in diverse environments and in several locations successfully. I gained a lot of specific research methods experience, such as interviewing different stakeholder groups and experts, and using content analysis to work through a substantial amount of documentary evidence.

Upon finishing my doctoral research, I started a role as a post-doctoral researcher, leading on a longitudinal study that explored student experiences at a British university. This project utilised administrative data to explore the patterns across the student body, as well as yearly interviews with a subset of 40 students. My published work from this project ranges from student loans, part-time work and budgeting, to extracurricular activities and career planning, as well as student experiences of the link between research and teaching.

In 2019, I gained a research fellowship at the University of Nottingham, which brought together my aspiration to conduct research internationally, as well as my newfound interest in higher education more broadly, and the research and teaching nexus specifically. In this role, I get to work across several national settings, in England, in Norway, and – after 10 years of absence – in Hungary. Of course the COVID-19 pandemic meant substantive changes to my original plans, for instance the majority of my interviews had to be conducted online, rather than face-to-face. Nonetheless, I thoroughly enjoy exploring different national systems again! I am also currently working with four doctoral students across three smaller-scale research projects relating to my work, and I get very excited exploring different sets of data with these colleagues.

Why might this type of research be easier now?

Due to the technological change that has occurred in the past ten years, this type of research would be much easier to conduct, with some aspects becoming speedier too. When I attempted online interviewing in 2012, there were crucial issues with software stability as well as sound quality. Nonetheless, where I could not meet interviewees face to face, I had to use this approach. Ten years later, there is a much-improved choice of software for online calls, and in the face of the COVID-19 pandemic most of us are more familiar with their use. These tools mean that interviewing online has become considerably easier to organise. As such, you can both minimise the cost of fieldwork and have the option of a longer and more flexible timeframe for data collection. Of course, I recognise that my interviewees for the PhD were professional adults – and that not all potential participants can be approached online. Further, there has been substantial development in speech recognition software and several online systems have automatic subtitling modes now, too. These can be used to speed up transcription, although only in major languages. Similarly, the translating capacity and quality of a diverse array of online tools will aid the work with documents, and internet browser plug-ins can be used to translate whole websites to the desired language.

I would very much encourage prospective doctoral students to entertain this kind of research if it fits with their broader research aims, given the learning and skills development process, and the important results it is likely to produce.

References

Hantrais, L. (2009). *International Comparative Research: Theory, Methods and Practice*. Basingstoke: Palgrave Macmillan.

Hordósy, R. (2014). Who knows what school leavers and graduates are doing? Comparing information systems within Europe. *Comparative Education*, 50(4), pp. 448–473. doi: 10.1080/03050068.2014.887370

Hordósy, R. (2016). "Tracing" Europeanisation: School leavers' and graduates' information systems as an example. *Research in Comparative and International Education*, 11(2), pp. 135–147. doi: 10.1177/1745499916632978

Hordósy, R. (2017). How do different stakeholders utilise the same data? The case of school leavers' and graduates' information systems in three European countries. *International Journal of Research & Method in Education*, 40(4), pp. 403–420. doi: 10.1080/1743727X.2016.1144740

Ladrech, R. (2010). *Europeanization and National Politics*. Basingstoke: Palgrave Macmillan.

Lawn, M., and Grek, S. (2012). *Europeanizing Education: Governing a New Policy Space*. Oxford: Symposium Books.

Phillips, D., and Schweisfurth, M. (2006). *Comparative and International Education: An Introduction to Theory, Method and Practice*. London: Continuum.

Raffe, D. (2008). The concept of transition system. *Journal of Education and Work*, 21(4), pp. 277–296. doi: 10.1080/13639080802360952

Vink, M. (2003). What is Europeanisation? And other questions on a new research agenda. *European Political Science*, 3(1), pp. 63–74. doi: 10.1057/eps.2003.36

CHAPTER 18

Evidence translation strategies to promote the use of research results in schools: What works best?

Caner Erkan

Introduction

This chapter presents a brief summary of doctoral research investigating how research evidence can be best translated into use for teachers. It begins with a rationale for the study, then presents methods used in the study, and concludes with the findings and their implications.

There is increasing interest in using evidence in practice, and this is nowadays regarded as an international movement in education (Siddiqui, 2020). In schools, evidence can show what works in a particular context, which can help teachers decide on their teaching approaches and strategies (Scott and McNeish, 2013). Also, research evidence can show what does not work, which is crucial not to waste money and time by implementing ineffective strategies (Gorard, 2020). Therefore, using evidence in education is regarded as an important factor contributing to improved student attainment (Cook and Odom, 2013). The use of evidence in schools is being encouraged so that teachers can decide on the most promising teaching strategies (See et al., 2015). For these reasons, many attempts have been made to generate more robust research evidence, such as the Evidence for Policy and Practice Information and Coordinating Centre (the EPPI-Centre), What Works Clearinghouses (WWC), the American Institutes for Research (AIR, www.air.org), and the Education Endowment Foundation (EEF). Despite these efforts and considerable progress in producing robust evaluations providing more secure evidence (Gorard et al., 2020), the use of evidence in schools by teachers is still very limited (Dagenais et al., 2012; Walker et al., 2019).

One issue to consider, in order to facilitate the use of research evidence in schools, is how evidence is best presented to practitioners. There have been efforts to summarise research findings better, such as in the EEF Pupil Premium Toolkit, summarising research evidence on different programmes and interventions, with estimates of their impact, the strength of

DOI: 10.4324/9781003201366-21

231

the evidence, and costs (See et al., 2015). More radically, Segedin (2017) proposed that instead of using traditional dissemination approaches like workshops, creative and innovative ones like theatre should be preferred.

However, the impact evidence of such dissemination methods on teachers' take-up of research is still unclear. Although there has been considerable progress in producing research evidence, little attention has been paid to providing equivalently good evidence on the effectiveness of dissemination approaches (Gorard et al., 2020). My PhD study contributes to this literature through a systematic review of the existing evidence on the most effective ways of disseminating research evidence to teachers, and a randomised control trial (RCT) to evaluate the most promising intervention based on the review findings. In the findings of systematic review, one of the most promising interventions was workshop training with ongoing support and evidence-based resources. The development and planning of teacher training workshop was feasible given time and resources available. The intervention workshop and outcome measures were chosen considering the findings of the review and other factors such as training budget and timeframe.

The review and subsequent evaluation questions addressed in the study are:

- What is the existing evidence on the most effective ways of disseminating research evidence to teachers?
- What is the impact of workshop training with supporting evidence-based resources on teachers' attitudes towards use of research evidence in schools?
- What is the impact of workshop training with supporting evidence-based resources on teachers' use of research evidence in schools?

A systematic review of the most promising interventions

The first research question was addressed via a systematic review.

Methods

The search involved a primary and complementary search. In the primary search, the studies were identified through 10 electronic databases and Google Scholar in February 2019. The search was for studies about research use (or similar), its quality, in education, and not health sciences (where most of the studies are). For information about evidence in health sciences and other fields see Gorard et al. (2020). Search strings were created, tested, and refined. An example for use with the ERIC database is:

(("Research knowledge" OR evidence) N/2 (use OR used OR using OR utilis* OR utiliz*
    OR uptak* OR transf* OR translat* OR modif* OR engag* OR summar* OR access*
    OR disseminat* OR mobilis* OR mobiliz* OR implement* OR present* OR bring* OR
    push* OR shar*)) OR (research N/1 (use OR used OR using OR utilis* OR utiliz* OR
    transf* OR translat* OR disseminat*)) OR ("evidence into practice" OR "research into
    practice")

AND
facilitate* OR improv* OR promot* OR increas* OR develop* OR support* OR effective*
    OR better OR best OR strateg* OR pathway* OR intervention

AND
education OR school* OR college* OR classroom* OR teach* OR learn* OR educator*
    OR student* OR children OR pupil* OR achieve* OR attainment OR exam* OR
    attendance

NOT
health* OR dent* OR medic* OR nurses OR nursing OR clinic*

The number of studies found from each database and Google Scholar
appear in Table 18.1. A further 1,237 records were identified through
complementary searches, including suggestions by experts and looking at
the references used in other reviews. A total of 68,308 pieces were considered
by title alone, or title and abstract.

Screening was conducted with selection criteria that included the following. I was looking for:

- Intervention studies such as RCTs, quasi-experimental, regression discontinuity, or any evaluation studies involving cross-sectional or pre-post
  comparisons to test an intervention
- Studies available in English
- Studies published between January 2000 and May 2019

Table 18.1 The number of records found in each database

Database/engine	Number of hits
Applied Social Sciences Index and Abstracts – ASSIA	2,262
Australian Education Index – AEI	1,717
British Education Index – BEI	457
Educational Resources Information Center – ERIC	9,477
International Bibliography of the Social Sciences – IBSS	5,607
PsychINFO	6,717
Scopus	13,888
ProQuest dissertations and theses global	15,087
Social Services Abstracts – SSA	1,090
Social Science Citation Index – SSCI	7,820
Google Scholar	2,949
Total	67,071

There were no restrictions on the location of the study, or the age groups taught in school.

Pilot screening was conducted with a second independent reviewer, using 2,750 randomly selected reports, and the titles and/or abstracts were screened. Inter-rater reliability calculated for Cohen's kappa was 0.91, which means there was a strong agreement between two reviewers (McHugh, 2012). After the pilot, all records were screened by the author, and 24 studies fitting the criteria were identified for the synthesis.

The "sieve" approach suggested by Gorard et al. (2017) was used to judge the quality of the studies in terms of generating secure evidence. This provides guidelines for reviewers to help them rate studies from 0 (the weakest) to 4 (the best realistically possible) by considering their design, scale, missing data, and data quality. Full details of the screening and data extraction, including quality judgements, are in the thesis.

Findings

Among the 24 studies there was evidence of evaluations relevant to improving teachers' knowledge of or attitudes to research, increasing their use of research evidence, and whether student outcomes improved as a result. Each type of outcome is dealt with separately. Where a study has more than one of these outcomes these are handled separately, and the study may have different quality ratings for these different outcomes. For example, a study with the same design for two outcomes may have different amounts of missing data for each. Or one outcome (such as attitudes) may be measured on a less robust scale (than statutory tests perhaps).

Table 18.2 summarises the review findings on nine studies with knowledge/attitude outcomes. Perhaps the first thing to notice is that there are no robust studies (graded 3 or 4) on these outcomes. As have been found in reviews before, the weakest studies tend to have positive outcomes. It is not

Table 18.2 How to improve attitudes to research?

Study	Quality	Approach	Impact
Ely et al. (2018)	2	Technology	Positive
Lord et al. (2017b)	2	Research summaries	Null/negative
Purper (2015)	2	Active single component	Positive
Rose et al. (2017)	2	Active single component	Unclear/mixed
Griggs et al. (2016)	1	Active multi-component	Null/negative
Briand-Lamarche et al. (2016)	1	Research summaries	Positive
Mady (2013)	1	Technology	Positive
Ogunleye (2014)	1	Collaborative	Positive
Speight et al. (2016)	1	Active multi-component	Positive

clear whether this is due to publication bias, or even conflict of interest for the evaluators. Focusing on the studies rated 2 or higher it seems that the results are very mixed.

In a study, involving 22 pre-service teachers, Ely et al. (2018) tried to improve teachers' knowledge regarding research evidence on reading through a classroom simulation. After the intervention, teachers had improved their knowledge somewhat. The scale of this study (only 22 cases in total), and its weak design (before and after scores) illustrate how poor the studies rated 1 are. These very weak studies are largely ignored here, as providing no useful evidence.

In another RCT by Purper (2015) involving 96 teachers (control 48, intervention 48), teachers were given information regarding five websites disseminating evidence and training. Although teachers showed more positive attitudes towards research, the intervention made no difference in teachers' actual use of the websites.

Table 18.3, on increasing research use among teachers, again shows no especially robust studies, and again with the weakest studies disproportionately positive. One of the positive impact outcomes came from Doabler et al. (2013). This trial by involved 129 classrooms (61 control and 68 intervention) covering about 2,700 students. The study examined the impact of the intervention on teachers' use of research evidence in mathematics. The students of the intervention teachers showed more positive results than control teachers.

Table 18.3 How to improve research use?

Study	Quality	Approach	Impact
Doabler et al. (2013)	2	Embedded	Positive
Ely et al. (2014)	2	Technology	Positive
Lord et al. (2017b)	2	Research summaries	Null/negative
Purper (2015)	2	Active single component	Null/negative
Rose et al. (2017)	2	Active single component	Positive
Walker et al. (2019)	2	Active multi-component	Positive
Griggs et al. (2016)	1	Active multi-component	Null/negative
Kretlow et al. (2011)	1	Active multi-component	Positive
Kutash et al. (2009)	1	Collaborative	Unclear/mixed
Briand-Lamarche et al. (2016)	1	Research summaries	Unclear/mixed
Learmond (2017)	1	Active single component	Positive
Maheady et al. (2004)	1	Active multi-component	Positive
Ogunleye (2014)	1	Collaborative	Positive
Sawyer (2015)	1	Collaborative	Positive
Schnorr (2013)	1	Active multi-component	Positive
Speight et al. (2016)	1	Active multi-component	Unclear/mixed
Vaughn and Coleman (2004)	1	Active single component	Positive

The study by Ely et al. (2014), involved 49 pre-service teachers randomly allocated to one of two treatment groups. It examined the impact of a multimedia-based approach consisting of video and advanced podcasting on evidence-based vocabulary practices on teachers' behaviours. The intervention teachers implemented more evidence-based practices than the control group teachers who simply read the same material.

Rose et al. (2017) used school-based evidence champions and workshop training for teachers as an intervention. The study involved 119 schools (59 control, 60 intervention) and found some positive changes in attitudes, but there was no evidence of impact on teachers' use of research or on their pupils' Key Stage 2 reading outcomes.

Four studies (Walker et al., 2019; Kretlow et al., 2011; Maheady et al., 2004 and Schnorr, 2013) used professional development for teachers in the form of workshop training with follow-up support. All reported improved teachers' use of research evidence, although only one of these studies is rated 2 in quality. Lord 2017 is discussed below.

The strongest studies in the review appear in Table 18.4. And, probably not coincidentally, none of these has reported positive impacts. The strongest studies show that merely providing teachers with summaries or digest of research, however well-constructed, will not improve their students' attainment.

Lord et al. (2017a) involved 12,500 primary schools, randomly allocated to four intervention and one control group. It examined the impact of disseminating various evidence-based resources and research summaries on pupils' Key Stage 2 English scores. None of the interventions led to improved student attainment.

Lord et al. (2017b) involved 823 primary schools (60 for each of nine intervention groups and 283 for the control). The interventions were similar to those in Lord et al. (2017a) but added ongoing support to use the summaries, or not. It investigated the impact of interventions on Key Stage 2

Table 18.4 How to improve student outcomes?

Study	Quality	Approach	Impact
Lord et al. (2017a)	4	Research summaries	Null/negative
Lord et al. (2017b)	4	Research summaries	Null/negative
Rose et al. (2017)	3	Active single component	Null/negative
Wiggins et al. (2019)	3	Active multi-component	Unclear/mixed
Clarke et al. (2011)	2	Embedded	Positive
See et al. (2015)	2	Collaborative	Null/negative
Abbott et al. (2002)	1	Collaborative	Positive
Kutash et al. (2009)	1	Collaborative	Unclear/mixed
Maheady et al. (2004)	1	Active multi-component	Positive

English scores and teachers' use of, and attitudes towards research use. None of the interventions was linked to significant improvements.

The only 2-rated study with a positive impact is Clarke et al. (2011). They conducted an RCT, involving more than 1,300 students, to examine the impact of the Early Learning in Mathematics (ELM) curriculum, which is based research evidence embedded within it. It is intended for students at risk in mathematics, and it improved their attainment compared with other students. Coupled with another study using embedded evidence outlined above, this appears to be a promising route. It is also simple. Instead of trying to get teachers to engage with research, they can simply be provided with programmes and resources that are robustly evidence-based.

Wiggins et al. (2019) conducted an RCT, involving 40 secondary schools (20 randomised to each group), to examine the impact of an intervention based on supporting research leads from schools with Continuing Professional Development (CPD) sessions. The intervention students made only small progress in mathematics and English compared with the control group.

In a quasi-experimental study by See et al. (2015), teachers in the intervention group read and discussed a research article on classroom feedback. They were supported with extensive training in their own departments to develop action research cycles for improvement. There was no evidence that the intervention pupils made more progress than the comparator pupils.

An impact evaluation of training with further support

The second and third research questions were addressed with a RCT.

Methods

One clear message from the review was that simply presenting research summaries does not work. Following the review, it was decided to adopt an intervention based on workshop training with supporting evidence-based resources (Figure 18.1). The study involved nine local primary schools, randomly allocated to the intervention (n = 4) or control (n = 5). Before the intervention, teachers who took part in the study from the intervention (n = 25) and control group (n = 21) completed a pre-survey asking about their attitudes to and use of research evidence. The survey was adapted and modified from The Evidence-Based Practice Attitude Scale (EBPAS) by Aarons (2004), and the Teachers' Utilization of Research Findings Questionnaire by Ogunleye (2014).

Figure 18.1 Workshop on assessing the trustworthiness of research findings

Participating teachers were offered a two hour workshop based on helping teachers to understand research evidence. It was led by a research professor at Durham University in February 2020. The workshop was recorded and shared with intervention group teachers via headteachers at the beginning of March 2020. This allowed teachers unable to attend to take the workshop, and also allowed participants to refresh their memory. Teachers were also given supporting evidence-based resources in the form of handouts (also supplied electronically).

Due to the COVID-19 pandemic emerging after March 2020, teachers were given extra time to complete the follow up survey. However, this still led to considerable dropout. Dropout is common in pre-post evaluations, but the pandemic made it worse for this study. Table 18.5 shows participants for the baseline and outcome. Full details of the initial responses by those who dropped out, and more comprehensive analyses, are shown in the thesis. Overall, pre-survey mean scores of teachers who missed the post-survey did not differ much from those who still responded.

Table 18.5 The number of participants for the pre-survey and post-survey

	Schools	Teachers pre-survey	Teachers post-survey
Intervention group N	4	25	12
Control group N	5	21	13
Total	9	46	25

Findings

Teachers were asked eight questions about their general attitudes towards research evidence. Table 18.6 shows the pre-survey and post survey results for 25 teachers (control 13, and intervention 12). It also shows the changes from pre- to post, and the difference in the changes between the two groups as an "effect" size (the difference in gain divided by their overall standard deviation).

The results are not encouraging. The intervention group are now less likely than the control group to report that that they would try new research-based interventions, or indeed any new intervention. And they are less likely to say that programme protocols are more important than their experience, or that academic researchers could know better than them how to care for students. Of course, these items may not be interpreted in the same way as in a US context, or perhaps "care" would be better expressed as "improve my students' attainment". But the changes in Table 18.6 are relative to the control group faced with the same items.

A further seven questions were about the influences that might affect teachers' use of a new intervention. The intervention teachers were now less

Table 18.6 Comparison of the pre- and post-intervention survey results, attitudes

Item	Group	Pre mean	Post mean	Gain	SD	Effect size
Research-based interventions/ methods are not useful in practice	Control	1.54	0.77	−0.77	1.77	+0.72
	Treatment	1.08	1.58	+0.50		
Experience is more important than using manualised interventions/methods	Control	1.62	1.92	+0.30	0.90	+0.04
	Treatment	2.08	2.42	+0.34		
I am willing to use new interventions developed by researchers	Control	3.15	3.15	0.00	0.99	−0.34
	Treatment	3.17	2.83	−0.34		
I like to use new interventions to help my students	Control	3.15	3.00	−0.15	0.65	−0.15
	Treatment	3.08	2.83	−0.25		
I am willing to try new interventions even if I have to follow a manual	Control	2.69	3.00	+0.31	1.07	−0.30
	Treatment	2.76	2.75	−0.01		
I know better than academic researchers how to care for my students.	Control	1.46	1.62	+0.16	1.17	+0.22
	Treatment	1.58	2.00	+0.42		
I would not use manualised interventions/methods.	Control	0.67	0.38	−0.29	1.26	+0.29
	Treatment	1.00	1.08	+0.08		
I would try a new intervention even if it were very different from what I am used to	Control	2.92	3.08	+0.16	0.97	−0.60
	Treatment	2.92	2.50	−0.42		

likely to use an intervention based on evidence, or indeed under any other circumstances (Table 18.7). Some of these "effect" sizes are quite sizeable.

Participants may have been concerned about the complexity of research reports, assuming that they had to read them:

> *Yeah I think there is a lot in there that you feel does not need to be there potentially.*

Or simply the vast choice of different interventions, and the difficulty of getting good information about them:

> *I think if you didn't know anything about any of them, it is really difficult to choose which is best.*

In practice, it is easier to do what others recommend:

> *I heard about it and heard it works well.*

The workshop and materials did emphasise the importance of judging the quality of the research evidence. Not all evidence is equal. And real-life examples were discussed which presented evidence for approaches that might actually not be trustworthy. This may have made the intervention group actually more wary of trusting and using research, without giving

Table 18.7 Comparison of the pre- and post-intervention survey results, attitudes

If you received training in an intervention that was new to you, how likely would you be to adopt it if:	Group	Pre mean	Post mean	Gain	SD	Effect size
Evidence said it worked?	Control	2.92	3.15	+0.23	0.84	−0.48
	Treatment	3.17	3.00	−0.17		
It was intuitively appealing?	Control	2.46	2.69	+0.23	1.04	−0.29
	Treatment	2.65	2.58	−0.07		
It "made sense" to you?	Control	2.62	3.08	+0.46	0.98	−0.39
	Treatment	3.00	3.08	+0.08		
It was required by your school (head teacher, principal etc.)?	Control	3.08	3.38	+0.30	0.84	−0.86
	Treatment	3.42	3.00	−0.42		
It was required by law?	Control	3.46	3.46	0.00	0.79	−0.10
	Treatment	3.58	3.50	−0.08		
It was being used by colleagues who were happy with it?	Control	2.77	3.15	+0.38	0.84	−0.25
	Treatment	3.08	3.25	+0.17		
You felt you had enough training to use it correctly?	Control	3.15	3.54	+0.39	0.73	−0.77
	Treatment	3.42	3.25	−0.17		

them sufficient confidence to make informed judgements about the quality of evidence.

Teachers were also asked 18 items regarding their (self-reported) use of research evidence (Table 18.8). The results are mixed. Intervention teachers are now more likely to report using research to prepare lessons, and to be effective in delivery and use of materials. But in all other respects they are now less likely than the control group to use research for any other reason. Perhaps they have become more discriminating, and realising what research evidence can and cannot do for them. Or perhaps these responses reflect the kind of real-life examples of research use in the workshop.

Conclusions and implications

The study set out to review the existing evidence on the most effective ways to disseminate research evidence to teachers, and then evaluate one of the promising approaches according to the review findings.

The review identified 24 studies, most of which are weak in terms of providing high-quality evidence. They also cover a wide range of possible outcomes from changing attitudes to improving student test scores. The best studies providing the most secure evidence were only about passive approaches to encouraging evidence use (sometimes with light active support). And these clearly did not work for their intended outcomes.

Rather than wasting resources on passive dissemination, we should focus on more promising approaches to evidence use. Technology-supported routes, embedding evidence in curriculum, collaborative or multi-component approaches can be considered for new evaluations. Even if the studies did not provide high-quality evidence on these approaches, at least there was no high-quality evidence that shows they did *not* work. The study confirms that, as Gorard et al. (2020) claim, there is lack of secure evidence on dissemination routes. Hence, further studies, particularly large-scale trials on different routes, need to be done to make better comparisons. Getting evidence-into use is not straightforward. It requires more and considerable attention.

The impact evaluation found no clear positive impact of the intervention on teachers' attitudes towards research evidence use – rather the reverse. So one possible conclusion is that attitudes may not matter very much. We need to focus more on use of evidence, and its impact. Of course, the evaluation was affected by COVID lockdown, and should be repeated at a larger scale. The instrument was probably too long, especially given that it did not eventually produce responses that could be neatly summarised in factor analysis. Perhaps the whole section on attitudes could be dropped.

Table 18.8 Comparison of the pre- and post-intervention survey results, behaviour

Level of agreement with "I utilize information from research":	Group	Pre mean	Post mean	Gain	SD	Effect size
to get acquainted with effective teaching strategies	Control	2.54	2.85	+0.31	1.04	−0.78
	Treatment	2.83	2.33	−0.50		
to help in improving my learners' progress	Control	2.85	3.08	+0.23	0.97	−0.75
	Treatment	3.00	2.50	−0.50		
for innovations in school curricula	Control	2.54	3.00	+0.46	0.94	−0.40
	Treatment	2.67	2.75	+0.08		
on how to improve my learners' interest in schooling	Control	2.62	2.75	+0.13	0.83	−0.46
	Treatment	3.00	2.75	−0.25		
to source better evaluation techniques for day-to-day activities	Control	2.31	2.62	+0.31	1.02	−0.51
	Treatment	2.67	2.46	−0.21		
in order to prepare my lessons well	Control	2.77	2.62	−0.15	1.01	+0.62
	Treatment	2.33	2.81	+0.48		
to help me in effective delivery of instruction	Control	2.85	2.76	−0.09	0.74	+0.32
	Treatment	2.75	2.90	+0.15		
for effective use of instructional materials	Control	2.31	2.46	+0.15	0.89	+0.30
	Treatment	2.25	2.67	+0.42		
to become knowledgeable on recent theories of child development	Control	2.00	2.46	+0.46	0.89	−0.43
	Treatment	2.67	2.75	+0.08		
for theories behind various new teaching strategies	Control	2.38	2.67	+0.29	1.10	−0.18
	Treatment	2.58	2.67	+0.09		
to improve my content knowledge of school subjects	Control	2.38	2.54	+0.16	0.97	+0.07
	Treatment	2.75	2.98	+0.23		
for the acquisition of more pedagogical knowledge	Control	2.62	2.85	+0.23	1.01	−0.23
	Treatment	2.50	2.50	0.00		
for more effective classroom management techniques	Control	2.31	2.85	+0.54	1.07	−0.74
	Treatment	3.17	2.92	−0.25		
for skills at motivating and reinforcing my learners in learning	Control	2.77	3.00	+0.23	1.04	−0.37
	Treatment	2.72	2.57	−0.15		
to acquire knowledge and skills in using modern questioning techniques in class	Control	2.54	2.67	+0.13	0.75	−0.35
	Treatment	2.80	2.67	−0.13		
for further verification of research findings	Control	2.15	2.31	+0.16	1.29	−0.12
	Treatment	2.00	2.01	+0.01		
to increase the level of classroom interaction i.e. teacher-student, student-student and student-material interactions	Control	2.46	2.54	+0.08	1.12	−0.29
	Treatment	2.83	2.58	−0.25		
to assist me in planning and carrying out research involving my learners	Control	2.23	2.62	+0.39	1.09	−0.28
	Treatment	2.33	2.42	+0.09		

Future work should also use more resource-intensive methods, such as observation, to assess the extent to which teachers really are using evidence.

The findings of the study further support the need for more and better evaluations. Researchers can adopt their interventions by taking account of this study.

References

Aarons, G. (2004). Mental health provider attitudes toward adoption of evidence-based practice: The evidence-based practice attitude scale (ebpas). *Mental Health Services Research*, 6(2), pp. 61–74. doi: 10.1023/b:mhsr.0000024351.12294.65

Abbott, M., Walton, C., and Greenwood, C.R. (2002). Phonemic awareness in kindergarten and first grade. *Teaching Exceptional Children*, 34(4), pp. 20–26. doi: 10.1177/004005990203400403

Briand-Lamarche, M., Pinard, R., Theriault, P., and Dagenais, C. (2016). Evaluation of the processes and outcomes of implementing a competency model to foster research knowledge utilization in education. *International Journal of Higher Education*, 5(3). doi: 10.5430/ijhe.v5n3p168

Clarke, B., Smolkowski, K., Baker, S., Fien, H., Doabler, C., and Chard, D. (2011). The impact of a comprehensive Tier I core kindergarten program on the achievement of students at risk in mathematics. *The Elementary School Journal*, 111(4), pp. 561–584. doi: 10.1086/659033

Cook, B., and Odom, S. (2013). Evidence-based practices and implementation science in special education. *Exceptional Children*, 79(3), pp. 135–144. doi: 10.1177/001440291307900201

Dagenais, C., Lysenko, L., Abrami, P., Bernard, R., Ramde, J., and Janosz, M. (2012). Use of research-based information by school practitioners and determinants of use: A review of empirical research. *Evidence & Policy: A Journal of Research, Debate and Practice*, 8(3), pp. 285–309. doi: 10.1332/1 74426412X654031

Doabler, C., Nelson, N., Kosty, D., Fien, H., Baker, S.K., Smolkowski, K., and Clarke, B. (2013). Examining teachers' use of evidence-based practices during core mathematics instruction. *Assessment for Effective Intervention*, 39(2), pp. 99–111. doi: 10.1177/1534508413511848

Ely, E., Alves, K., Dolenc, N., Sebolt, S., and Walton, E. (2018). Classroom simulation to prepare teachers to use evidence-based comprehension practices. *Journal of Digital Learning in Teacher Education*, 34(2), pp. 71–87. doi: 10.1 080/21532974.2017.1399487

Ely, E., Kennedy, M., Pullen, P., Williams, M., and Hirsch, S. (2014). Improving instruction of future teachers: A multimedia approach that supports implementation of evidence-based vocabulary practices. *Teaching and Teacher Education*, 44, pp. 35–43. doi: 10.1016/j.tate.2014.07.012

Gorard, S. (ed.). (2020). *Getting Evidence into Education: Evaluating the Routes to Policy and Practice.* Abingdon: Routledge.

Gorard, S., See, B.H., and Siddiqui, N. (2017). *The Trials of Evidence-Based Education.* Routledge.

Gorard, S., See, B.H., and Siddiqui, N. (2020). What is the evidence on the best way to get evidence into use in education? *Review of Education*, 8(2), pp. 570–610. doi: 10.1002/rev3.3200

Griggs, J., Speight, S., and Javiera, C. (2016). *Ashford teaching alliance research champion: Evaluation report and executive summary.* Education Endowment Foundation. https://educationendowmentfoundation.org.uk/public/files/Projects/Evaluation_Reports/EEF_Project_Report_AshfordResearchChampion_1.pdf

Kretlow, A., Cooke, N., and Wood, C. (2011). Using in-service and coaching to increase teachers' accurate use of research-based strategies. *Remedial and Special Education*, 33(6), pp. 348–361. doi: 10.1177/0741932510395397

Kutash, K., Duchnowski, A., and Lynn, N. (2009). The use of evidence-based instructional strategies in special education settings in secondary schools: Development, implementation and outcomes. *Teaching and Teacher Education*, 25(6), pp. 917–923. doi: 10.1016/j.tate.2009.02.016

Learmond, K. (2017). *Evaluating the use of instructional coaching as a tool to improve teacher instructional strategies at a Title 1 middle school: An action research study* (Publication No. 10621891). Doctoral dissertation. Capella University. https://eric.ed.gov/?id=ED579858

Lord, P., Rabiasz, A., and Styles, B. (2017a). *"Literacy Octopus" dissemination trial: Evaluation report and executive summary.* Education Endowment Foundation. Retrieved 10 July 2020 from https://files.eric.ed.gov/fulltext/ED581230.pdf

Lord, P., Rabiasz, A., Roy, P., Harland, J., Styles, B., and Fowler, K. (2017b). *Evidence-based literacy support: The "Literacy Octopus" trial. Evaluation report and executive summary.* Education Endowment Foundation. Retrieved 10 July 2020 from https://files.eric.ed.gov/fulltext/ED581248.pdf

Mady, C. (2013). Reducing the gap between educational research and second language teachers' knowledge. *Evidence & Policy: A Journal of Research, Debate and Practice*, 9(2), pp. 185–206. doi: 10.1332/174426413x662509

Maheady, L., Harper, G., Mallette, B., and Karnes, M. (2004). Preparing preservice teachers to implement class wide peer tutoring. *Teacher Education and Special Education: The Journal of the Teacher Education Division of the Council for Exceptional Children*, 27(4), pp. 408–418. doi: 10.1177/088840640402700408

McHugh, M. (2012). Interrater reliability: The kappa statistic. *Biochemia Medica*, pp. 276–282. doi: 10.11613/bm.2012.031

Ogunleye, Y. (2014). *Impact of collaborative intervention programme on pre-primary and primary school teachers' awareness, acquisition and utilisation of educational research findings in Oyo State, Nigeria* (Publication No. 88641). Doctoral dissertation. University of Ibadan. http://ir.library.ui.edu.ng/handle/123456789/3661

Purper, C. (2015). *Study of early childhood teachers' use of federally funded websites that disseminate information about evidence-based practices* (Publication No. 3680792). Doctoral dissertation. USA: The Claremont Graduate University.

Rose, J., Thomas, S., Zhang, L., Edwards, A., Augero, A., and Roney, P. (2017). *Research learning communities: Evaluation report and executive summary.* Education Endowment Foundation. https://files.eric.ed.gov/fulltext/ED581267.pdf

Sawyer, M.R. (2015). *The effects of coaching novice special education teachers to engage in evidence based practice as a problem-solving process.* Doctoral dissertation. The Ohio State University. https://etd.ohiolink.edu/apexprod/rws_olink/r/1501/10?clear=10&p10_accession_num=osu1436464651

Schnorr, C.I. (2013). *Effects of multilevel support on first-grade teachers' use of research-based strategies during beginning reading instruction.* Doctoral dissertation. The University of North Carolina at Charlotte. https://ninercommons.uncc.edu/islandora/object/etd%3A703/datastream/PDF/download/citation.pdf

Scott, S., and McNeish, D. (2013). *School leadership evidence review: Using research evidence to support school improvement.* National Centre for Social Research for CUBeC. https://www.dmss.co.uk/pdfs/evidencereview3.pdf

See, B.H., Gorard, S., and Siddiqui, N. (2015). Teachers' use of research evidence in practice: A pilot study of feedback to enhance learning. *Educational Research*, 58(1), pp. 56–72. doi: 10.1080/00131881.2015.1117798

Segedin, L. (2017). Theatre as a vehicle for mobilizing knowledge in education. *International Journal of Education & the Arts*, 18(15). Retrieved 14 July 2020 from http://www.ijea.org/v18n15/

Siddiqui, N. (2020). Generating research evidence in teaching practice. In Gorard, S. (ed), *Getting Evidence into Use* (pp. 100–109). Abingdon: Routledge.

Speight, S., Callanan, M., Griggs, J., Farias, J.C., and Fry, A. (2016). *Rochdale research into practice: Evaluation report and executive summary.* Education Endowment Foundation. https://files.eric.ed.gov/fulltext/ED581418.pdf

Vaughn, S., and Coleman, M. (2004). The role of mentoring in promoting use of research-based practices in reading. *Remedial and Special Education*, 25(1), pp. 25–38. doi: 10.1177/07419325040250010401

Walker, M., Nelson, J., Bradshaw, S., and Brown, C. (2019). *Teachers' engagement with research: What do we know? A research briefing.* Millbank: Education Endowment Foundation. https://educationendowmentfoundation.org.uk/public/files/Evaluation/Teachers_engagement_with_research_Research_Brief_JK.pdf

Wiggins, M., Jerrim, J., Tripney, J., Khatwa, M., and Gough, D. (2019). *The RISE project: Evidence informed school improvement.* https://educationendowmentfoundation.org.uk/public/files/Projects/Evaluation_Reports/RISE_Report_final.pdf

Conclusion

CHAPTER 19

The implications of these studies for new researchers

Stephen Gorard and Nadia Siddiqui

Introduction

High quality ambitious doctoral studies, that offer real-life knowledge contributions, *are* feasible. Strong projects can help the academic development and progression of early career researchers. Ambitious and high quality studies are also intrinsically more ethical in their conduct than those that are not (as explained in Gorard, 2002). These points are amply demonstrated by the 17 substantive chapters in this book. This final chapter looks, generically, at how these fledgling researchers achieved what they did.

What are the common ingredients of these successful PhDs?

The obvious place to start, when considering these 17 substantive chapters and what sets them apart from much research in social science, is in the formulation of their research questions (see Gorard, 2013, Chapter 3).

Their research questions

All of the projects start with real world, topical, policy and practice issues. Underlying each example is a genuine concern that education (their field of interest) should become better or fairer in some way. The projects are not (only) concerned with people's perceptions, or with what some group of stakeholders think or say about some issue. Instead, examples include how or whether a policy is actually influencing education, and how or whether we can improve student learning experiences and outcomes, at school or beyond.

Of course, several of these new researchers initially misaligned their research questions in relation to how they intended to address them. The usual problem of this nature is to have a causal question like "does this teaching approach [or new policy or whatever] improve learning [or other outcome]?" But then the PhD researcher suggests asking stakeholders whether they *think* that there has been an improvement. Or perhaps the plan starts with a descriptive question like "has an attainment gap [or whatever] grown over time [or does it differ for sub-groups, or whatever]?". And then the PhD student suggests just asking people if they think the gap has grown. If you read more, and analyse what researchers (even some very senior researchers) actually did, then you will see how common this error is. We are not sure why it happens. We blame doctoral supervisors who are probably doing the same thing in their own "research". This apparent ignorance among doctoral supervisors then perpetuates through their doctoral researchers. It is (or should be) the role and responsibility of the supervisor to nip this in the bud. The PhD research plan has to include actually evaluating the new teaching approach, or comparing the attainment gap over time, to continue these two examples. Of course, the study can include asking people for their perceptions as well (as many studies here illustrate), but these perceptions are addressing a different and usually subsidiary research question.

As the authors chapter have explained, some research questions arose from their own experiences. Some emerged from a rapid review of the literature. Some wanted to evaluate a topical or controversial policy. All had elements of theory at the outset, such as what morality is, or how group work could improve attainment (sometimes called a theory of change). And all adapted those theories in light of their findings. In fact, it is almost true to say that testing an initial theory, however informally it was expressed, was the purpose of all of these studies. There was no room however for what can be termed "Grand Theory" (deliberately capitalised here), either as a "lens" to examine the social world, or a set of concepts to "explain" findings by distorting them to fit. Something called a "Theory" which is not being tested by the research is not actually a theory at all. It is kind of religion and has no place in social science. Researchers need to be genuinely curious and open to being surprised by what they uncover.

None of these PhDs starts by considering the nature of knowledge itself, or whether the real world exists, or what their "identity" is as a researcher (whatever that means). These, and other philosophical questions, might be perfectly proper as the basis for new work in philosophy. But they are not relevant to everyone undertaking new work in education. It is anyway not feasible, with the time and resources they have available, for doctoral researchers to address such questions in any meaningful way, and *then* continue to a full original research programme of their own. What usually happens instead, because misleading resources or inexperienced supervisors might insist on it, is that doctoral researchers in the social sciences merely pay lip service to some of these fundamental philosophical ideas. They usually do so without any real understanding, presenting complex terms as though they were stances, that a researcher can choose to adopt or not at will. A bit like fashion accessories. Please avoid this.

An important lesson that new researchers need to heed is that results are often "negative". Most of the plausible interventions that have ever been evaluated properly do not actually work in practice (Gorard et al., 2017). There are examples in this book. Indeed, some may be harmful. Many supposed differences between sub-groups or "effect" sizes in social science are volatile, and of no substantive importance. Of course, there must then be no dredging of data to try to find differences and so claim "success". Rather, new researchers must come to realise that apparently negative findings are valuable and can be among the most interesting. Knowing that something is not really a problem, or that a widespread policy or programme does not work, means that (often public) time and money can be saved, and life chances improved otherwise.

Methods choices

In real-life, outside academia, when conducting a skilled or important task, everyone has been observed to behave in much the same way (Gorard with Taylor, 2004). When crossing a busy road with their young children, not even social science researchers behave as though the car bearing down on them is just a matter of perspective (or only relevant as text, for example). They will try to avoid the car, and would be correct in doing so. When renting an apartment they will not neglect to enquire about the rent, and claim that they do not "do numbers". They will not ignore the smell of a gas leak in their apartment because they are a "positivist" and prefer not to deal with sensory data. And so on.

Education is surely as important as these examples. When young children do not learn to read, the likely damage to their life chances is real, but it can usually be overcome. When a child has a disability, this is a real thing – although the lifelong impact of the disability depends on a wide range of factors, including the nature of the society they live in. There is a genuine difference between being accepted or rejected, when applying to attend university – even though we may not know what that difference will be until later. So, as supervisors, we ask our doctoral researchers to behave and think as they would in their real lives. And not to adopt spurious ideas and terms that will just make their research harder to conduct, and more difficult for others to read.

Research paradigms, at least as the concept was developed by Kuhn (1962), are the result of translating scientific problems into puzzles that can then be solved by more normal approaches. They are clearly independent of, and make no mention of, the specific methods to be used. The technique of observation might be used to help create the idea for a new paradigm, and also may be more used for more routine empirical work (normal science). Or not. The same applies to any method of data collection or analysis.

The idea that research projects can be separated into two distinct purported paradigms known as "qualitative" and "quantitative" is plain wrong. It is also unhelpful. None of the studies in the foregoing 17 chapters uses these Q-word terms, or could be described as having the characteristics of one or the other. Nor should the projects be thought of as being "mixed methods". The idea of *mixing* methods must depend on the methods having been separated beforehand. In our much simpler view, there is nothing to mix because no distinction has or should be made in the first place. Researchers can use any approaches that they foresee as being useful in answering their real-life research questions.

Research designs

So far, many of the points have been about what not to do. This is useful because it saves new researchers' time (by encouraging students not to waste time doing them). More positively though, all of the authors have considered appropriate research designs for their research questions (Gorard, 2013). The 17 main chapters include a wide range of case studies, time series analyses, regression discontinuity, simulations, cross-sectional, comparative, longitudinal, and experimental designs. Sometimes, there are several of these designs in one study, because all of the studies have more than one research question.

All good research studies will have an underlying design even if this is not reported, just as a well-built house has a foundation and an architectural plan even if these are not visible to people living in the house. The research design should stem from the research question(s) to be addressed by the study, and should suit the type of question being asked. Conducting research without considering its design is as ill-advised as trying to build a house without foundations (Gorard, 2021).

Sources of data

As the chapters in this book portray, good research looks for evidence wherever possible to address the key research questions. Most of these studies involved observation and interviews of some kind. Some also used surveys. Some looked at documents and websites, and several others designed their own instruments or tests.

Several of the studies here used existing large-scale datasets like the National Pupil Database (NPD), often linked at an individual record level to other datasets. Some used this kind of dataset descriptively with associated documentary analyses, field observations and interviews. Some present interrupted time series analysis, or regression discontinuities, based on existing data. Some use these datasets in a quasi-experimental design to evaluate policy. The possibilities are almost endless. Using existing data usually saves time and money. It (inadvertently) helped researchers to maintain social distancing during COVID-19 lockdown, but is always invaluable. The datasets are generally larger, more authoritative, richer, independent resources and have less missing information, than anything a PhD researcher could hope to generate on their own.

Many studies also use the existing literature in a systematic (or similarly structured) review of evidence, in combination with, or preparatory to, other forms of data collection. Just like existing and archived data, the research literature as an empirical resource appears to be under-used or even largely ignored in too many PhDs. We are not talking about the partial, uncritical and usually cherry-picked so-called "literature review" chapter common in a PhD. We advise you not to have such a chapter that just ticks off the need for some citation of literature. Instead, have chapters on what the issue is, and why anyone cares, what current policy/practice is, how the issue has been researched so far, and what is known and not known about it. The last leads to your chapter on what you plan to do to fill the gap, and so to the methods used in your PhD.

A review of literature, whether rapid, to scope the field, or extensive, ought to be structured and as inclusive as possible. It should not, of course, ignore material because of its source, author or the methods used. That is a further reason why there should be no schismic paradigms, and no researcher identities, and why all researchers and supervisors need be to prepared to examine evidence of any type. To do otherwise would lead to partial, biased reviews. For example, imagine omitting from a review of evidence, everything that used numbers or everything that did not!

The focus must not be only on the famous or published pieces. This also leads to bias, at least partly because of the well-known publishing bias towards positive results. Perhaps most importantly, as well as describing the research of others fairly, you have to make a judgement about how much to trust it. And you must explain and be prepared to defend that judgement. Several of the chapters refer to using a simple "sieve" we developed to help them do this, rating each piece that they read in terms of the fit between research questions and design, scale, amount of missing data, quality of data collected, and other factors. Again, these judgements are needed regardless of the methods used in the study. For example, if you would require research to be of a certain scale in order to trust its findings on what some people report, then it does not matter whether the data was recorded, observed, or collected face-to-face, or on-line.

Simple analyses

Another feature of the work in all of these PhD studies is the relative simplicity of their analysis. Of course, some analyses are more complex than others, given the nature of the research being undertaken (comparing different models for value-added analyses, or assessing fuzzy regression discontinuity, for example). But even here, what is revealed is that the more complicated analyses are unhelpful, and/or produce the same substantive answers as simple ones. In which case simpler is better. Simpler analyses are easier to do, easier to complete without error, easier for supervisors to check, and much easier for a wider audience to read.

In these studies, data was usually examined using a mixture of pre-specified hypotheses or planned codes, and *post hoc* considerations, whether the research involved content analysis of policy documents, statistical modelling, or arranging informal observations made during fieldwork.

Another reason that the analyses are simple is the prior use of research design (see above). The design does the hard work in the research. For example, in the experimental studies in Part II, the fact that the design is a randomised control trial means that the researchers can simply present the difference between the intervention and the counterfactual control groups. This is so whether the difference is based on observation, opinion, or measurement. No dredging is possible or needed. Of course, if the randomisation was subverted, or there was high dropout, or evidence of bias from the process evaluation, then we need to report this, and be very cautious about any reported differences. But a more complex analysis still cannot help, because it cannot address any of these issues either. The authors are better off spending their time thinking about the safety of their findings, and what they might mean.

Linked to this is the absence of significance tests and related approaches (p-values, standard errors, power calculations, confidence intervals, and so on). These widely abused approaches are useless here for two reasons. They assume that the cases in the analysis have been completely randomised. None of the studies described, and none of the studies we have ever encountered in real-life, meet this assumption. These studies are quite properly based on convenience or opportunity samples (taking whatever these ambitious PhD students could get!). *Statistical* generalisation is therefore not possible, and would not make sense with these data. Even when the cases have been allocated randomly to groups in the experimental designs there are missing cases, and cases with missing responses. These make the cases no longer random.

The second problem is that even if we found a study with fully randomised cases, the significance test would only tell us the probability of a difference (pattern, trend) being due to chance, assuming it was only due to chance. It is like computing the chance of rolling a six with an unbiased die. Easy, primary school maths. But, this probability is of no use for any of the projects here, or indeed any applied social science. If possible, we would want to know instead the probability of the result that we found actually being due to chance. This very different probability is not possible to compute (Gorard, 2021). It would be like trying to decide on one roll of die whether a six meant that the die was biased or not. Impossible.

Another element that all of these studies had in common, although restrictions of space did not allow all of them to focus on it in their chapter, was the importance of respecting missing data. Missing data was coded as such, and used in descriptive analyses and as a possible predictor in regression models. As discussed in some chapters, authors also ran sensitivity analyses to see what the possible impact of missing data could be on their findings. This is a key step in judging the trustworthiness of your own or others' published results.

Conclusion

In a research doctorate, you can do so much more than merely asking a few people what they think or perceive about something. You can do it in less time, and with less disruption than is usual for a PhD. And the research can then make a real difference somewhere. There will be implications to draw out other than – "it is all more complex than it seemed", and/or "we now need more research", and/or "I am sure Bourdieu [replace as needed] would have had something to say about this".

Not only that. There appears to be a link between ambitious research and completion of a PhD on time, and the link is the reverse of what you might expect. All of these authors completed, or are clearly on course to complete, their theses bang on schedule. And this is despite COVID intervening for perhaps half of them. Not for them the so-called "writing up" year(s), or endless extensions, that we have seen happen for other students doing far less research. It is almost as though the real struggle for too many doctoral researchers lies in finding something, indeed anything, to write to fill their 80k words. If you have something more substantial to say, there are few or no writer's blocks.

A final point. We realise that some of what we say will be controversial, or even a blow to those who are unambitious, and expect much less from themselves or their doctoral researchers. Our comments on methods, philosophy, and even on the purported qualitative/quantitative divide, are anyway not what many existing PhD texts portray. Maybe your (potential) supervisor disagrees with us as well. And the advice is commonly given to PhD researchers to listen to their supervisors. On these issues, however, we say do *not* necessarily do that. As with many things, it depends.

Whenever you come across a methods dispute, with one party saying try this, and another saying do something entirely different, look first at what the parties have done themselves with the approaches they advocate. You would not want to learn cooking from someone who was unable to cook a decent meal, or to learn driving from someone who was unable to drive properly. Such training would be very unlikely to work. In the same way, look at real-life examples of good, robust, trustworthy research for a template of what to do. We hope that the chapters in this book can act as examples of what is possible, and powerful. We also hope that you enjoy your research as much we all do.

References

Gorard, S. (2002). Ethics and equity: Pursuing the perspective of non-participants. *Social Research Update*, 39, pp. 1–4.

Gorard, S. (2021). *How to Make Sense of Statistics: Everything You Need to Know about Using Numbers in Social Science*. London: SAGE.

Gorard, S. (2013). *Research Design: Creating Robust Approaches for the Social Sciences*. London: SAGE.

Gorard, S., and See, B.H. (2013). *Overcoming Disadvantage in Education*. London: Routledge.

Gorard, S., See, B.H., and Siddiqui, N. (2017). *The Trials of Evidence-Based Education*. London: Routledge.

Gorard, S., with Taylor, C. (2004). *Combining Methods in Educational and Social Research*. London: Open University Press.

Kuhn, T. (1962). *The Structure of Scientific Revolutions*. Chicago: University of Chicago Press.

Index